FATHER HUNGER

EXPLORATIONS

with

ADULTS AND CHILDREN

FATHER HUNGER

EXPLORATIONS
with
ADULTS AND CHILDREN

James M. Herzog

THE ANALYTIC PRESS

2001   Hillsdale, NJ   London

Published by The Analytic Press, Inc.
101 West Street, Hillsdale, NJ 07642
www.analyticpress.com

Typeset in Adobe Sabon by CompuDesign, Charlottesville, VA

Library of Congress Cataloging-in-Publication Data

Herzog, James M., 1943-
    Father hunger: explorations with adults and children / James Herzog.
        p. cm.
    Includes bibliographical references and index.
    ISBN 0-88163-259-7
    1. Father and child. 2. Psychoanalysis. I. Title.

    BF723.F35 H47 2001 150.19'5—dc21

    2001033496

Printed in the United States of America

10   9   8   7   6   5   4   3   2   1

ACKNOWLEDGMENTS

I WOULD LIKE TO THANK MY PARENTS, Henry James Herzog and Hilde Salomonski Herzog, for their initial and shaping contribution; my children, Noah Alexander and Eve Elana, for their reflecting, enduring, and enabling roles; my friend Mark E. O'Connell for our playing, working, and thinking together; and my wife, Eleanor White Herzog, for everything. Leni *is* everything to me.

John Kerr from The Analytic Press was more than an editor. His role in helping this book to achieve its present status is immense. Eleanor Starke Kobrin copy edited the manuscript with grace, elegance, and precision. Steven Cooper, Alison Potter O'Connell, Elliot and Barbara Schildkrout, Lora Heims Tessman and Arnold Modell, Steve and Gridth Ablon, Chris and Jill Lovett, Bob Muellner, Fred Meisel, George W. Goethals, John Nemiah, Julius Richmond, Herb Goldings, Paul Myerson, Joe Nemetz, Helen Tartakoff, Sam Kaplan, Tony Kris, and many other colleagues, teachers, and friends at Harvard, BPSI, and in Boston also made invaluable contributions. Arthur Valenstein deserves special mention in this regard. In New York, John Munder Ross, Susan Coates, Judith Kestenberg, Eleanor Galenson, and Martin Bergmann were and are pivotal helpers and influences. Rosemarie Berna in Zürich and Lotte Köhler in Munich also belong on this list.

Because this book is about development of the self in the family, it seems more than appropriate also to mention my wife Leni's parents, Harmon S. B. and Ruth N. White. Their role in our lives and in our children's lives has been very great and their support of this project of equal magnitude.

I thank all of you very much.

NTS

RAISING CHILDREN BOOKSTORE

We offer the largest selection of
resources for parents, families
and professionals for
raising children and the many
topics related to
children's mental health.
~

PARENTING
ADOPTION
FOSTER CARE
CHILDBIRTH
NUTRITION
HOMESCHOOLING
EDUCATION
TRAUMA
DEATH & GRIEF ISSUES
ASPERGERS SYNDROME
AUTISM
ADD, ADHD
TOURETTES SYNDROME
DEVELOPMENTAL DISORDERS
LEARNING DISABILITIES
DOWN SYNDROME
OBSESSIVE COMPULSIVE
DISORDER
REACTIVE ATTACHMENT
DISORDER
CHRONIC ILLNESS

Ask about our
**FREE VIDEO LOANING
LIBRARY**

www.raisingchildrenbookstore.com

PREFACE

MY MOTHER'S FATHER, MARTIN SALOMONSKI, was a liberal rabbi in Berlin. In 1943, he was sent to Theresienstadt together with his son, Dolph, and youngest daughter, Ruth, who had remained in Germany with him. Later that year, when Dolph, then 14, was told that he would be transported to Auschwitz, my grandfather, who did not have to go, would not let him go alone. He accompanied his son and subsequently, like countless others, was lost. I never knew my grandfather, and the horror of his particular circumstances and of the Holocaust generally defy comparison, but the identification with him is strong. To accompany, even in terror; to refuse to extract myself, even at a cost; and to try to help so that a person who requests my assistance, and with whom I have forged an alliance, need not do it alone—has been my guiding and abiding principle. To extend the historical antecedent: that one may be endangered in such a journey is always a possibility; that both people survive and that the patient knows himself better is always the goal. Toward this aim of "full-deck" (Herzog and O'Connell, submitted) functioning for the patient and the continued capacity of the analyst to work, love, and play, my work is directed and this book is brought forth. In all these ways I hope to honor the memory of Martin Salomonski.

1 | INTRODUCTION

INFORMATION OBTAINED IN THE ANALYTIC SETTING is different from that emanating from biography, autobiography, random sampling, structured interviews, philosophical contemplation, or other modes of data collection. It seems to bear a stronger resemblance to actual developmental processes than to scientific pursuits in that absolute truth is less an ultimate goal than is the making of meaning and the finding of sense in what has transpired and in what is occurring and recurring. Continuity as a principle of the ongoing life of the mind pulls for the construction of causal sequences and meaningful patternings. The veridicality of these constructions may be limited to the conceptual framework in which they are devised and divined.

Practitioners from other disciplines have cautioned about the generalizability of data from the analytic situation and stressed the particularities and limitations of insights and conclusions drawn from such a setting. Their caveats are well taken but need not result in the exclusion of analytic data from the palette of information available to theoreticians or students of human development or behavior. Rather the special significance of psychoanalytic data is in what I have called "the domain of personal meaning," the construction of reality that features both conscious and unconscious process, thought, and fantasy and is to be distinguished from data bases I have called the level of videotaped reality and the level of interrogative reality.

By videotaped reality, I mean data the camera can see and record. Currently, much is being learned by filming mother–infant interaction, father–child interactions, and actual therapeutic encounters. One sees what is happening. Interrogative reality refers to direct questioning of a child, his parents, or any individual. This approach yields consciously considered material thought to be appropriate in response to the query in a particular circumstance. As has been noted by Mary Main (2000; Hesse and Main, 2000) and others (e.g., Slade, 2000), this level of inquiry can also yield data about underlying neuropsychological linguistic strategies of cognition and affect tolerance that are highly correlated with an individual's attachment history.

In this book, I use primarily psychoanalytic information, with all its robustness and all its fragility. Each individual whose story unfolds in conversation with the analyst illustrates the ways in which the unraveling and reconstruction of the past as it is encountered in the present allows for a coconstructed version of individual development and derailment and for a fresh perspective on what is entailed in restitution and even in repair. I call the intermediate space that analyst and analysand create together the *Spielraum*, or play space; what is unique to this setting is a collaborative finding of ways in which two people can play, albeit asymmetrically, in a manner that is safe enough and contained enough that the most profound personal pain and conflict is assured admission and respectful regard.

The fresh perspective on the self and its history is unique to the analytic setting and to the opportunity for new play that arises out of a kind of interplay that features not only replay but also an examination of how and why the replay has occurred.

I am always trying to explore the ways in which the self, especially the masculine self, develops as a self-seeking entity using sameness and difference as a way of harnessing, knowing, and owning his own attributes, both facultative and problematic. I try to show that the boy self is concerned with learning how to do it, as well as mastering the concomitant tasks of being, doing, bearing, working on, working with, working out, and working though. How these processes are reencountered, recapitulated, and reinvented in the analytic setting is a continued focus. My emphasis on the masculine self grows out of several decades of research on the role of the father in child development. This focus has multiple determinants, not the least of which is autobiographical.

The self, as it is constructed of accrued experience and subsequent representation of self with father, with mother, and with father and mother together, is, optimally, a self endowed with multiple playmode options and resiliency in the face of overwhelming or underwhelming environmental input. Such a self has a greater capacity to "roll with the punches" and thus a greater capacity both to manage trauma and to integrate its accoutrements. This thesis, which addresses the primacy of triadic experience at every developmental stage, is a fundamental postulate of my work. On it I base the notion of internal enactments as fundamental to the neurotic process and instrumental in the recovery from the derailments in the play function that trauma may occasion. Such derailment features the emergence of external enactments and of interactive enactment as primary psychological modes of functioning. The ubiquity of these modes is very impressive; their integration into the recovery process is often complex and problematic. By presenting detailed analytic data, I hope to illustrate the ways in which each of these processes appears, influences both analytic and reparative developmental play, and influences the lasting and shiftable contours of the individual inscape as it is seen in an interactive *Spielraum*. Within this developmental triad, I often highlight the self-with-father representation and its particular function in the management of aggression and in the toleration of trauma.

This book is not intended to be a textbook of psychoanalytic theory or technique. Yet problems of both will be evident as it is read. Rather, it is intended as a window on processes of development, derailment, and repair as these are accessed, uniquely, in the analytic modality. Simultaneously, by looking at the contributions of developmental reseach and observational study, an attempt is made to fit the analytic perspective together with data from other avenues of investigation. For better or worse, I utilize my own work in this regard. I thus compound the possibility that my own biases and indiosyncracies will be communicated in undiluted form. I also want to mention that I have gone to great lengths to protect the confidentiality of my patients who have so generously given me permission to share some of their inner lives. In order to insure their anonymity I have at times resorted to the simple but effective device of manufacturing red herrings by replacing specific, but inessential biographical details with details taken from my own biography and the biography of close friends and colleagues.

> For the waking, there is one world,
> and it is common; but sleepers turn aside each
> one into a world of his own.
>
> —Heraclitus

2 | MICHAEL: No Face

"MY SON DAVID IS SMALL IN THE DREAM. He is thrown by my wife, Anne, onto a sharp fence and then to the ground. He screams. My daughter Angel is dancing. I am devastated and feel that I cannot be in a world which is like this. This dream reminds me of the first dream of my analysis which featured David in a concentration camp, fires burning. He clearly stands for me in both dreams. The dream from my analysis was 21 years ago; he was three then."

Two dreams, separated by 21 years, begin this book. They are both from a man whose relationship with his own father was deeply scarred and whose relationship with his first-born son was deeply fraught. The themes of danger, intertwining identifications, and the concomitant but wholly nonameliorative presence of women are idiographic and, of course, closely related to this man's early life experience. Given the content of the dreams, one may suspect the impact of trauma, both historical and intrafamilial. One may note too the aspect of helplessness, or at least of inactivity, on the part of the dreamer in both recitations. We might ask, where in the manifest content is the father, or at least a paternal presence, who might protect or serve to organize and modulate aggressive drive or fantasy? Why I nominate the father for this role will, I hope, become clear as I present more of our dreamer's thoughts and some of my own as well.

In waking life, our dreamer, Michael, is a highly accomplished professor of philosophy; four years ago, he returned to analysis after a hiatus of 17 years. His son David, now 24, is a medical student on good terms with his parents and not overtly threatened by historical calamity or his mother's outbursts. The mother is an attorney, not distinguished by either her violence or her passivity; and the daughter, Angel, 22 years of age, has been known to dance, but mostly writes poetry and studies French.

Michael recently presented a paper during a trip to Europe and experienced a reawakening of some of his family's Holocaust history. His parents emigrated from Vienna in 1939, and many members of their Jewish family perished. His area of specialty is Nietzsche, and he is often theoretically preoccupied with the strength of men, the dimensions of power, and questions that might be regarded as bordering on misogyny. Of late, he has become quite interested in French philosophy, too, and the issues of deconstruction or, as he is inclined to put it, how to interrupt the continuity of meaning and allow for revision, reworking, and spontaneous association.

He is deeply gratified by his wife's good nature and vibrant presence as these are differentiatable from his mother's postwar depression and inability to intercede for him when his father was out of control. He is an active and involved father, always trying to help his children. Both, in fact, rendezvoused with their parents on the recent European journey. They are a close-knit family, perhaps too closely knit. Our dreamer feels himself to be as different from his own father as it is possible for a man to be; and yet, he is always fearful that he will either actually become like him or, worse yet, manifest all those negative qualities his father always said were there in him, qualities that are understood alternately as manifestations of character pathology and as "innate badness."

Michael is 50 years old. He has been married for 27 years to Anne. Their marriage is good in that both can work and play, but it has not been without incident. Anne has brought her own issues to the marriage. Life has not been neutral as the children have grown, as work lives have evolved, and as anxieties have mounted. Twice over the years, Michael has fallen in love with male colleagues. Both relationships were confined to work; neither ever entered the actual sexual realm and each was intensely painful. Both men admired Michael and his work enormously and sincerely. Each idealized him as a father-mentor. In Michael the longed-for relationships evoked resonances of their developmental reciprocal, a father loving his son; Michael came to love each of the men ardently. He suffered tremendously when each relationship came apart in what might be called the almost natural chain of events. Love does not always go smoothly, especially when fueled by developmental deprivation.

Neither Erik nor Hans, the objects of Michael's love, ever really knew that he had been chosen; certainly neither knew that he stood for Michael's unresponsive father. Sometimes during lovemaking with Anne thoughts of Erik or Hans might enter Michael's fantasy. These thoughts are not explicitly sexual but, rather, take the form of a present, benevolent, and supportive man helping him, being with him, looking out for him. He shares these occurrences aloud with his wife, who is accepting and not dismissive. Both understand the connection between Michael's "forbidden" homosexuality, never enacted, and his *father hunger*.

Father hunger is a term I first introduced when working with young children whose fathers were unavailable because of divorce. The typical dreams of these children, and my thoughts about them, we take up in the next chapter. In Michael's case, his father did not leave him, but their relationship bore all the manifestations of the father's history and pathology and was thusly significantly strained.

When Michael's father died after a long illness, Anne hoped his death would constitute a kind of liberation for her husband. The mourning period was in many ways as convoluted as the earlier relationship had been. Michael comforted his mother and siblings, wife, and children and then rushed back to his university so as not to disrupt his teaching schedule. He redoubled his efforts as mentor and guide for his students. He could not free himself from the conviction that to father others was his mission; nor could he surrender the hope contained in this very activity that somewhere there might be a father for him. This hope hovers in his consciousness but does not constitute a cure for his pain or for his longing. Michael, though tormented, is highly functional and has fathered a whole generation of graduate students and, in a sense, a school of philosophical thought. His preoccupation with the father's role, with trauma and repair, and especially with the topics of replay, new play, and interplay occasion his appearance as this work's frontispiece.

I view fathering from the perspectives of internal reality and of external reality—I treat the inscape (after Gerard Manley Hopkins, 1937) as a continual component, both idiographic and nomothetic, of all psychological functioning and interactive competence. The inscape, or inner landscape, is the realm of internal experience, both actual and phantasmagorical, as it exists in each person's self-reflection and internal play space. Because I am a psychoanalyst, I draw heavily on data available to me both clinically and personally. My interest in fathering will be seen to be conjoined with thoughts about trauma and repair, about play and intrapsychic development. What emerges is my own blend, compromised, complicated, but, I hope, of heuristic value. I return to Michael repeatedly as this book unfolds. He will be joined by a number of other women and men, girls and boys, who have afforded me the privilege of sharing their innermost process, meaning, pain, and efforts at repair in the psychoanalytic *Spielraum* or play space. Their companions, in my thinking, are the poets, among them Rainer Maria Rilke and Wallace Stevens, T. S. Eliot and Paul Celan. Each in his work articulates the issues with which I am absorbed in a manner that far more directly than my prose evokes and illumines the feeling and the essence of these matters. I am immensely grateful for their companionship and for their music. For the most part, they are silent companions in this book; they are not the less present for that.

Let me provide a sample of what Michael has to say as he and I are together, listening, experiencing, trying to understand his dreams, his feelings, "the music of what happens" for him, as the poet Seamus Heaney (in Vendler, 1988) would put it, when Michael is with me and we are listening together. I have selected only a very few sequences from a long and productive piece of analytic work. My selection has been tutored by the applicability of Michael's material to the themes of this book.

One day in the current round of the analysis, 17 years after his first round, Michael speaks with great feeling about a symptom that is not new. He has read in the *International Herald Tribune* a report from 1879 detailing a guillotining and describing the struggles, in vain, of the two men who were being executed. There is some hint that one of the condemned men was innocent and of a possible sado-masochistic relationship between them. Michael's thoughts turn, as they often do, to the cruelty of man to man. He speaks of his tendency to obsess about reports of atrocities or, in this case, of executions. Then he remembers a childhood fantasy about guillotining a chicken, something he had thought he could do successfully if the blade were to descend after he had fled from the scene, only to discover afterward that, even though he had engineered the decapitation from a distance, he was still the executioner.

At this point, I, the analyst, remind Michael of our interest in his reluctance to hurt, what we have called his extreme worry about his aggression. Our code for this is his reluctance to kill mosquitoes, which we first learned about with reference to a childhood scene in which his father was jumping on the bed in his efforts to rid their hotel room of the buzzing of these insects. This scene of the father jumping on the bed has interested us from a number of perspectives. Michael responds to my comment by saying, "I could do more to the chicken than to the mosquitoes, but here it is men doing it to men." I agree that what men do to men is of enormous concern to Michael. Often, I add, we are concerned with what one man did to him and sometimes, indeed oftentimes, what did not happen between them. Michael sighs and then says that he is smiling to himself, sort of. "What heralds the international tribunal?" he says, "It heralds that I wonder how to manage this question of who will hurt whom."

Who will hurt whom? How is hurting to be managed? How is the result to be judged? I wish to emphasize the recurring nature of these questions in our dreamer, even after their roots have been understood, their origins reconstructed. Our topic is again the father's role in the modulation and organization of aggressive drive and fantasy, how he teaches his son to manage the hurting. In the analysis, Michael chooses to "comanage" some of these repeating refrains with me. What does this mean? Does this make me a kind of substitute or surrogate father? If it does, is that an acceptable solution or resolution, or does it proclaim something about the gravity of the assault he has sustained or the inadequacy of our therapeutic endeavors? Are we in the realm of a neurotic history being recalled or of a traumatic past being reenacted? What does each signify? What are the expectable sequellae of each intrapsychically, interactively, and as therapeutic possibilities? How general is this process of a man needing another man to help him manage issues of hurting and being hurt? What are these issues really about? Since most men are not in analysis, are there correlates in the social order for this function. What are its developmental *Anlagen*? Do we observe in Michael the sequellae of a developmental deprivation, or is it a more normative need?

I hope that the conceptual road map now begins to become clear. I shall tell you of Michael's life and struggles, of his analysis and our relationship, and of the ways in which we—he and I—have understood the origins and the meanings of his way of being. That Michael has studied psychoanalysis, too, is an immeasurable help in this endeavor. That he consents to allow his inscape and our explorations to serve as the text is but another manifestation of his extraordinary generosity. What we have figured out together is further elaborated by the commentaries of others, patients, poets, theorists and observers. I place it in the larger context of meaning, of etiology, and of derailment and repair; of treatment, hope, new play, and interplay. Let us, then, together learn more of Michael's inscape as it emerges, is recognized, and is mutually understood in the analytic situation.

Michael married Anne when he was 23. Anne's background was totally different. She was sunny in history and personality and had, from Michael's perspective, an untroubled family story. He had met Anne when she was 18 and had just arrived at the Ivy League school he thought was paradise. It was so different from the small mid-Western town where he had grown up. His was the only Jewish family in the town, as Michael told me in the first hour as he was trying to explain his concentration-camp dream: "We never went to Europe when I was a child and, although its recent history was very vivid in our family—I mean the Holocaust—it was hard to picture. Sometimes when we went to New York, I would see old men in Hassidic garb. I wondered, was this the way it looked, them, me? There is another part to this too; I always used to think of Europe as green hills and flowing water, a kind of idyllic Switzerland."

When Michael first began to tell me his story, during the first hour of the first phase of analysis 21 years ago, he interrupted himself to say, "You know, I think that I am really frightened to be here. My head began to hurt early this morning and it is killing me now. I don't know what frightens me, but something does." I listened, noting that he had spoken of his head's killing him while not knowing yet what this might mean. Minutes later Michael spoke of his involvement in the peace movement and his conviction that aggression was reactive rather than innate. Oddly, he told me, his headache was becoming worse by the second. He made reference to an aneurysm and joked that, were he to have one in his brain and were it to burst in the first seven minutes of the analysis, it might be the shortest treatment ever conducted—"barring some of Lacan's methods," he continued, joking.

I felt that I needed to say something both acknowledging and reassuring. "You make references to deadly things within your mind," I said, "Our job will be to learn about them in a way that seems bearable to you as well as meaningful." Michael's response to this intervention, which was meant to be supportive, was to begin to cry: "Bearable and meaningful, is that what you said? Do you think that both are possible? Could they be?"

My response was already, in the first hour, influenced by Michael's pain and his ability to communicate it to me. I was being supportive and trying to explore his meaning. Being supportive and allowing for exploration are not contradictory; rather, both are essential and facultative.

Michael reports another dream. This is from the second piece of analytic work in which we are now engaged. He had the dream in Europe after a recent Holocaust conference. The dream thus came shortly after the dream of his son's being impaled reported at the beginning of this chapter. In the dream, his daughter, Angel, reports that his son David has been beaten with a belt by a man—a father—who has blond hair. "Poor David," she states in the dream, but without too much emotion. Michael goes on: "I rush in and find David in the shower. There are welts all over his bottom and the backs of his thighs and also red marks on his face—cheeks? I remember that Angel said something about his face. David does not seem too upset either. The dream takes place in a familiar house. It is often in my dreams. It is not the house we live in now. But I know it to be a former house of ours. Not in reality, but I know it in the dream. There is a feeling of nostalgia. We should have stayed in this house as it is in someway preferable to where we now live."

"As you know," Michael continues, "I am interested in spanking, both as a potentially erotic activity and as a form of aggressive discharge far preferable to killing. In fact, I raised this issue at the German meeting. How are punitive practices toward children and genocide related? But this dream was really strange. It was neither erotic nor was anyone disturbed, that is, but me. I felt that I had not protected David from this blond man. I used to have blond hair. My pubic hair is still blond. It was the marks on his face that really upset me. I think that he had been hit with the belt on each cheek. It was the face." I ask Michael about the face. "I can't face it," he says and begins to cry, "I know that David feels that he has a father. He does. I am even a good father, but I am so afraid that I will be 'in his face,' or fuck him over in some way."

"Perhaps that is why your blond pubic hair comes to mind," I say, "There is some confluence of body parts and different kinds of fucking or fucking over."

"Now, I think that welt means world in German," Michael continues, "It's like the blond man, me, imposes the world, or worlds, on David's backside and face. I feel so close to David. Our relationship is so different from what mine was with my father. I feel scarred by my past and, I guess, petrified that my aggression toward David will scar him.

"You know, the amazing thing again was that David was not upset, nor was Angel, although she told me about it. It's like they were saying your *Weltanschauung* has its impact. It shows and it is definitely from another house, but the sting is more in the mind of the dreamer than on the body of his son. I just thought of how Rilke uses the phrase *nicht Gesicht*, no face, in his work. I translated it because I don't know whether you speak German. No actually, because I just had the feeling that you couldn't possibly bear or understand this dream. It now feels intolerably horrible to me, the beating of David. This is really quite strange as it wasn't so horrible in the dream. As I said, no one was disturbed but me. But there is something in telling you about it, there is something between us that horrifies me or something not between us, I'm not sure which it is. It's like I have no idea how to be with you as this comes out, this confusion between loving and hurting or to put it another way this way that I have tried to eroticize my uncertainty about aggression."

"It can't have been easy for you to either bear or understand what you felt and even what happened," I reply.

"So you aren't going to check out on me if I am interested in the worlds of cheeks and can't even be sure if this is a face or a backside phenomenon. I thought 'cheek out' when I said 'check out.'" Michael sighs. "Isn't it strange, no it isn't, that this uncertainty about us emerges just now. I say that it isn't because I understand how much I needed my father's help with these matters and how unable he was to provide it."

"Why didn't you say, 'cheek out'?" I ask.

"I think because it would have sounded, no, been too exciting, invitational or something. You see that's the bind. By eroticizing this stuff I have made it tolerable, but I also am inclined when I feel safe to want to go with the erotic. I think that means to do something or to have something done to me."

"With David?" I ask.

"Maybe, but at the moment, I think, it was with, is with you."

"Now more is coming to mind. It is very embarrassing. I might like to be involved in spanking with you or in a face–butt conversation with you, be that close. Please tell me if it is unacceptable to say that here. I have never talked about this with anyone except Anne. I like my own butt and the smell there. I wonder how other men smell. It's weird. I've never smelled another man there. Of course, I have smelled Anne. She smells great. Not like me. I feel very embarrassed, bare-assed saying this. I feel an inhibition about wanting to get that close to David, just as I wouldn't want to spank him and certainly not strap him with a belt. I know that these feelings of inhibition may cover their opposites, but I feel them. It's amazing to me that I am telling you this and even going further and involving you and your butt, aroma, or belt and spanking. I apologize; it is unacceptable. I think that it's because you said that thing a few minutes ago about bearing and understanding. I hope that this is O.K."

"Why wouldn't it be?" I inquire. "Only if I were to stir up so much excitement that we both couldn't control it," is Michael's response.

Once again we are encountering the danger of excitement and its enactment. Analytic work often moves between the historical and the here-and-now, between a description of interaction among others and something going on between analysand and analyst. This sudden olfactory, aggressive, and anatomical wish directed to me requires that I shift gears and try to hear what Michael was saying on both a manifest and latent level about faces and backsides and "no faces" and about not checking or cheeking out.

Michael speaks about something else that he feels is very profound and perhaps too painful to reveal. It involves his sexual relationship with Anne. Michael and Anne make love often, very often. Usually they have intercourse every evening. This pattern has persisted throughout their almost 30 years of being together. There have been interruptions around the birth of the children and when each of the spouses has traveled, but when they are home or away together, they make love.

When Michael first began to discuss this aspect of his life in the analysis, he expressed the conviction that this activity and Anne's involvement with him sexually were the cornerstone of his capacity to continue. I inquired what his thoughts about this involved. Using his knowledge of analytic theory, specifically of the British pediatrician-turned-analyst, D. W. Winnicott (1968), who emphasized the child's need for a maternal environment in order to experience continuity of being, he explained, "I mean that this is in someway the essence of my going on being, in the Winnicottian sense. There is something of finding my essence or reestablishing that I have it in our love making." He continued by telling me that he could no longer masturbate. He tried it a few times when he has traveling but it was neither exciting nor, in fact, did it work. He became so bored that he could not make his hand stroke his penis long enough for anything to happen. For Michael this inability was particularly noteworthy because masturbation was the anlage of his sexual life with Anne. He used to masturbate every night, just as he now makes love every night. What seems so interesting, he says, is that there is no connection between these two forms of ejaculating, masturbating and coming inside of Anne.

"This doesn't explain why I can no longer do the former, but I want to make that perfectly clear. When I used to masturbate, I would have some exciting fantasy and when I would come it would feel very good, the build up, reaching the point of inevitability and then shooting. I loved it. Once Jay, my friend in childhood, said that he couldn't imagine that real sex could be any better. I disagreed with him, I was always hopeful, but I knew what he meant. We were 15 then and had gone with his parents to Colorado."

"I am having an intrusive thought now," Michael says, "It is about Jay and me. When we were much younger, we would sometimes talk together about killing a chicken. I had concocted in my head a device to behead the chicken from a distance, so that I could actually do it but not have to see it. It reminds me of that story I told you about in the *International Herald Tribune* that bothered me so much, you know the one about the guillotine. This makes me think that my masturbation, now impossible, is related to aggression or to Jay and me in some way."

"Didn't that story have to do with two men and with something that you felt was unsavory between them?" I ask. "Yes, like a sadomasochistic something with the execution of the framed guy being the ultimate sadistic act even though the top guy was going to die too." "The top guy?" I ask. "You know, as in top and bottom. That's the vernacular of male S and M homosexuality. It seems extraordinary that my thoughts turn to this. I want to get back to Anne." (I thought that one motivation for wanting to get back to Anne was the evident anxiety that this content elicited. I elected to say nothing.)

"When Anne and I make love, it is totally different. I am attending to her body and to what she feels. I love that. I come after her orgasm when she says, 'You, You.' It isn't such a strong physical sensation as I remember feeling when I was 18 and masturbating, but it is infinitely better. I drift off afterward. I feel totally safe, at peace and good. And then I have a cool feeling, which I think is like a total relaxation response or some manifestation of endorphin relief. It is quite remarkable and wonderful. As I said, it seems unrelated to the way I used to come. The odd thing is that it's still exciting, more exciting. Everything about Anne sexually is a turn-on. I don't quite understand how this all can be or what would happen if we had to stop. I don't even know why that comes to mind. The only reason I could imagine our stopping would be if something terrible happened, like if one of us were ill or, this is odd, I feel quite anxious and as though I can't even think about this."

Some of this material had been shared in the first round of the analysis, and Michael and I talked about the relationship of his sexual relationship with Anne to other aspects of their being together. Anne was there for Michael in almost every area. She seemed to admire his work, his body, his neuroses—every aspect of his being. She was, Michael said, his sunshine, and this seemed true. We explored the way in which this intense involvement seemed to flow from his relationship with his mother and that it was hypertrophied by the pain in what did or did not transpire between his father and him. As we tried to tease out the nature of the masturbatory conversation with Jay and Michael's later love for Erik and for Hans, we wondered together about the way in which this intense and gratifying lovemaking with Anne might help Michael with his homoerotic longings and even with some of the feelings that had emerged regarding his wish for physical closeness with me. Michael seemed open in his consideration of all these ingredients of what he called "the determinants of this remarkable adaptation." That there was not only a homoerotic but also a sadistic-aggressive component beneath the defensive invocation of the lovemaking seemed clear.

During the first phase of the analysis he had told me about the issue of birth control and their decision to use an IUD. Anne got urinary tract infections when they used a diaphragm, and he had always had trouble with rubbers. What was the trouble? Well, it seemed that there was this strange worry that he would lose his erection in the time that it took to put a rubber on. They hadn't really worked on this very much because Anne had gotten this thing put in. It worked really well if you didn't think about the mechanism of action except that sometimes the string poked him. Anne's obstetrician had said that he must have a really sensitive penis if he felt it, and the doctor had to cut the string extra short.

Michael was still quite interested in this phenomenon of fear of losing his erection, and now he surprised himself with the thought that this was one advantage of masturbating, that one did not have to worry about this happening. "I think that I worry about something having to do with my father at those moments. He is the most unwelcome visitor when Anne and I are together. I can't say how he would join us if I were putting on a rubber, but that's what I think I don't want to have happen. I just had a thought that seems improbable to me, maybe that is why I can't masturbate anymore. Having a man's hands on my penis, including mine, arouses my homosexual anxiety, but I think I mean—that means—having my father right there. Something about this seems too intellectual; that seems like a strange word too. Well, anyway, when Anne touches me, its clear that her hands are not a man's hand."

"A man's hand," I repeat.

"Yes, like letting the guillotine blade fall. No, releasing it. No, causing it to descend and behead the victim," Michael says, "This is about that, although I am inclined to say that it couldn't be, about the difference between an execution, totally unwarranted at the hands of a sadistic man, and feeling sheltered, safe, loving. You know my father was not really a sadistic executioner. He was a cultured, helping man."

"That may not be how it felt to you when he glared or thundered," I respond.

"It's eerie, David used to call him Grandpa Thunderbolt," Michael says and begins to cry. I am thinking of the relationship between these thoughts and what Michael has told me of sometimes thinking about Hans or Erik when he is making love with Anne. A man could be with him in a threatening and sadistic way or in a loving and holding way. Were the thoughts about my aroma connected to this need for a man? Would my smell reveal danger or safety? Elicit excitement or portend dread? In such a primal-limbic way of taking in information about the other, could one tell what the other actually was and differentiate a good-enough father from a very dangerous one? I thought of how rough-and-tumble play between fathers and children allows for close enough contact so that the scent of the father in action is known to his son or daughter.

Let us pause for a moment to take in what has happened. Michael had a dream about his son's being beaten and having welts on both his face and bottom. In talking about the dream, he has become concerned about my reaction in quite a vivid way, so vivid that, almost as a way of getting away from the moment, he switches to talking about his wife and their lovemaking. But no sooner is he on that track than thoughts of masturbation and his childhood friend Jay come to mind. And from here, as he zigs back to his wife once more, a new worry emerges, that a man's hand, even his own, would bring his father into the bedroom—a possibility that evokes some unclear mixture of dread, plainly, and also excitement.

This is how matters sometimes go in analysis. Michael is a very talented analysand, if one may put it that way. He is pursuing the analytic task, exploring his own thoughts and associations. Yet, as he does so, there are odd, disconcerting juxtapositions in the inscape. More, there is a threat that something may become actual in the analysis between him and me, though it is not quite clear what that might be.

As Michael zig-zags through the inscape, I try to follow, each step of the way consulting my own associations, but also, with caution, my store of suppositions. In this instance, associations and suppositions are converging toward the figure of the father in my mind. Why this is so may not be clear at the moment. Partially it is because issues pertaining to the father are a recurrent theme in the work with Michael. Michael's material is redolent of work with other patients, children and adults, where issues pertaining to the father were likewise prominent, but also reminiscent of observations made outside analysis on children whose relations with their fathers failed them in some way. Much of the rest of this book is taken up with spelling out these parallels and echoes. Here let us say only that they enter my mind as I attempt to follow. But let us also be clear that their presence as concepts does not fill the gaps in Michael's inscape as he has presented it so far. As of yet, the matter remains an enigma. It is not clear what aspects of the usual father–son bond, perhaps longed for and perhaps also feared, are being invoked, assuming that the father–son bond is indeed what is at stake. Nor is it clear which aspects of the actual relationship between Michael and his father are critical here. Nor is it clear which parts of each wing of possibility, the actual father or the imagined one, may be potentially informing and shaping, for better or worse, the analytic relationship.

Michael presents another dream: "I was sitting during my office hours with Hans. Anne was with me, I don't know why. It went on for a while, and then Hans started to say something disturbing, something like that he was upset about our relationship. I wanted to say something back that seemed just right, but I noticed that I was naked and needed to get dressed. Then it seemed that I was stuck in my undershirt and needed to get out of it in order to put on a tee shirt and shorts. It all seems very strange. I haven't seen Hans for some time, you know. He is on the West Coast now, but what he was saying in the dream is just what he said when he and I parted; I almost said 'broke up.' God, was I broken up about that. His leaving and deciding to study with J_____ was one of the hardest things that ever happened to me."

"I know," I reply, "You thought that you had wrecked it again."

"He writes to me regularly," Michael says, "And I enjoy getting his letters a lot, but I have to keep myself from going where I would like to go with him. It feels so strange and I think that no one really knows about it except you and Anne."

"She was in the dream," I note.

"Yes, that was strange. She was in my office. We have been having an especially exciting time in bed lately. I seem to be even more interested in her breasts than usual, and of course she loves it."

"You said something about a chest or the upper part of the body."

"I did? I don't remember."

"Oh, yes, it was that you were stuck in your undershirt."

"This is so interesting. Anne has been wearing an undershirt to bed instead of a nighty. It's been fun to take it off, and last night she got sort of stuck in it."

"Just like in the dream."

"So, do you think that this is another of these dreams in which sex leads to something else. I just had the thought that my sexualizing seems to lead to very interesting things here, with you. I mean that we can share it. I feel embarrassed, but I think that I am saying that we can tolerate this aspect of my mental life together, but of course I can hear that Hans and me could also be you and me and that I seem to be Anne as well as me in the dream, which gives me still another way of being with you, right?"

In these few dreams and in his associations, it is clear that Michael tackles many things as he tries to unravel what is going on inside of him. That what is inside is constantly impinging on the outside and his interactive existence is evident. Moreover, that he has been tackled by many things is also apparent. Together, he and I are careening down the football field, mostly as teammates, comrades in arms; but sometimes the action shifts so that it is between us as well as a coordinated effort conducted by both of us. Analysis is this way, works this way, and helps this way. Michael needs someone really to be there as well as to think with him about where he has been and what he has made of his experience, his pain, and his progenitors.

As I have portrayed selected aspects of Michael's inscape in these several excerpts from our work together, I have not shared very much of what was happening within me. This is always a critical part of the analytic experience, differentially conceptualized and weighted by differing analytic schools, but always a relevant factor. The very act of listening, not to mention accompanying, is contoured by the who-with-whom dimension of the analytic Spielraum. As I tell you more about our work together, Michael's with me, I shall share more of what is touched within me, how I listen, what I understand of the overlap and the lack of overlap between us, and how each of us factors these variables into the experience.

Sometimes these areas converge confusingly and dramatically; sometimes they diverge with corresponding amplitude and intensity. For Michael and me, the historical and biographical overlap was often remarkable although our individual domains of personal meaning were frequently quite disparate.

In general, I propose that the way in which analyst and analysand are together, including what is felt by each in response to the other, not only affects significantly what happens or does not happen in the analysis, but also is directly related to developmental processes that the analytic experience may seek to reproduce. Clearly, the analyst is not the same with each analysand, and the nature of the mix—some might call it match—is a powerful factor in what is elicited and how it is understood. Here, too, there are parallels with the developmental process. How these parallels relate in manifold ways to a child's actual experiences of father, and of mother, and of mother and father together—that is the subject of this book.

FATHER HUNGER AND CHILDREN'S DREAMS

Who is riding so late through dark and wind?
It is the father with his child.
He has the boy snug in his arms
He holds him safely; he keeps him warm.

"My son, why are you scared and hiding your face?"
"Father—can't you see the Erlking, the Erlking
with crown and robe?"
"My son, it is a wisp of cloud."

"You, darling child, come, go with me!
I will play lovely games with you.
There are heaps of bright flowers on the shore,
my mother has lots of golden clothes."

"Father, father, can't you hear what the Erlking
whispers and promises me?"
"Hush, don't fret, my son, it is the wind
rustling in the dry leaves."

"Pretty boy, will you come with me?
My daughters shall look after you nicely,
Every night they will dance the round
And will rock and dance and sing you to sleep."

"Oh, father, oh father, can't you see the Erlking's
daughters over there at that dismal place?"
"My son, my son, I can see it plain;
it is the old willows that gleam all gray."

"I love you, your beautiful shape excites me,
and if you won't come willingly, I will use force."
"Father, father, now he's taking hold of me!
He has hurt me, the Erlking has!"

The father is terrified, he rides fast,
he holds the groaning child in his arms
it is all he can do to reach the farm;
in his arms the child was dead.

—Goethe, "Erlkonig"

IN MICHAEL'S INSTANCE WE HAD TWO DREAMS separated by 17 years. Both dreams featured a boy in desperate circumstances, facing violence, needing rescue. In neither dream did a rescuer appear. I have nominated the father as the missing rescuer—in Michael's dreams, and in the dreams of other adults like him, suffering in one way or another from *father hunger*.

I first came to think this way, about father hunger, when I was treating a group of small boys who were faced with nightmares that also featured terrible threats of violence. For these boys, the precipitants for the nightmares seemed clearly to entail the recent loss of their fathers. Accordingly, we are about to move quite a way from Michael. His father was physically present and abusive. His father's "absence" was an emotional one, compounded by what he brought to the scene when he actually interacted with his son. Yet, I contend, we can learn something from these boys and from their nightmares and from their other concerns about beatings and bodies that can help us understand something about Michael's predicament.

Here I draw on my experience working as a child psychiatrist in a hospital setting and as a consultant to a suburban school system. My sample involved over 70 families from the hospital setting where parents were divorced or divorcing and over 100 families in similar straits in the school setting. In both settings, problems of behavior and adaptation appeared to me to reflect the absence of paternal involvement and participation as this affected both children and mothers. I was struck, among other things, by how this lack impinged on the little boys' sense of their own aggression. Without a father to help him integrate and modulate it, a boy's aggression typically appeared as a foreign force in his dreams and fantasies. I came to postulate that the father's careful use of his own aggression as a part of his paternal functioning constituted an opportunity for the consolidation of the boy's masculine sense of self and a beginning basis for his own management of drive and fantasy.

Various symptomatologies announce the presence of father hunger. In young children, the presence of nightmares and night terrorlike phenomena is pathognomonic. One sometimes sees in older children other symptom pictures, including both hypertrophied attempts to manifest and manage aggression and an inner deadness resulting from defeat. I begin this chapter with Goethe's poem *Erlkönig* to highlight the fact that underneath all these phenomena a child desperately seeks help from his father. Absent nutritive experience with the actual father, restitutive fantasies and overwhelming hunger are likely to become a prominent feature of a boy's evolving sense of self. Father hunger is also seen in girls, though it may take a different form.

GARY

Gary was 18 months old when his mother brought him to the clinic. She explained that he had awakened every night for the past week, screaming as if something were after him. Gary and his mother had been sharing a bed since the departure of his father one month earlier. The mother therefore observed each episode in its entirety. "Gary wakes suddenly," she reported. "He seems to jump off the bed. He screams uncontrollably, sometimes for 20 minutes to an hour. There is a look of fear in his eyes. He cannot be reached."

The mother's pregnancy and early developmental history of this little boy were entirely within normal limits. He was the first child of a 23-year-old mother and a 25-year-old father. The three months preceding the father's departure had been most tumultuous and involved considerable affective display in the household. When Gary's father shouted at his mother, the little boy would cover his ears or begin to cry. There had been no contact between Gary and his father in the intervening month. As Gary's mother was finishing her description, she suddenly looked quite angry and said, "Oh, I forgot to mention that when Gary wakes up and starts screaming, he calls for his daddy. I don't know whether that should make me angry or make me sad."

Gary was a tall, blond, attractive boy who separated easily from his mother and ran smilingly into the playroom. He immediately got into my lap. Staying in constant physical contact with me, he began to play with some clay. He rolled it into long, loglike pieces and then broke them into smaller parts. He laughed, seemingly with pleasure. I introduced a puppet into the play who picked up one of the pieces. The puppet could be taken for an adult male—a daddy perhaps. Gary looked very frightened and said, "Daddy hurt. Daddy hurt." I thought that Gary was indicating that the daddy was hurt, and I said, "What is the matter?" There was no response. Then I asked, "Who can help?" To this Gary brightened and said, "Daddy help Gary—please." He hugged me hard at this point. At a later time, a little boy puppet was sleeping in the same bed with his mommy. Suddenly, he jumped up. I got out a pencil, called it a dream-machine, and put it on the little boy puppet's head. "What's happening?" I said, "Let's see if we can see what is happening to him." Gary peered through the pencil dream-machine and then looked very frightened. "Scare," he said. "Scare me—Daddy hurt. Quick get Daddy—Daddy help Gary." I had the mommy puppet get up and try to comfort the little boy puppet. "No, no," shrieked Gary, looking very afraid. "Daddy hurt. Get Daddy." I then introduced the adult man puppet. Gary put him next to the little boy. Then he had the man put the little boy in a separate bed and return to his wife's bed. "All better now," Gary said happily.

In real life, Gary's sleep disturbance lasted for about one month. His father did not come back and make it all better. Gary and I met twice a week during this period, at the end of which Gary's affection for me began to wane. The play seemed very similar in our eight meetings. Our work was interrupted when Gary's mother decided to move back to the city she came from. She wrote me a note saying that she would look for a new daddy for her son and for herself.

IRA

Ira was 28 months old when his mother, a physician, brought him to the clinic. He was the youngest of three children. Four months earlier, his father, also a physician, had announced that he was in love with a female colleague and moved out of the home. Both parents were "working on the situation" in couples' treatment, and Ira saw his father on weekends. Ira's previous development had been unremarkable. Because both parents worked, however, he had been cared for by a devoted housekeeper from the time he was three months old until the present. His two older brothers, almost five and almost seven years old, were functioning quite well. The mother attributed the continuing smooth functioning of the family to the steadying influence of the housekeeper, who accompanied them to the clinic.

The chief complaint was that Ira had been awakening every night for the past two weeks, screaming and tearful. He had his own room and would come darting out as though being chased. Neither the mother nor the housekeeper could comfort him at these times, and the situation was deteriorating rapidly. Ira had begun to refuse to go to bed and for the previous three nights had not fallen asleep until well after midnight. On the weekend following his first symptomatic week, Ira had been with his father. He had awakened screaming as usual. His father had come to him, held the screaming child, and said, "It's a dream, Ira. Do not be afraid." The little boy had sobbed, "Daddy, Daddy," and clung to his father with all his might. "They are after me. Please don't let them hurt me," he cried. The following week, in his mother's home, the nightmares continued. "Daddy said it's a dream," the little boy would say before going to sleep, as if to give himself courage. When he awoke in the night, he would scream for his father and could not be comforted by his mother. The housekeeper informed me that she had spoken to the boy's father and told him he needed to come home; if not for his wife's sake, then he must for his son's.

Ira was a very tired-looking boy with big, sad eyes. He separated from his mother and babysitter with great ease, taking my hand and saying, "You will help me. Are you a daddy?" We began to play, and before long a scenario evolved with a little boy puppet. I took out my pen, called it a dream-machine, and placed it on the little boy puppet's head, saying, "Let's look into his head and see if we can see what he is dreaming." Ira said, "This little boy is having a bad dream. I have them, too. He is dreaming Big Bird. He eats the boy's head. The boy is scared." "What can we do to help the boy?" I asked. "Get the daddy," Ira cried. The little boy was literally in tears. "Why the daddy? How can he help?" I asked. "He is like the boy. He can because he knows the boy. He is not a mommy," Ira cried.

Ira's father did come back, and his nightmares abated. I continued to see Ira in psychotherapy. He is greatly concerned about a number of Big Bird's blatantly aggressive proclivities and continues to employ phobic displacement as his principle defensive maneuver. He is not, however, seriously symptomatic.

Ira's parents had been married for 10 years. His mother appeared to be a sad but competent woman who felt that her husband was "sowing his wild oats." They had met and married in medical school, and he had "never really had a chance to fool around." Ira's father seemed to fit the part. He was delighted initially with his new liaison and the fact that the new lady in his life was 10 years his junior and a beautiful blonde. Ira's daddy, however, was disturbed by the effect his escapade had had on his youngest son. When he returned to the family, he also embarked on psychoanalysis. The parents had not been able to serve as totally adequate monitors and receptacles for each other's sexual and aggressive drives. Yet it must be said that neither was severely disordered and the children had not been exposed to unbridled passion or other excessive stimulation.

MARVIN

When Marvin's parents separated, he, too, developed a syndrome resembling night terrors. He would awaken screaming each night. He said he was being pursued by a dog that would bark and then bite him. In happier times, Marvin and his father had played a "doggie" game. The father would get down on all fours, begin barking ferociously, and then chase the little boy. The child would flee amidst squeals and howls of what was thought to be mock terror. Sometimes, the roles were reversed and Marvin would attack, bark, and bite.

Marvin's mother did not seek assistance when her son's sleep was initially disturbed. She concluded to her satisfaction that Marvin's symptoms were a response to her husband's departure. When three weeks later, however, Marvin, who was then 22 months old, developed a daytime phobia of dogs, his mother decided that professional assistance was indicated. Marvin became afraid of Baba, his word for dog, and would shake with terror whenever a dog or Baba was mentioned. He refused to attend his nursery school and grew ever more frightened and restricted. His previous history was more complicated than that of any of the other boys in the treatment group; he had a chronic mental illness, and his mother had a psychiatric illness.

Initially, Marvin was wary of me, as was his mother; but by the second interview both had become very attached and Marvin began to refer to me as Bubu, a name that to my ears was quite similar to Baba. At this time, the little boy's language was quite impaired and he said very little. Whereas he previously had been able to leave his mother easily, both he and she now considered this an impossibility to a degree that far exceeded any such phenomena observable in normal rapproachment. Marvin presented a full-scale phobia. His entire day revolved around the avoidance of Baba. Initially, the play was comparably monothematic. Baba was a merciless creature who attacked, and attacked, and attacked. Over time (a 10-month period), a modification occurred: Baba could be controlled by Bubu. Bubu originally and for a long time stood for me but ultimately became a part of Boy-Boy. Marvin said that Boy-Boy needed to have Bubu control Baba in order not to be afraid of Baba. Bubu could become part of Boy-Boy because they were *alike*—not the same, but alike. Eventually, we learned that Baba was a part of Boy-Boy, too. At the end of the treatment, Marvin, then four years old, said that Boy-Boy should now be called Bart. Bart was big and well and he contained Boy-Boy (sometimes now called Bye-Bye), Baba (sometimes called Angry or Mad), and Bubu (frequently called You-You).

Development affects mental process and necessarily the evolution of symptomatology. Older children respond to father hunger with mechanisms not available to their younger confreres. Thus, where previously phobic defenses predominated, we now encounter the emergence of identification, hypertrophied caricaturing, and the inevitable appearance of affective imbalance. In children manifesting father hunger this may initially present as a manic defense but almost always assumes increasingly depressive coloring.

JOEY

Joey was almost five years old (58 months) when his parents separated. His younger brother, Anthony, was three years old (36 months). Joey's mother contacted me with the chief complaint that her son was completely uncontrollable. "He hits and hurts Anthony at every opportunity," she explained. "He always says that Anthony needs to be spanked and punished. I tell you, he is downright strap-happy."

Joey's previous developmental history was unremarkable. A product of a planned pregnancy, he was born when his mother was 27 and his father 31 years old. He was described as an active, outgoing child by both parents and had not been symptomatic in any way according to his history. His response to Anthony's birth when he was 18 months old had been to become more clinging and to want a baby bottle like his brother's; however, this lasted only a short time and then he wanted to be a big boy and use the "toidy" (toilet) just like his dad did, according to his mother. Joey had gone to preschool from the age of two and half years and was now in a nursery school setting. Recent reports from the school suggested that Joey's anger and "aggression" were interfering with the smooth functioning of the classroom. One mother had angrily protested when Joey hit her son quite hard with a table-tennislike paddle, proclaiming, "He needs a good spanking right here and now."

The parents were involved in a bitter custody fight when I saw Joey, and they could barely tolerate each other's presence. Neither acknowledged the physical violence in their relationship with each other, but they stated that they had occasionally spanked both Joey and Anthony for misbehavior.

Joey separated easily from his mother and joined me in the playroom. He told me he liked to draw and produced a picture of a man. The man had very large hands, which I inquired about. "Oh, he needs them to spank with," Joey told me. "How come?" I asked. "A boy needs his dad for that. A mom won't do. I spank Anthony. He likes me to do it because our dad isn't around. I'm like my dad."

Before our next meeting, Joey's mother told me that Joey was continuously ordering her around. "He says, 'Do this, do that.' I find it maddening. He is worse than Vittorio [her husband] ever was. Boy, is he going to give some woman a hard time some day." Joey and I played in the dollhouse that day, and Joey played out a family drama in which the father spanked everyone in sight and ordered everyone around. "They like it," Joey maintained. I took the roles of the subservient members of the household and suggested that each might have experienced resentment about being beaten and regimented. "Oh, no," said Joey. "Well, maybe the mother doesn't like it and will get divorced; but the little boy needs it. Otherwise, who knows what might happen?" This question interested me, so I tried to find out what might happen without the strict punitive control. "He could hurt someone," Joey said softly. "He could hurt the mommy or maybe the daddy. Oh, no, not the daddy. The daddy would whip him." With that comment, the anxiety that had briefly stirred in him seemed to quiet.

In another meeting, the little boy in the doll family was going to sleep. I produced my dream machine so that Joey and I could investigate what he was dreaming. The boy was dreaming of a volcano, "like on television," Joey told me. He was very close to it and wished someone had made him stay further away. A big fireman appeared. He was very angry with the boy for going so close to the fire. "I will punish you," he said. Joey's voice showed great excitement. "No, no," the boy said, "I have a father." "Is it a happy dream?" I inquired. "Yes," said Joey, "That boy has a father."

Over the next several months, Joey's behavior toward Anthony, toward his mother, and in nursery school continued to be hyperaggressive. In the play, the daddy spanked and spanked, and the little boy felt warmed and safe. He would not dare get out of line, Joey said. Then the inevitable occurred in the play. The mommy and daddy separated. The little boy was frantic. He was terrified that the fireman of the dream would reappear or not appear. He was very naughty with his mother, but she did not know what to do. Finally, a new baby appeared in the doll family, and the little boy started spanking him. According to Joey, he felt better now because someone was keeping things in line. "A boy needs someone around to do the spanking. The big brother can do that. He has the biggest hands," Joey reported.

Joey's psychotherapy was prolonged and involved his anger and despair at losing his father and his understanding that controlling himself did not necessarily mean tormenting Anthony. By the time he entered kindergarten, he was no longer a menace at school; it took another year of work, however, before he stopped punishing Anthony. "I still think about spanking, though," he told me, "especially before I go to sleep at night. It gives me a good feeling to think about it."

Joey's parents, Angela and Vittorio, were quite different from Ira's parents and from each other. Their marriage had been shaky for some time. Each accused the other of terrible transgression, and each felt compelled in some way to act out those accusations. Both parents had trouble with impulse control but tended to act out outside of the family rather than inside it. Angela went into psychotherapy during the time I was seeing Joey. Her therapist saw her as a primitive hysteric whose caretaking abilities were only partially intact. She could nurture but had grave difficulties with limit setting. Vittorio was also seen by a therapist. He, too, could be very giving to the children, although some of this was in the service of winning the children to his side. He was the product of a restrictive, extremely religious family, and he felt very uncomfortable with his sexuality. He frequently visited prostitutes and felt that only they should be "fucked." His therapy focused on the relationship of his feelings about sex to his own marital situation and the notion of excluding marital relations from the marriage. Both parents did well in treatment. Both decided to seek new adult partners.

BRENDA

Brenda was six and half years (78 months) old when she first came to my attention. I had been asked by her first-grade teacher to consult with regard to this "obviously bright" girl who seemed to have slowed down and become uninterested in the classroom. On the day of my visit she was sitting in her seat and playing with her long blond hair, a sad, distant expression on her face. She looked very tired. When we met together after class, she shook hands with me quite mechanically and then looked away. I said that she looked tired; she yawned and said she didn't sleep very well. She had terrible dreams. I wondered what she dreamed about and she just looked away. I asked her what she would like to do. "Not much anymore," she replied. I picked up on the "anymore" and asked her if it used to be different. "Yes," said Brenda, "when we were all together as a family." Then very quickly she blurted out that Mommy and Daddy didn't love each other anymore and were divorced. "My dad's gone," she said. I learned that they had been apart for almost a year.

Brenda then started talking about school. It just did not seem interesting to her. I took out a book and asked her if she would like to read. She shook her head and then gave me the book. "You read," she said. I noticed that she began to play with her hair again and looked off into the distance. As I read to Brenda, she nestled her body against mine and seemed to doze off. After a few moments I stopped reading and she opened her eyes. "You must be very tired," I said. She agreed.

At our next meeting, Brenda began playing in the dollhouse. I noticed that she kept placing the little girl doll all by itself. I wondered why this happened. "That's the way it is," Brenda replied. As a scenario developed, the daddy had to go to work. The little girl wanted him to stay home but he wouldn't. "Who cares what she wants. Daddies just go away," Brenda had the little girl say. "Now the mommy and the daughter can be together," I suggested. Brenda looked at me quizzically. "No," she said. "The mommy is too busy. Besides, she doesn't want to be with the girl; she wants to be with Daddy, but she can't. He doesn't love her anymore." She halted a minute and then said, "I mean he has to go to work."

In another session, Brenda put the little girl doll to bed. "Who will read her a bedtime story?" I inqured. Brenda looked blank, then smiled a little and said, "Maybe the daddy, but he's not there; or perhaps you, you read stories." Soon the little girl doll was asleep and I got out my dream-machine, held it up to the doll's head, and asked Brenda to look through it and describe what she saw the little girl dreaming. Brenda looked up and said, "Let's do something else. Will you read to me?" I said yes and read, this time from Sendak's (1963) *Where the Wild Things Are*. Brenda did not drift off as before, but listened intently. At the end of our time, she gave me a little smile.

At our next meeting, she again put the little girl to bed. I again offered her the dream-machine, and she looked in. "They are all sick," she said, "the whole family. Oh, the daddy just died. He's gone.

Now the mommy. Poor little girl, she died, too."

"You mean the little girl is dreaming the whole family is dying? She is even dying herself?"

"Yes," said Brenda.

"But what kind of disease is it? Why are they dying? What has happened? Who caused it?"

"She did," said Brenda, "Now will you read? Without the daddy being there, she did. She killed them all. Please read to me again."

As she left my office that day, Brenda said, "I am like the little girl, not like Max [of the Sendak story]. At night, I die, too."

Following this session, I met with Brenda's mother and strongly urged that she make arrangements for Brenda to continue psychotherapy. Her mother told me that Brenda had already talked about meeting with me at school, that I had read to her, and that we had talked about sleeping and dreams. The mother confessed to me that she had been very worried about Brenda, who seemed slowed down and not there. "It's not surprising, though," said the mother. "I've been so upset and so busy since the divorce that I haven't had any time for her. Since Brad [her husband] left, I have been afraid to do anything, really anything. Why last night Brenda asked me if I would read to her before she went to bed, and I realized that I haven't done that for over two years."

Susan, Brenda's mother, was 28 at the time I saw her daughter. She was clearly depressed. She was in her sixth year of graduate study: "A project as old as Brenda," she told me. She had been in psychotherapy for a year but could not yet overcome or integrate what had happened to her marriage. Her husband had received his doctorate five years earlier and was teaching at another institution. According to Susan, their marriage had been good until she got her master's degree, which was when Brenda was four years old; since then, however, it had just not worked. "I couldn't handle everything," she said, "I couldn't sort out my priorities. I lost Brad; now I feel as if I have lost Brenda too." Susan's therapist told me that themes of loss and worthlessness and worries about "having enough to manage" had plagued this woman for many years. Brenda's father came to see me only twice. He was an attractive, composed man who discussed the difficulty of putting a bad marriage behind him without abandoning his daughter too. "I found someone new," he said. "We can give to each other and take from each other. Susan and I used to be able to do that. Then we couldn't. Now that I have someone new, I hope I can be a better father to Brenda. Poor Susan, however, will have to fend for herself."

DISCUSSION

The cases presented here are drawn from 170 similar ones. In each case, the separation and disunion of what was previously closely united (Webster's definition of divorce) resulted in demonstrable symptomatology and suffering on the part of the involved children. As previously mentioned, this sampling is particularly noteworthy in that in the two younger groupings (i.e., 18 to 28 months of age and 36 to 60 months of age) the vast majority of children seen were male. In the second grouping all but two were boys. My third grouping of children, between 60 and 84 months of age, consisted of approximately half boys and half girls.

Children react to loss in many ways. Other investigators (Wallerstein and Kelly, 1960; Tessman, 1978; Hetherington, 1979) have demonstrated a number of behavioral changes of varying duration. By focusing on the child's affect, fantasy, play, and dreams, I hoped to be able to learn something of how divorce and father loss felt to the child and what the intrapsychic ramifications of such an experience might be. Ira's case is more or less typical of the first age group (Herzog, 1978). In this age group, children develop nightmares, and their play reveals a precocious use of phobic processes. I understand the Big Bird dream and comparable material from other children to be manifestations of displaced aggression. There are, of course, other meanings as well. The absence of the father was perceived simultaneously as the child's own doing and as depriving him of necessary protection. The father's return was considered a treatment of choice.

Joey's case is drawn from the second age group. Here again, the drive that is experienced as unleashed, frightening, and out of control is the aggressive drive. The need for a fireman is most compelling. That the fires to be quenched are both libidinal and aggressive seems more probable with Joey than with Ira. The spanking motive appears to be progressing toward an eroticized masturbatory status, and the possibility of a negative oedipal resolution seems apparent. There is also an inability to see the father as both nurturing and disciplining (cf. Mussen and Distler, 1960, who reported that masculine boys have fathers who are both nurturing and disciplining). It seems that Joey is employing a manic defense and splitting, a kind of hyperidentification with the aggressor. To be the limit setter in a kind of grotesque caricature of male discipline emerges as a common way of dealing with the loss of a father and the disruption of what previously was experienced as intact. Tooley (1976) and others have commented on this phenomenon, which I think is well known to all who work with preschoolers who come from father-absent families.

Brenda manifested all the symptoms of childhood depression. Here, too, we see a mixture of libidinal longings and aggressive concerns. Yet, from my viewpoint, it is the aggressive fantasies and fixations that are pathogenic. Brenda's aggression is turned against herself. She is the cause of the family disease and is struck down by it. The child in her play dies in her dream as well. I have called this typical disturbance the *Erlkönig* syndrome, after Goethe's poem immortalized in a song by Shubert. The poem tells of a little boy pursued by a monster, the Erlking, or elf king. The exact Danish etymology of the word suggests old woman or menacing woman as the root. The little boy begs his father for help—to be saved from the Erlking. The father cannot perceive the threat and therefore cannot comply. In the end, the boy lies dead in his father's arms, a victim of the Erlking—or, according this book's themes, a victim of his own aggression. In my experience, as well as that of others (Lucas, 1977), such a finding is pathognomonic of childhood depression. Other researchers as well as I have also found the incidence of childhood depression to be quite substantial among latency-aged children of both sexes whose parents are divorced.

What I am suggesting here is that the modulation of aggressive drive and fantasy is a leading concern, perhaps an omnipresent one, in children of divorce. It appears that the material presented by the children substantiates this formulation in a number of ways. The separation of what was previously united seriously discombobulates the inner world of the developing child: this circumstance alone might produce extreme distress. In each case, however, the father, through his absence, is linked in the child's mind with the emergence of aggressive material, and his return is seen as being restitutive. That mothers are often bereft and thoroughly overtaxed in the postdivorce situation must clearly be critically important. It is noteworthy, however, that even in situations where the mother is competent and proficient and is ostensibly pleased by the dissolution of the marriage, one finds the symptomology and material similar to that described in the three cases.

Why the great predominance of boys in the first two groupings? The answer may well lie in a number of contributing areas. Boys probably have a greater aggressive endowment from birth (Maccoby, 1996) and a greater subsequent need for mentorship in its management. Every study of postdivorce adjustment acknowledges the greater morbidity in preschool-aged boys. "I'm hot," a four-year-old said to me, "Daddy's hot, too. That's how we guys are." This sentiment has been voiced in more or less direct form by many boys I have seen. The recognition of sameness with the father, the need to manage a mutual concern, and the need to be shown how is common. I have come to consider this need to be "shown how" a hallmark of the preoedipal boy's relationship with his father. Of course, girls need their fathers too. It may be, however, that either they need them more when they reach oedipal age or they can make out better without them before that time. Certainly much cognitive research supports this interpretation (see, e.g., Inhelder and Piaget, 1958), as does Abelin's postulation of earlier generational triangulation in girls and a critical need by them for their fathers in the oedipal period.

The material presented has briefly covered the character structure, marital relationship, and intrapsychic organization of the parents. Some attempt has been made to convey a "flavor" of who they are. Clearly, divorce seldom occurs in a smoothly functioning, mutually satisfying marriage. All the marital relationships studied had by definition serious, even irreconcilable failings. Therefore, because the adult–adult interaction was impaired, the adult–child interaction was probably also affected. Nevertheless, the most compelling finding is that similar concerns and pain occurred, albeit in different guises, in a large number of the children, even though the parental personalities, conflicts, and modes of separation and divorce were quite diverse. To paraphrase Tolstoy, unhappy families may be very different, but certain kinds of effects of divorce and father loss may be the same.

Children without fathers suffer father hunger, an affective state of considerable tenacity and force. The children studied in this chapter all appear to evince father hunger. They feel that they lack something they vitally need. Mothers and others can mediate the effects of actual father absence or psychological father absence. When the father is absent but revered (idealized or presented as an important and valued family member), as in times of war or following death, the resulting state of father hunger seems less pronounced.

The ambivalence, hurt, and hatred characteristic of divorce seem to maximize for the child the felt absence of a masculine parent and to exacerbate father hunger. There is currently an epidemic of divorce and with it, sadly, an epidemic of father hunger. It is far from clear what the long-term ramifications of this state of affairs will be.

4 | MICHAEL: The Strange Nurse Dream

"I HAD A DREAM LAST NIGHT WHICH FEELS quite important. I want to tell you about it," Michael (whom we met earlier) begins the hour with emphasis and excitement. "I had gone to see Dr. L, but it was about some kind of abnormal, pigmented growth on my face. I guess that means that he was a dermatologist or facial surgeon, I thought of saying 'face doctor.' He or we thought that it was a good idea to remove it even though, I think, he said that it was not malignant. I don't think that I consulted with anyone else but went right to see this woman. She was a nurse. She said that she was from Latvia or Lithuania when I asked about her accent. She also told me that she had a sister living in some other country and that Geneva was like their shared city. This had something to do with my bringing up Switzerland, but I don't know what." Michael and I have often talked of his verdant and idyllic image of Switzerland as a place of forested hills and lovely rivers.

Michael's father had returned from an extended absence when Michael was two years old and upon his return became quite psychotic. In this state, he was abusive both to his wife and to his son. These assaults reached egregious proportions and included throwing Michael against a wall and fracturing a number of his bones, among them his hip and his collarbone. His mother was also injured in some of these outbursts, although Michael remembers trying valiantly to protect her. The period when his father was away involved his discovering and confirming the family's Holocaust losses. His decompensation followed on these discoveries, although its exact causes were unknown to Michael or his mother, and the father would not seek psychiatric care. A fresh injury that Michael sustained working out at the gym has reawakened the memories of earlier injury and its circumstance at a deep and profoundly painful level, which, however, he cannot entirely consciously access. A partial anesthesia still prevails. In the session, he continues with the dream.

"She looked very strange. Especially her hair, it was blonde and layered, maybe a wig. I almost said *perücke*, the German word for wig. I was not actually certain that she was female. She began to inject the side of my face with anaesthetic, Novocaine, I guess. I noticed that she was injecting very close to the eye. Then this man, actually more like a boy, entered the room. I recognized him immediately. It was Rick; I've told you about him. [Rick is a student.] He was to be the surgeon. I walked with him to another room. It was a little difficult to walk, maybe because of the anesthesia. I couldn't exactly figure out why that would be. We entered the room, and Rick began his preparations. He was exactly as he is in real life. Unrelated, autistic. I thought, 'This is inappropriate. I am not going to let my student, who is autistic, perform surgery on my face. There are boundary issues. This is an abuse of the transference.' I left the room with difficulty. Then I tried to find my way back to the main office. This was enormously hard. Eventually, I got there and I told someone, a person whom I did not recognize, that I needed to stop the procedure. I had trouble speaking, but I think I was successful. Then the phone rang and I awakened."

Michael finished telling me the dream and then began: "The most striking person in the dream was the nurse, but I think that this is more about how much I went through with my shoulder. That's why Dr. L is here. [Dr. L treated Michael for his recent shoulder injury at the gym.] I now feel that the climactic part of this analytic work has been triggered by what I did to myself in the gym and why. Remembering what actually happened with my father is, as you have said, an essential ingredient of stopping or at least modifying these endless diatribes by him within me."

"Yes," I said, "You mentioned that you think that the nurse was very striking." My comment was intended to echo Michael's word, which evoked his father and the remembrances to which he had just referred—his father's striking him and his beating on himself in his unremitting working out at the gym. In fact, he was injuring himself;

so strenuous were his workouts that I, as his analyst, thought I should be suggesting that he modify his gym practice and that we should consider its severity to be a symptom. Finally, it took the evidence provided by an MRI to persuade him that he was injuring himself; the same MRI documented the residual damage from his childhood injuries.

We discussed further the nurse's ambiguous gender and accent and place of origin. Michael's thoughts turned to his father, one who struck, one who injected him often with antibiotics into his posterior. "I think I got more shots than most boys," he said.

This recollection led to his thinking about the face as here representing the buttocks and was followed by a series of thoughts about his interest in spanking and bottoms. "You know, I just thought of something strange," Michael went on, "When my dad used to give me a shot, I wouldn't feel it. It was as if I anesthetized my butt. I think that this is connected to not being able to walk so well after she injected me and somehow also to my way of dealing with the pain, in my shoulder and in my hip, before."

"In a way, you were the nurse anesthetist for yourself, of necessity," I offered.

"I think that it is true."

"And did you say that in the dream she was injecting very close to your eye, possibly jeopardizing your vision, anesthetizing your eye, almost, so that something abnormal could be removed?"

"Yes, my thought is that this is about my having to see. You know, I felt that I had to see the MRI and X-ray in order to fully retrieve, resee what had happened to me. I couldn't see it. It's as if something anaesthetized my seeing almost as well as the pain.

"The strangest thing about the nurse was that the pieces didn't entirely fit together, especially her hair. It was like there were several hairpieces or sets of hair one on top of the other. She didn't look altogether real. It reminds me of how my mother looked when she and my father made their first trip back to Europe. She was wearing a dress over pants, a sweater, and a parka. It was long before the layered look was in and she looked, well, as though not all the pieces fit together. This is strange, but she was dressed to withstand the coldest weather—or maybe to protect herself from terrible things, like a concentration camp. I just had the thought that she told me once, a long time ago, that the people from those Baltic states were very nice. Maybe it was something about the Hanseatic league, I can't quite remember."

"How do you connect that thought?"

"I don't except with another thought. My mother told me that she—he—was O.K., to go along with what was being administered. I think that is actually true. She represented my father to me as a good and fine man. That was part of the problem. I had her reality as she told me of it and mine as I saw him with her and experienced him with me. And, of course, here is the rub—as I wished for him to be with me and struggled to fit the way he was into something that made sense.

"I am just remembering again that time when he threatened her, I must have been 15. I've told you about this before. How strange it felt standing up and saying, 'You can't do that—I will protect her.' And then hearing him laugh. Now I remember his story about going out with the ambulance in Vienna and arriving at a house where a man was beating his wife. When he and the police tried to intervene, the woman shouted, 'How dare you stop my man from beating me?'"

I commented on the intricacies of the relationship between his parents and how he, Michael, had tried to sort it out. Now all these intricacies were represented within him, and we were learning ever more of his dynamics, how all this fit together.

"I had a funny thing—actually not funny at all—happen this morning with Anne. She asked me if I would do an errand with her before we both went to work, and I said sure. I was watching the clock as I have a 9:10 class, and she began to wrap some presents for her friend Jacky's birthday. I felt very irritated. She always does that. Her departures are always delayed because there is something else to do before going out. I started to say something about either we go now or I won't be able to go, and then I stopped myself. You and I have talked about this before, but I think that I took it somewhat further. I thought, it is I who have something going on here, not just Anne. I need to leave right away when I decide that I am going somewhere. This is just as striking as is the fact that Anne always needs to do something first."

"And what is your thought about why you must leave immediately?" I inquired.

"Well, right now, something like, if I don't go immediately then I won't be able to go at all. It's connected to my mother's wearing all those clothes, maybe, like fleeing from Austria and not having time for the bread to rise, you know like matzoh and Passover. I am thinking that I carry their, that, anxiety with me. Get moving now or you won't get a chance to move at all. This feels connected to the working out, too. After all those years, I got moving again. And to how terrible I felt when I injured myself, like now you will never move again, you are doomed. It's also about the hurting business, who hurts whom, who protects whom. I feel hurt when Anne dawdles, as though she is riding roughshod over my need to move. Somehow this is being mired in my father's hurting my mother or me and—I hate to say this—being attached to it. This is what I have to recognize."

I started to say something about the abnormal pigmentation and the question of how to deal with it when Michael said, "You know it's a part of me, the way they were, the way we were, but I also always tried to see things on my own. I mean, even though I couldn't remember it. I did know that my shoulder hurt and that my hip did, too. That I had been hurt, not taken care of, and that it was wrong. I just had the thought that I am piggish. Both my parents referred to masturbation that way—piggish. I shouldn't be sounding so self-righteous. My father had more than enough reason to be as he was, given his losses and my inability to heal him."

"I suppose that that is one of the origins of the *pig*mentation in the dream. It is also the case that your capacity to 'explain' their actions protects you from getting too angry."

"Like not killing a mosquito," Michael replied.

This reference to work from the first round of analysis reminded Michael of a dream that he had had around the age of four. In the dream he needed to choose between the entreaties of a tiger and those of a large snake. He chose the tiger and immediately felt that he had made a terrible error. The snake slithered away, and Michael felt that he had lost something very important. Shortly thereafter, he had a febrile hallucination as he was coming down with chicken pox. He thought that his blanket was woven entirely of serpents and, when his father tried to examine him, he felt bitten by him as by a snake. We had discussed this dream often, but now Michael said, "You know I have reason to be very angry with both the tiger and the snake as these represent each of my parents. The problem always was that I felt that, if I really got angry, they couldn't take it. And then I'd be some kind of lesser creature, I guess a pig, because I felt so furious with these two people whose emigration after all was the reason that I had a life at all. Maybe that is the reason that I have tried so hard to substitute spanking for killing and to sexualize it, too."

"You connect the piggish and the pigment on a number of levels and to the dream from when you were four and to the dream from last night," I said.

"They seem almost continuous, like that dream about David's being thrown on the fence and the first dream of the analysis about the concentration camp," Michael responded.

Michael thought that his autistic student Rick's appearing as the surgeon was also multidetermined. His thoughts turned to another student, Anthony, whom he had liked very much and who had almost joined the pantheon of those men he had loved secretly. He had resisted taking Anthony into this secret place within him, feeling that doing so might compromise his abilities to be his teacher and mentor. Anthony, like the other men whom Michael had loved, was not a neutral or innocent bystander in this drama. He extended himself and was inviting for his own reasons, but Michael had maintained his boundaries. Now he thought about boundary violation and the ways in which his father was autistic, here meaning doing what he did because of his own trauma or narcissistic pathology rather than being a good father or caretaker. Michael also thought about his own "autism," the way in which he had disregarded the opinion of Dr. L in the dream because he felt that the opinion might not emanate really from Dr. L but, rather, was projected onto him from Michael. He had not believed Dr. L when told that he was, in fact, recovered. There was something unrelated about his repression of the memories of his injuries and maybe even about his not being able to secure help for himself.

At this thought, Michael became quiet and then said, "I don't think that that is the way it goes here, at least anymore." Michael's next thought was that the procedure, or nonprocedure, in the dream had taken place at the Biedersteiner Clinic in Munich. His father had done some of his training there, and Michael had visited it on a trip to Germany.

"Now that is really strange, I am not sure that that's what the clinic was called or if Biedersteiner refers to an architectural and design period in Germany. You know, a place or a fashion," he said.

"This is what we struggle with, I think: how to differentiate between the way things were fashioned and how you place them now, and not to be mired down in the former," I said.

"Thanks," Michael laughed. "The style is *Biedermeyer*, as in mired down. The clinic is Biederstein. I agree this is the Biederstein-Biedermeyer sorting out."

Michael and I continued to sort. Using the dream of the almost surgery and its strange but recognizable cast of characters, we again formulated together. We thought about how unmetabolized, not to mention unintegrated, traumas and anxieties of each of his parents had affected him. Using the model of his anxiety around not being able to get out, to get moving, we constructed the ways in which he had built on this historical calamity in his parents' lives and its repercussions in his own upbringing and developed a style in which he always kept moving. Against the backdrop of this modus vivendi, his troubles moving in the gym or on the athletic field appeared as a symptom, or even a kind of ongoing signal reminder, of what was being defended against and what had been forgotten. Caretaker to all, Michael was shouldering the pain of the parental generation and of all his students and children. He glimpsed that there was more going on when he found that he could move on the sports field and then again when he really got moving in his workout program, only to injure himself to the point where he could not continue. This was another reason that Rick, perhaps the most impaired of all his students, appeared in the dream. Michael had been unflagging in his efforts to help this young man, who sounded very much as though he had been an atypical child with some of the classical signs of pervasive developmental disorder.

Being forced to stop working out was the precipitant for major anxiety and for major reworking. Something similar characterized the analysis. He was always moving, analyzing, making meaning, keeping the process going. We understood after much work that his statement at the end of the dream that he needed to stop the procedure referred to this "autistic" way of keeping on going in and even conducting the analysis. This autistic process coexisted with his

MICHAEL: THE STRANGE NURSE DREAM | 43

working very hard in the analysis, constantly striving to understand, to recognize, and to bear.

"I can't do it all," he finally said. "I have tried. I have many successes, now even including my more muscular physique. I am not a boy anymore, strong enough to hobble off the field and keep on no matter what; nor do I need to. As I look back, it feels as though I had to then—to avoid total humiliation or worse. I am a middle-aged man. I can't shoulder everything, but my shoulders are broad enough. I don't think that I will be disqualified from membership in the human race because I have not tried hard enough."

As always, Michael's statement was a compromise formation showing both the dread and the wish, the tapestry that retains its fundaments even when each thread—or at least many—have been recognized and sorted out by place, fashion, and origin—the Biedermeyer and the Biederstein.

5 | FATHERING DAUGHTERS AND FATHERING SONS

FOR SEVERAL YEARS, I CONDUCTED A HOME-BASED naturalistic study of eight families. When I began, each family consisted of a mother, a father, and a child in the second year of life. Four of the children were boys; four were girls. All were first children. The parents, all volunteers, were middle-class professionals. In six of the eight families, there is now a second child. It has thus become possible to compare the behavior of some fathers and mothers with children of each sex, although not to control for some birth-order effects or the possibility, as some epidemiological data suggest, that parenting improves with practice (Rutter, 1979).

In this chapter I present observations from two families, which I have selected because, in a particular way, they balance some of the demographic variables one must consider. In the first family, my initial observations involve a triad consisting of mother, father, and first-born son; 37 months later a daughter was born. In the second family, the original constellation was father, mother, and first-born daughter; 38 months later a son was born. As you will see, these families, though matched for age, socioeconomic status, religion, occupation, cultural interests, and even training institutions, encompass great variability in parental behaviors, particularly on the interrogative and meaning levels of reality. On the level of what I call videotaped reality (what a camera would record), there is, however, considerable overlap.

I wish also to comment briefly on the interesting reaction to genital discovery and manipulation. There was much variation, but, in my admittedly unrepresentative sample, both mother and father

44

applauded genital play on the part of the boys. Fathers were more enthusiastic than mothers about this phenomenon in girls. Mother most often mentioned dirtiness and the proximity of the anus when discussing this matter—a cloacal reference, perhaps. Obviously, the enthusiasm of the fathers for their daughters' self-exploration may be determined by culture, class, and time. It would be hard to imagine a Victorian parent approving of any such behavior in either a son or a daughter.

In presenting observational data in this forum, it seems useful to point out that home-based data contain information from various strata of functioning. Often "seeing what goes on at home" raises questions about private and public modes of playing and being (Goffman, 1959). Analytic home-based observation perhaps calls forth play and fantasy that reflect the observer's interests as well as the agendas of all the members of the family. Looking for and at, as well as looking away, are defensive and adaptive stances that characterize all functioning, including data collection. Put another away, the kinds of things that are observed here tend to go on in families, but not in public; and when they do go on in public, most adults tend to look away out of a feeling, as one student put it, "That's private."

FIRST FAMILY

Daniel is the first-born son of 30-year-old parents. David, a lawyer, and Miriam, a pediatrician, had been married three years prior to his birth. They described their relationship as close and growing. The pregnancy had been planned and had proceeded smoothly. The delivery had been uncomplicated, and 7 lb. 12 oz. Daniel was welcomed, seemingly unambivalently. Miriam went back to work when Daniel was three months old. She worked part-time until he was nine months old and then decided to stay at home full time. "He will only be a baby once, and I want to be here," she said, arranging a leave of absence. Miriam seemed warm and friendly toward her husband and toward her son, although she was occasionally critical of her husband's indecisiveness. She was a careful, mildly obsessional woman, clearly invested in her mothering. David, Daniel's father, seemed even more obsessional than his wife. When I began my Sunday afternoon visits, he seemed quite nervous. He would advance very strong opinions and then, under his own scrutiny or his wife's, he would reconsider. He felt that someone interested in fathers might find fault with his fathering. By my third visit, however, he had noticeably relaxed. A typical observation follows.

Danny is 17 months old. He and Miriam are sitting on the floor playing with some blocks. Miriam is following Danny's lead. He is sort of arranging the blocks. Some are placed on top of each other, some next to each other. Miriam tries to be the assistant contractor-engineer. David is on the phone. He hangs up and comes barreling over. Danny looks up. David gets down on his hands and knees. He tousles Danny's hair and says, "No, no, come on, let's go." He pushes over the assembled blocks. Danny squeals with laughter. Miriam's face breaks into a smile. Now Danny starts to hit the blocks. Both father and son are pushing them around. About a minute later, Danny picks up a block and throws it. It doesn't travel very far. Miriam says, "Oh no!" David says, "Stop it, Dan." A second block is picked up. "I said stop it now. That's dangerous." His father speaks more quietly than he did when playing raucously. He sounds very serious. Danny puts down the block. He smiles, as do his parents. Less than 30 seconds later, David gives the blocks another jab. Round two has begun, and almost immediately Danny is once again convulsed by giggles and squeals of delight.

Subsequent observations revealed many different kinds of interactions, but the pattern just described was often repeated. David would disrupt what Danny was doing. Danny would welcome the assault, and his spirits would rise dramatically as the active and exciting play commenced. Often the intensity of his affect would escalate until he lost control. At this point, his father, who had initiated the sequence, would bring it to a close. Whereas at 17 months these second and third rounds of play were initiated by David, by 24 months successive rounds were initiated by Danny himself.

Now Danny is 21 months old. He is playing with the vacuum cleaner. He is in high spirits, making whooshing sounds as he goes about his work-play. He bangs into some plants. David says, "Easy does it, cowboy." Danny regards him with an intense look and resumes his play. David intervenes again. "If you want to be a Boston Bruin, you'll have to go into the living room," he says. Danny puts down the vacuum cleaner, begins to suck on his thumb, and then puts his hand into his diaper and begins to masturbate. Miriam, who has been reading during the preceding dialogue, now looks up as her husband says, "That's the spirit, you big stud. Take matters into your own hands." He smiles at Danny, who smiles back. Miriam remarks, "You're a good boy, Danny."

SECOND FAMILY

Rachael is the first-born of her parents, Arthur, a 34-year-old psychiatrist, and Nora, a 30-year-old researcher. Rachael was a planned child, and the pregnancy was uneventful, but a Caesarean section was performed after 16 hours of labor. Although Rachael was observed in the neonatal intensive care nursery for 48 hours, she went home with her mother at six days of age. Unlike some of the other families, the transference reaction evoked by my presence was not obvious with Arthur and Nora. Arthur did not appear to be either competitive or compliant. As a dynamically oriented psychiatrist of adults, he remarked that the relevance of normative data to reconstruction was quite critical. Nora was often quiet during my visits. She seemed less uneasy than retiring. Both parents told me at the beginning of the study that Rachael was enormously committed to her mother and would go to no one else, sometimes not even to her father. Both grandmothers had expressed concern about the tightness of this bond. Arthur said, in Nora's presence, that she had found her niche as a mother, that she loved being at home, that he loved her being there, and that Rachael was the luckiest little girl in the world.

At the beginning of my observation, Rachael, at 14 months, would often look warily at me as she held tightly to her mother. They played together or Nora read to her. Arthur sometimes waved at his daughter or drew close to mother and daughter to complete the family tableau. Rachael would smile attentively at him and sometimes draw closer to her mother. Occasionally Arthur did something that created noise. During my first observation of this sort of event, he put on some music and invited Rachael, who was being quietly read to, to dance. Rachael looked perplexed. Her father, on his knees and smiling, waltzed her gently around the floor and then lifted her up into the air. "Be careful," Nora cautioned, noting that the little girl's smile diminished as she became airborne, "She's not such a great flier." Arthur responded to his wife's suggestion and stopped. Rachael did not immediately toddle back to mother, and as the music played on, Arthur resumed the waltz. "You lovely dancer—what a joy to squire you," he said and then looked over at me with obvious embarrassment.

Now, at 18 months, Rachael is lying somewhat dreamily with her mother while Nora reads her a story. Arthur gets up from his reading (it is about 30 minutes into the observation) and heads over toward them. He hums—the tune is "Who's Afraid of the Big Bad Wolf?" "What's my beautiful girl up to?" he asks. Rachael looks up and smiles. "Beautiful dreamer," the musical Arthur begins to sing. Rachael rises and walks toward her father. Mother smiles. As Rachael approaches, her diaper falls off. "Pretty girl," says Arthur. "Put the diaper back on," says Nora. "Da Da," says Rachael, "Da Da." She is beaming now as she reaches her father. He sweeps her up in his arms and waltzes her around the room. Nora follows with the diaper. "She'll get you all wet," she says to her husband. Rachael is very excited and tries to sing along with her waltzing, crooning papa. This continues for about a minute, and then Nora puts on the diaper and says, "Let her calm down, Art." The oomph in father's singing is decelerated. His volume decreases, and the speed at which he is going around the room diminishes. Rachael also quiets down. Arthur puts her down. She stares expectantly in his direction. He smiles, first at Nora and then at Rachael. "May I have the pleasure of the next dance?" he asks, bowing archly and speaking with a mock English accent. Rachael squeals in delight, resumes singing, and rushes toward her father. Once again she is transformed by the excitement of the situation.

Rachael at 21 months is approaching her father, who sits at his desk. Her hand is at her crotch. Arthur looks up. "Do you need to go to the bathroom?" he inquires, smiling. "Uh, uh," smiles Rachael. Arthur gets up and goes to her. She puts her arms around his legs. "Hey, little one, want to play?" asks Arthur. Rachael smiles in assent. Arthur leans down and picks her up. "Ay, ay," she says. "That's right, fly," responds her father and whooshes her around his head. "Ay, ay," laughs Rachael, "Ay, ay." Notice that daughter approaches father.

Two weeks later, Rachael is sitting quietly between her parents on a couch. One parent after the other is reading *Goodbye Moon* to her. Rachael's hand is in her diaper. She appears to be masturbating. She pulls out her hand and smells her finger. She then puts her finger in front of her mother's nose. Her mother frowns and says, "Don't do that, Rachael. It's not nice." Rachael looks troubled, then moves her hand over to her father. "My pretty girl," he smiles, "My fetching fragrant filly." Rachael smiles, then looks back toward her mother somewhat questioningly. Nora seems not to notice and continues reading. Rachael snuggles up close to Arthur.

Now let us observe each of the families with the second child. An important aspect of these observations is that they often involved four people, both children usually being at home during my Saturday or Sunday afternoon visits. First, father David and family.

Rebekah is 15 months old. Danny is four years, four months. He is very much an oedipal child, attached to his mother, often quite rivalrous of and angry with his dad. Miriam, who has still not gone back to work, is reading to Rebekah. They are sitting on the couch. David and Danny are tossing a football. "Throw it right, Daddy," Danny shouts when he misses the ball. The football game continues until Danny gives up in at least mock disgust and switches to TV. David then approaches the couch with the football. He tosses it gently toward Rebekah. "What are you doing?" asks Miriam. "Just playing." Rebekah reaches for the ball. She smiles broadly and leans over to her father. She applies her body to his. The reading is over. Miriam puts down the book and goes to the kitchen. David, who has appeared somewhat rattled, seems to relax as he and Rebekah snuggle. Shortly thereafter, he asks her if she wants to play horsey. She nods excitedly and he picks her up, neighing noisily as both go galloping across the floor. "Be quiet, I can't hear," shouts Danny from the front of the TV. Rebekah is giggling and excited; she seems to be enjoying herself immensely. Two minutes later Miriam returns from the kitchen. "Whoa, Horsey," she says with a smile, "That little girl needs to take her nap shortly."

Rebekah is now 21 months; Danny, 58 months. Danny has just been naughty, throwing something at his sister. He has been sent to his room, from which loud bangs occasionally issue. Rebekah is sitting between her parents. She and Miriam are playing with some loops of material with which one can weave potholders. "Pretty one, come here," her father says. "I can't believe it. You're not only beautiful, but you can sew." He scoops his daughter up. All the potholder material falls on the floor. Rebekah laughs and grows excited. Shortly thereafter, David puts her down. "She is so beautiful," he says to his wife, "and so easy to be with." Miriam nods assent and then notices that Rebekah is wet. David goes to get a diaper. He returns and watches as Rebekah touches herself while her mother is changing her. "She is so beautiful," he murmurs, "She'll make some man a lovely wife." "Move your hand, dear," says Miriam to her daughter. "I need to fix your diaper." She gives Rebekah a kiss. Then she turns to her husband and says, "And she'll make a certain father a wonderful daughter, particularly in comparison to what you're going through with Danny." The last words are practically drowned out by a loud crash from Danny's room. Everyone rushes in that direction.

We return to father Arthur and his family. Gideon is 17 months; Rachael is four years, seven months. Nora is at home full time. She is editing a book in the evenings. Arthur is now an academic psychiatrist and has become an analytic candidate. Rachael and her father are sitting, talking. Gideon and Nora are on the floor playing with blocks. Rachael is talking to her dad about how cute Gideon is. "Babies are wonderful," she says, smiling. This grouping, father with daughter, mother with son, continues for about 15 minutes. All eyes are on Gideon. Then Rachael (who is a very good reader and often wants to read to me) gets up and says she will read. Arthur joins Nora and Gideon. "So you want to be an architect," he says to his son, "Gideon, the builder." Gideon stares at him intently. "Let's see," Arthur continues, "Shall we build a skyscraper?" He piles block on block. Gideon is still staring. "Nah, this is no good. Let's start again," says Arthur, and he knocks over the tower. Gideon laughs and knocks over some blocks too. "That's fun, old man, isn't it?" says Arthur, "Can you push it farther?" Father and son are now both pushing blocks quite vigorously. "Art, he was playing so nicely, so quietly," says Nora, "Rachael won't be able to read." "Gideon, we've got to cool it," says Arthur, "You heard mother. Let's build our Empire State Building." The construction recommences, and one can almost feel Arthur's urge to knock over the building. There is a look of excited anticipation on Gideon's face. "One, two, three—now!" shouts Arthur and the building goes over. "Boo, boo, boo!" shouts Gideon and begins pushing the blocks. "Shh," says Rachael loudly.

"You see," says Nora to her husband, "She can't read," and then to Rachael, "Boys will be boys, my dear. Why don't you go to the library and close the door?"

Six months later, Gideon is walking around the room holding his penis. "My wee wee," he says. Rachael looks up, "Mom, tell him to stop." "Gideon, no." Gideon says, "Da Da wee my wee. Da Da wee wee, my wee." He beams. Nora looks uncomfortable. "Let's do something, Gideon," she says, "Would you like to read?" "My wee Da Da wee," sings Gideon. Arthur is smiling broadly. "If you've got it, flaunt it," he says, "Yes, Gideon, we wee wee the same." He then turns to Rachael, who is quite upset, and explains, "Little boys like Gideon are just figuring out important things like whether they're boys or girls." "He's so stupid, Daddy," Rachael answers, "Everyone knows he is a boy and I'm a girl." "And I am delighted that you are, a wonderful girl who brings her mother and me much joy. Carry on, you wee wee soldier," he says to his son and simultaneously hugs his daughter. Nora smiles.

DISCUSSION

Despite the fact that many children today grow up without one, there is much clinical evidence to support the idea that children need a father. In a previous chapter, I introduced the idea of father hunger—an affective state experienced when the father is felt to be absent. I postulated, on the basis of the symptoms, play, and dreams of father-less children, that the father's principal intrapsychic role was as the modulator and organizer of aggressive drive and fantasy. Much earlier, Hans Loewald (1951) had posited another critical but related function as a protection against the threat of maternal engulfment. Mahler's (1955) seminal contribution on psychological separation-individuation also favored this paternal function. Ernst Abelin (1975) followed this fecund lead in his research and theorizing on the father's role during this important period of late practicing and rapprochement.

The father is the organizer and modulator of intense affect paradigms. He beckons to the child like a knight in shining armor, not only pulling him or her out of, or assisting in the dissolution of, the intense mother–child relationship that Mahler called symbiosis, but actively intruding on it; he breaks up the intimate, homeostatically attuned, resonating empathy (Herzog, 1979). The disruptive care-giver, when asked what he is doing (the interrogative level), often portrays himself as such times as a sibling. He can play with his child under the benevolent auspices of the mother. She remains the adult. "It's fun," David said, "just knocking around like a kid." "Boys will be boys," the astute Nora observed. This pattern is more true for isogender interactions, fathers with sons.

On a deeper level, there is often a simultaneous raging against the mother–child union and a desire to be included in it. "If I am an 18-month-old, too, maybe Maria will take me to her bosom," a 40-year-old physicist in analysis told me. He had dreamed that two peas in a pod were warm and snug in the palm of the jolly green giant. This dream followed closely upon his telling me that he felt young and free when he romped with his 17-month-old son, as he had been before all the trouble in his family of origin began. The green giant also signified his envy of his wife's power and fecundity and his fear of her disapproval that he was endlessly a little boy and not an adult.

Fathers of sons disrupt by the use of gross motor activity, which introduces escalating affect. Fathers of daughters tend to use less disruptive large motor modes of entrée and to key their pitch to the protoheterosexual aspects of the exchange. There are thus numerous uses of terms referring to physical beauty, invitations to dance, and other descriptions of courtship. Some of these ways, as well as some of the ways in which fathers interact with boys—"So you want to be an architect, do you, Gideon"—have an almost peculiar, out-of-synch temporal quality. It is as if the father were disrupting with context that reveals his future plans or aspirations for the child. That there should be sex-typing in these aspirations is highly interesting. All the fathers of girls in my study roundly insisted that they favored total freedom of choice for their daughters professionally, but they tended to interact with them predominantly in the model I would call protoerotic endorsement. Notice, however, that David tossed a football to Rebekah as he had with his son as his initial invitation for her to leave Miriam and join him.

As I talked in considerable depth with the fathers, I found that on the interrogative level this future-oriented empathy was fairly prevalent. Fathers see their children not only as they are (and per-haps not so clearly as they were; cf. Earls's, 1980, work, which shows that fathers are not very good observers of their children), but as they would like them to be. Their empathy seemed in part to be focused on a developmental goal. Sometimes this aim was explicit. Arthur said, "My dad is an architect. If I hadn't decided to study psychoarchitecture, I would build buildings. It would be nice if Gideon wanted to do that too." Dorothy Burlingham (1973) reported about this aspect of fatherhood:

> According to my own experience in direct observation and analytic treatments of a number of fathers, their fantasies concerning the expected child were built around the wish that the boy should be a powerful male like the ideal of himself: if a girl, that she would respond to his own loving feelings [p. 30].

So the disruption of the father is Janus-like, It appears to have regressive determinants—identification as a rival, as a sibling longing to dislodge and longing to unite, fearing reengulfment and simultaneously courting it—and progressive ones—pushing or enabling development by introducing future-oriented content and attuning oneself with that part of the child which is gazing in the direction of further differentiation, individualization, and growth.

The situation is even more complex with a second child. The first child is still very much present, and his or her developmental issues exert a powerful effect on the father. Daniel's struggle with David affected his relationship with Rebekah. The same is true of the Rachael-Arthur dyad and the Arthur-Gideon interaction. In some ways there is a generalizable conclusion. First-time fathers of boys tend to be more large-motorish with subsequent children, either male or female. First-time fathers of girls tend to be less so with subsequent offspring, either male or female.

With the second child, there is another phenomenon of note. Father tends to have a special relationship with the first-born. Esther Shapiro (personal communication) reported that in middle-class families this phenomenon is related to the need for the father to care for the first child while the mother is occupied with the newborn second child. On the interrogative level and the level of meaning, there is a clear connection to the sibling motif and to the conflict over viewing and sensing the mother–infant unity—the wish to be one with the mother and the fear of being engulfed by her. Mothers do not report this fear when watching father and child together, in my experience, not even in analysis. Fathers report it frequently.

A brief vignette from an analytic patient is illustrative. "My father and I get doughnuts every Sunday morning," seven-year-old Tanya tells me. "He knows that I love them. He doesn't mind if my fingers get sticky. He likes my doughnut hands. Mommy doesn't. 'Wash your hands, wash your hands, don't be dirty,' she always says." Tanya is in her third month of analysis. She has an older and a younger brother. She fights with her mother constantly and longs for her father, who is frequently traveling, to be at home. Tanya is often ashamed of herself. She is always messy or messing up. When she draws pictures of faces, they always lack noses. "I don't like to draw noses," she says sadly, "Mommy says I stink." Analytic data are always multidetermined and draw their meaning from many levels, but I wonder about the connection between these constellations of feelings and my observation of father–daughter and mother–daughter interaction in the second year of life.

The following poem was written by a nine-year-old boy in his second year of analysis with me. In it he describes the son of a knight at the time of King Arthur. I take it to be a commentary on the antiquity of the issue:

> *The night swoops down*
> *It helps me get my guts up*
> *I want to stay at home*
> *But I have to learn to fight to grow up right*
> *My father loves to wrestle*
> *He can run fast too*
> *He shows me how to get my guts up*
> *Then I don't have to stay still*
> *If it gets noisy I won't be ill.*

6 | BART AND THE KILLER WALRUS

Will remain of those cities what went through them, the wind?

—Bertolt Brecht

OFTEN, BUT NOT ALWAYS, A CHILD BEGINS LIFE with two parents, a mother and a father. The sociological and psychological evolution of family structure and the care of the newborn is complex and variegated. In our time, a rethinking of the etiology of extant and idealized groupings is accompanied by experimentation, alternative family makeup, and a spectrum of politicization that reflects the damage of oppression and the burden of expanded opportunity. Even in our current climate, and without assuming a political stance, it is useful to note that men and women approach family-making differentially, with histories, biologies, psychologies, and role expectations that affect their availability, affects, and modes of attunement and attachment. The biorhythmicity of man with infant and woman with infant is a relevant ingredient in the way in which a father holds, regards, views, and interacts with his child; the same is true of the mother. These variations in the ways in which biology intersects with psychology afford, even without reference to varying life histories, an opportunity for the infant to have interactive, state-sharing, and state-tuning experiences with two different kinds of caregivers as well as two different people.

Although much more will be elaborated about the male-care-taking line of development and its impact on fathering and about the qualities of self-experience that are unique to the female and how this impacts on mothering, I wish here to emphasize a particular aspect of this dichotomy. Man and woman, father and mother may assume distinguishable protopositions with regard to the initial mode of both regarding and relating to the infant. The mother's initial stance is one of already being with and, in some sense, in. She perhaps needs to withdraw a little so as to establish a way of differentiating between inside and outside and conveying to her child something about the salience of the outside for the inside. But she begins from a sense of already being inside.

The father, on the other hand, needs to find a point and mode of entry into both the mother–infant dyad and his child's inner world. He must find the right spot to touch and needs to learn something of the inherent sensitivity and sensibility of his child. The sense of sameness, projection, and other forerunners of empathy need to be organized in terms of getting there and getting in rather than in terms of being there and finding a space. Just as the mother must, in a sense, withdraw, he must, in a sense, intrude, penetrate. These complementary modes become accessible to the child as they constitute the modal structures of the beginning dialogue between self and other and the initial representation of self-with-mother and self-with-father. They are also regarded by the child as he views them occurring between his parents and observes how each parent views him.

In the previous chapter, we examined how fathers typically go about entering into their children's world. As the paternal mode of entry can constitute an intrusion, we also noted how mothers typically go about restoring order after fathers' Kamikaze style engagements. A child obviously needs both. Were the child to be exposed only to these Kamikaze engagements, we would have a terribly overstimulated little person on our hands. Clearly, the mother's role in restoring the status quo ante is crucial. But the parceling of roles between the parents optimally also leads to the sharing of these roles. That is to say, the father, like the mother, must come to appreciate what is too much and how he and the child can learn to damp down and control excitement as well as shake things up. The mother, like the father, must be able to stimulate as well as modulate and to retain an age-appropriate view of her son. Where this sharing of roles does not happen, aggression does not become modulated. In place of masculinity, we see hypermasculinity or some other deformation of optimal "full deck" functioning (O'Connell and Herzog, 1998).

Take Bart, for example. Bart was conceived after his parents had been married for three years. They had waited until Howard, the father, had been promoted in his work and was about to become a partner in his law firm. Lisa, his wife, had been awarded her doctorate in modern Spanish literature and found a teaching job that would permit her to devote some of her time to mothering. The conception occurred after six months of pleasurable trying. Lisa was 33 and Howard 36. The pregnancy was unremarkable by obstetrical standards, although Lisa was thought to be a somewhat anxious mother-to-be, an opinion that was recorded in the notes of her prenatal office visits. There was no medical reason to undertake an amniocentesis, and the couple joked about the impact of a child of either sex. In fact, each acknowledged the wish for a boy.

Lisa wanted a boy, she said, because she so admired her older brother, who was fair and square, to use her own words. She also thought that boys had it easier in the world because they were less concerned with foolish things like weight and complexion and more focused on the important aspects of life like work and competition. Her own doubts about her femininity and the difficulties in her relationship with her mother also entered into this wish. A boy could get ahead, unencumbered by the internal conflicts and ambiguities that she knew so well from her own struggles. Her own academic success felt to her to have been achieved in spite of her gender rather than because of it. She admired her husband, whom she found intelligent and attractive, but especially she admired what she called his masculinity, the hardness of his body, his decisiveness, and the way in which he handled anger. When he was mad, it always showed. He made no attempt to hide it but seemed to accept it as a natural part of his being. Consequently, it did not linger. It flashed, was expressed, and then subsided. In Lisa's mind, this somehow corresponded to his erections, which followed the same pattern. When Howard had an erection, he wanted to come and she was usually very happy to oblige him.

Howard wanted a boy, too. He loved being a man—aggressive and sweaty was the way he thought of it. Lisa smelled soft and melting; he imagined that a girl-child would be the same. That might be a problem for him, for the way Lisa was made him want to get inside of her, be as close as possible, even melt in. This was the exact opposite of what it took to get ahead in the world.

It's a jungle out there, he thought. A boy could play hard, be hard, and get his way. He loved Lisa, actually everything about her, but he knew that his kid should be like him. Otherwise how would he manage. Of course, his younger sister, Babs, was O.K. but she had always been a tomboy and that was a hard path, too. No, a boy would be straightforward and easier for both of them. He could really help out because he knew boys, from his own experience, from the locker room, and from his firm. He knew how to be with them, how to beat them, that is, win; and how to be friends, that is, on the same team. He considered the possibility that they would have a daughter, as did Lisa. Howard worried that he would not know what to do or, worse, that he would be attracted to her and not be able to control himself. Lisa feared that a daughter would be moody, weak, and indecisive, the traits she most disliked in herself and in her mother.

The relationship between the couple was good for both of them, and this continued throughout the pregnancy. They both worked hard, worked out together until the ninth month, when Lisa sent Howard off to the gym without her so that she could work on a blue blanket for "our guy." "Don't take a shower at the gym though," she would say by way of send off, "I want all of your sweaty masculinity when you get back here." Howard loved Lisa's love of him as an active, wet, and aromatic stud. He thought often that they were a perfect pair and that a little guy would make them a perfect family. Howard had confided to his best friend, Ted, that he feared that Lisa would want him less as the pregnancy progressed, but it was exactly the opposite. She was as horny as ever, and the same was also true for him. He wondered about sex in the postpartum period, as this part of their relationship was absolutely vital to his well-being.

When Bart was born, both parents were ecstatic and relieved. Howard thought that his boy looked like a football player and would probably become a surgeon. Lisa was astonished by the baby's bigness and his hardness. He sucked vigorously and decisively at the breast, so much that Lisa's nipples soon became quite sore, but this condition was admired by both parents. Howard said, "He really knows how to take what he wants." Lisa felt confused by her mixed feelings. On one hand, she concurred with Howard totally; on the other, it hurt her to nurse Bart and she wished that he were a little less persistent. Howard felt very sexual and alive; Lisa was not quite in the same place, but she continued "to help" her husband to achieve orgasm several times each day.

The nursing style seemed to be echoed in sleeping, crying, and every other activity. Bart was strong and persistent and seemingly willful. Howard continued to applaud his son's masculine qualities; Lisa did, too, but she felt that she was on the front line and often as though she were in need of reenforcements. The couple worked on this dilemma, and when Bart was six weeks old they hired a house-keeper-nanny to assist Lisa in her mothering. Howard said proudly that his boy needed two women, he was so gutsy. Lisa felt somewhat defeated by the hiring of Jenny but had to concede that it was an absolute necessity.

Lisa was surprised that Jenny was not as mesmerized by Bart's erections as she was. Lisa could not take her eyes off his little penis when it became hard. When Howard was at home she would call him in to admire their son's erection. Howard said that it was a good one but then added that he didn't want Lisa to like it too much. She should concentrate on his erection and on his penis, on his alone, he said. Lisa reassured Howard but felt puzzled by his response. Why did he not celebrate this aspect of Bart's masculinity as she did? Was he jealous? Was she out of line? she wondered. It also passed through her mind that Howard might feel that her sexual interest in him was inadequate; it was to some extent true that a disparity had arisen between their sexual appetites, even though she did her best to meet her husband's "insatiable" needs.

When Bart was seven months old, Lisa took him to a play group that included three other boys and two girls. Their parents were all friends and associates. Lisa was a little nervous about Bart's behavior in the group. He strongly and confidently grasped whatever he wanted. He would not let go, once he took something, and seemed to ignore the protests of the other children. The other parents nick-named Bart the Taker. When Bart was 11 months old, the mothers of the two girls withdrew them from the group. They felt that it was too rough for their daughters and that Bart was a tyrant. Again, Lisa was quite concerned; Howard, for his part, thought that his son was a natural-born leader. When Bart was 15 months old, Lisa and Howard were asked to come to a meeting with the parents of Tommy, Rudy, and Steven, the other three boys in the play group. Lisa and Howard were quite shocked when the other parents told them that Bart was a bully, regularly terrorizing their sons, and that they thought he needed treatment. Lisa was less horrified than her husband, but she, too, felt that the other parents were overreacting. She was particularly surprised that Steven's father, Jim, agreed with the group. He had been a football player, was still a jock and, she thought, very much like her husband. Lisa had often felt very attracted to him, particularly when he picked up Steven directly after a workout and was very sweaty.

Howard was beside himself. He considered taking legal action and thought that the other parents in the group must be crazy. Bart was a perfect boy. He was aggressive and unafraid. A boy takes what he wants, and Bart *is a boy*, his father thought. He was particularly happy with a new game he and Bart were playing. Howard would chase his son, bellowing, "I am going to get you, really get you." Bart would run from his father and then turn around and try and kick him. A really tough kid, his father thought.

Despite their feeling that something was the matter with the group, Howard and Lisa decided to heed its advice. Lisa pushed hardest for this course as she harbored some concern about Bart's adaptation and also held a secret worry. She wondered if he had suffered from her persistent belief that he was a "man of steel." Often, when he cried, she would just let him cry—she thought that this was his natural exuberance and vitality but also had a feeling that his hardness hurt her too much, beginning with her nipples and continuing into his biting and hitting behavior, which was really quite excessive. She felt guilty about this neglect and fearful that her wish to retaliate had affected her son in a negative fashion. Her parents, too, thought that the evaluation was a good idea. They worried that Bart was too demanding and that his behavior was wearing their daughter down. She always said to them, he's just a boy's boy, but now she felt relieved that someone else's expertise could be brought to bear on the issue.

Howard obtained the name of a child analyst who saw infants, and an appointment was made. Howard consulted a friend to make certain that this shrink was not a wimp. "That's the last thing that we need," he stated. He was told that the analyst was a good guy and an athlete to boot.

In the initial meeting, Howard was straightforward about his son's masculinity and raised the possibility that the other parents were jealous. He also stated that to be hypermasculine was certainly preferable to being a sissy, and he knew which option he would choose. The analyst inquired about each parent's childhood. Lisa told of her closeness with her father and her difficulties with her mother. Howard discussed his father's coldness and distance and his mother's availability and how painful it had been for him that he was smaller than the other guys. In response to gentle questioning, he revealed his fascination for Charles Atlas and how he had begun lifting weights when he was 12. "It works," he said with a grin, "I'm big guy now, and I shall never be puny again."

The child analyst met four times with Bart. The boy insisted that his mother be in the room for the first three meetings, but for the fourth he allowed her to leave. He was interested in the analyst, explored easily and eagerly, and did not respond to the analyst's efforts to limit any action. It was as if he had never heard the word no. When he cried with frustration, while trying to reach something out of his grasp, the analyst noted that Bart's mother did not come to his aid and eventually, he, the analyst, himself did.

At 17 months Bart played the following game. He would take the analyst's hand and bite it. The analyst would withdraw his hand and say no, firmly. Bart would laugh and bite again. The analyst set about teaching Bart the meaning of no. He would take his hand away from Bart and then hold him so that he could not bite. Bart seemed angry and astonished by this intervention. Lisa felt embarrassment, but also great relief. Howard had always told her that saying no might inhibit their son's aggression.

At 18 months, in the very last session of the evaluation, Bart took two stuffed animals that the analyst offered. He called one Da Da. Da Da chased the other animal around the room. Da Da made loud and perhaps scary noises. He seemed to be enjoying himself. The other animal was hidden behind a chair by Bart. He seemed to be very frightened. The analyst said to Bart, "Shall we protect the little one from Da Da?" Bart nodded gratefully. Then Bart and the little animal, joined by the analyst, chased the Da Da. The Da Da seemed scared. He hid behind the chair. Bart laughed and jumped around. Then he looked at the analyst suspiciously, became quiet, and himself hid behind the chair, as if hiding from the analyst or from the scenario he had just created.

We can only conjecture about the contributions of the formerly puny Howard and the unhappily feminine Lisa's conscious and unconscious minds to Bart's situation at 17 months. It is possible, however, to see something of the evolving perceptions of the father's chasing, the son's fear, the efforts at reversal, and the conflict and anxiety that accompany this enterprise.

What do we learn of the content of Bart's mind when he is seen in analysis at age four? The recommendation grew directly out of the original consultation and the preceding psychotherapy.

Bart plays out a scenario in which a furious walrus kills everything it sees. "I only want everything dead," it says.

"Why," I ask, playing the role of a walrus doctor. "Otherwise I might get killed," the walrus says, "If I kill everybody else, then I am safe. Kill, kill, kill, that's what I do."

Indeed, the contents of Bart's mind were distinguished by the presence of unmodulated aggression, expressed as hyperaggressivity and experienced as continuous fear. A first-strike philosophy was felt to be the safest way to prevent terrifying and lethal retaliation. Bart remained in analysis for two years, and then his family moved to another city. Howard and Lisa had postponed, "perhaps indefinitely," having more children because Bart was "such a handful."

Many factors had contributed to what appears to have been a quite pervasive problem in the modulation and organization of aggressive drive and fantasy. Bart continued to be able to function, but his inner life and certain aspects of his behavior were very clearly affected by both his parents' conscious and unconscious issues and their subsequent behavior. By following his internal experience as it was elicited in the analytic playroom, we were able to follow the impact of parental and evolving self-formulations on what was to become his developmental line of personal meaning. I wish to emphasize that a considerable part of what emerged in the play was not known to Bart. It was unconscious, although elicitable through the technique of constructing a play space that he could utilize. Bart returned to analysis three years later, at age nine, when his parents returned to

Boston. In the interim, the parents had embarked on a treatment of their own that had apparently been extremely helpful.

In this second round of analysis, I began meeting individually with Howard. Together we worked on how he might help his son with his aggression by using his own strength and endowment for Bart. I proposed that, when Bart and his dad fought, a seemingly favorite undertaking, Howard should say to him, "I will help you learn to fight well and to manage your anger carefully. I know how to do these things better than you do because I am older, have more practice and experience, and am your father. You needn't worry that our fighting will get out of control because I am strong enough to manage the situation, and I will." This developmental help allowed Howard to interact with his son in a way that was less terrifying for the boy and more in keeping with Bart's developing internalized structure and better modulation.

In this piece of his analytic work, Bart continued to struggle with the impact of his own aggressivity and his need for developmental help. His play now focused on a sailor by the name of Jeb who had been cast off in a boat alone because he could not get along with anyone. Jeb tried valiantly to manage. He killed fish for food. That was easy. He invented a way to make the water drinkable. That, too, was accomplishable. His major problem is the presence of killer walruses in the ocean on which he sails. Here we return to the previous and persisting waters, so to speak.

Bart and I work on ways to "deal" with the killer walrus. Eventually a plan is devised to capture one. For this undertaking the boy allows me to be his partner. Jeb thinks that killing the walrus is the way to proceed. I wonder about anesthetizing him so that he and Jeb together might learn more about what makes the beast tick. Bart tells me that Jeb thinks that this suggestion is a trick. A dead walrus can't hurt him; a sleeping one may wake up. The truth of this statement is acknowledged and Jeb's fears are validated. A plan is devised to monitor the level of anesthesia and thus guarantee the boy's safety.

Thus began an incredible journey of discovery that featured the uncovering of the truth about how the walrus got to be a killer. The story turned out not to hinge on a basic or innate walrus quality but on the ways in which the father and the mother wanted the walrus, who came to be called Big Little Red, to be. Together Jeb and I, or more correctly Bart and I, devised a treatment, a neurosurgical and computer-age possibility. A new program was introduced into the walrus's hard disc. It featured a father walrus who did not need his son to be a killer because he had learned to manage his own aggression and a mother walrus who liked her boy even when he was not hard. Bart and I felt that this new program could "coexist" with the program that was already there, so that the walrus could "choose" which one to operate.

Following this highly successful treatment of the walrus, Jeb was welcomed once again into the Navy and now no longer needed to sail alone. Upon his return to his crewmates, he said, "I found someone to help me solve my problem and now I'm fit to be one of the guys."

The analytic work allowed in play for a new program to be introduced by virtue of extended opportunities for the analyst to accompany Bart in his fantasy and by the concurrent treatment of the parents. The parents were able to make substantial changes in themselves and thus allow Bart a little bit more space for his own growth and for the analytic process. In the play Jeb acknowledged a basic fact: that a new program can coexist with one already in place, but that the delete function is not extant in usual human (or walrus) functioning.

7 | MICHAEL: Doing It

*If I chance to talk a little wild, forgive me. I had it
from my father.*

Henry VIII

*What's madness but nobility of soul
At odds with circumstance? The day's on fire!
I know the purity of pure despair . . .
A night flowing with birds, a ragged moon,
And in broad day the midnight come again!
A man goes far to find out what he is*
—Theodore Roethke, *In a Dark Time*

LET US RETURN TO MICHAEL, THE 51-YEAR-OLD philosopher, who
has returned to do more analysis 17 years after doing an earlier piece
of analytic work. He is married and the father of two grown children. Much of the earlier work in his analysis centered on the troubled relationship that obtained between him and his father and the
variable presence of his mother as a buffering and ameliorating or
an abandoning and betraying force.

Michael is talking about Rob. The friendship with Rob is now
a year old. They are academic colleagues and have become good and
deep friends. They talk about everything. Each likes the other's wife,
and the wives are friendly, too. Michael has talked a lot in his analysis about the significance of this friendship and its impact on him
both in his day-to-day functioning and intrapsychically. How the
relationship is related to the analysis and what happens with the

analyst have also been topics of exploration. He has particularly focused on the way in which he and Rob track each other, by which he means that each thinks about the other, and how extraordinary this is. He has related this thinking about Rob to his experience of being thought about by the analyst. He has contrasted this experience with an aspect of his childhood in which he felt that his father could not think about him. The mutuality of thinking about another and the other's thinking about him seems particularly meaningful first in the analysis and now in his friendship.

Rob is in Europe with his family. He and Michael speak on the phone, and Rob tells him that he is grumpy. He has a cold, his adolescent daughters would rather not be with their parents on vacation, and his wife is feeling harried, preoccupied by the girls' hostility, and not very sexual. Rob expresses a wish to be back at home, at work, and talking with Michael. Michael develops a fantasy. It follows on a dream in which he and Rob are lounging on a couch together. Their legs touch. Rob says something about this is how guys can be together.

In the fantasy, Michael thinks about helping Rob with his grumpiness. He imagines giving Rob a blow job. He wishes to provide him with wonderful pleasure and a grumpiness-relieving orgasm. Instead, Rob expresses dissatisfaction with Michael's amateurish technique. Perhaps Rob will punish him for not doing it well. The fantasy is quite powerful. As Michael thinks about it, he considers two forms of *doing it*. He might tell Rob about the fantasy; it would extend their friendship to share this kind of material, and he thinks about actually proposing this as a remedy for his friend's grouchiness. This second version of *doing it* immediately elicits Michael's realization that Rob is not homosexual and that he is not interested in expanding his sexual repertoire in this direction. The fantasy is not one that Michael in his adult life has had previously about a man, although a variant of it has come up in his analysis. Thinking about the fantasy becomes quite absorbing. In reality, Michael has never given a man a blow job. In his early adolescence, he and a buddy experimented together, but nothing much came of it, either out of or for either of them.

Michael thinks about Rob's scent. He especially likes the way his friend smells. His consciousness of this aspect of Rob and of himself is something new. His thought is that Rob's scent would be even stronger in the center, the essence of Rob. This, too, is a very pleasurable thought. The second part of the fantasy, that Rob's grumpiness might be expressed by his being dissatisfied with Michael's expertise and punishing him, is much more familiar to him than is the first part. He has learned a lot in his analysis about the origins of this form of relating with a nonavailable and critical father.

In this chapter, I would like to broach the topic of *doing it* and *how do you do it* as these phenomena occur in father hunger and in perversion. Trauma, grievance, symbolization or its impairment, and interactive enactment, the play mode that features action and necessitates that the involved other also act, will be seen to be applicable concepts for this exploration. The relationship of father hunger to perversion is addressed as this relationship unfolds in the struggle that Michael conducts as he feels the pressure to do it, wonders about how do you do it, and how to take into account the reality of Rob's being. Michael's predicament is contrasted with that of Andrew, another analysand who wrestles with similar issues and with that of David, a man with yet a different pattern of searching for the father.

In analysis Michael speaks of his fantasy. The analyst may appear to be relatively absent. In this stage in the work, Michael is extraordinarily competent, partially because of the work, at sharing his thoughts and describing his process. I listen, with many thoughts and associations that parallel what my patient is saying but that also sometimes diverge in a quite interesting fashion from what is said. Much has occurred in the preceding work that has focused on my activity and its impact on him. It is important to get this right; indeed an earlier interruption occurred around Michael's feeling that an aspect of his being in the analysis interfered with his doing his own writing. The current phase of the work is characterized by a more far-reaching understanding of the self-righting function of his analyzing in the presence of the analyst. He feels comfortably tracked by me, which entails both that I be thinking about him and that his thinking be on track. He is open to my thoughts and interested in his own thinking and in his self-analysis with me.

In the material that follows there is, perhaps, a congruence between the shift in the primary locus of the analyzing function and the emerging capacity for a love in reality (related to but separate from the love for the analyst) that takes account of, but is not solely determined by, its antecedents in historical psychical reality. Again, the mutual tracking seems significant. In reality each of the men, Rob and Michael, thinks about the reality of the other, the areas of overlap and the areas of separateness. This pattern is not unheard of, I think, in a mature and long-lasting analytic undertaking; it may be the essence of not only a normative developmental process but also a genuine friendship.

"I can hardly believe how absorbing this is, this thought that I can help him with his grumpiness. I wonder who I think I am or how I feel entitled to such intimacy with him. Then I think that this is perfectly safe because I know that Rob would not want it to happen, I mean my blowing him, and because I care about him, I wouldn't want something to happen which he doesn't want to happen."

"Does that necessarily follow?" I ask.

"It seems to have major relevance for me, not the powerfulness of the feeling, but whether or not I act on it. I know that my wishes don't have to be governed by anyone else's reality, but that's what I am thinking. I couldn't bring myself to propose doing this with him, but I am considering talking about it with him. Wait, the way I said that just now is wrong. It's not that Rob's reality takes precedence over my reality. It's that Rob's reality has become a part of my reality. Because, because I love him. I feel his grumpiness when he talks to me about it. I want to help him with it. A part of me, actually one that is usually dormant, gets lighted up. It is part of us, him and me, although distinctly flavored, might I use that word, from within me. But then the me-with-him, or even the us part, is there. Now I'm getting confused." Silence follows.

I wonder what to say. I am feeling that the "us" part has often come up before in the analysis as something occurring between the two players in the analytic *Spielraum*. Michael has usually felt free to own the fantasy and to attribute to me prohibitive or safety-making positions, which, in a sense, enables him to continue the fantasy as fantasy. How is this the same or different from what is now happening inside Michael's head with regard to Rob? He does not speak because he thinks that Michael will continue when he is ready and does not detect the need to support or otherwise intervene in order for the process to continue. The option to make a transference interpretation is also considered. Much that Michael says of Rob can be related to feelings that have come up before between analysand and analyst. These were related to wishes and disappointments with his father. Michael has acknowledged this congruence. The analyst chooses not to articulate this connection again. This decision reflects his willingness to let Michael *play* in the way Michael has requested.

"My thoughts turned to Ezra by way of Jay," Michael recommences. Ezra is a childhood friend often encountered in the analysis; Jay, also known since childhood, is a current friend and close colleague. "I noticed my silence just then. It was like I was thinking about the intensely private part of this. These feelings are within me but are so much for Rob. The I and the we parts of this are both closer than ever and so distinct. It produces a feeling of extraordinary pleasure within me. I don't think that I was silent to exclude you. It's more like I was absorbed with the momentousness of this. It is wonderful to feel this wish to help Rob, to be that close to him and yet to know that doing it would not . . . ."

"What?"

"Please him, no please us, please me. This is not the final statement on this. But then my thoughts turned to coming home from New Jersey on the train three or four years ago with Jay. We had been at a meeting at Princeton. There was this drunk guy in our car. He took offense at the way I looked or was looking and threatened to hit me. He was completely looped, and nothing happened. Jay laughed and said something about the fact that this could only happen to me. I wondered about that. I also felt scared. What would I do in a fight? I don't know how to fight, how to do it. I started talking out loud again when my thoughts moved to there. That must be important.

"This is strange because—I feel like I am continuing to fill you in, that is, tell you what I was just thinking. But then I remembered a time in West Hampton, must be 35 years ago. Ezra and I had gone into town from the lake and we encountered this sort of gang, maybe six guys. They were townies. I can't remember how this happened, but they said that they were going to beat us up. I was really scared then. Ezra was no help. We went into this restaurant. In my mind it was a McDonald's, but I don't know if there were McDonald's then. We sat there for about three hours. I kept thinking about what it would be like to be hit by all those guys. It seemed absolutely terrible. It was a kind of paralysis. It felt like I was powerless. I couldn't get out of it. But even more striking was the feeling of not knowing how to defend myself. As I sat there picturing it, it was like I didn't know how to do it, how to use my fists or kick or anything else. I just have the thought—and this is current, not reporting on what I thought before, but maybe I am making it such with the annotation—that maybe I wasn't allowed to hit back, like being hit by your father. You know, a boy doesn't hit back when he's getting a spanking. This is, of course, a fantasy, too. I don't know about this really, but in my mind it has always featured a kind of contract, that the boy thinks that he should get it, so he does not resist. It is a form of submission."

"The fantasy with Rob goes in that direction, too?" I ask.

"Yeah, that he would spank me because I didn't know how to give him a blow job. That's old hat for me, for us, I think. But I, too, see the connection now, although I don't understand exactly what it means. With Rob, the fantasy is something like he would say, 'If you are going to do it, I want it to feel really good and I am going to shape your behavior with my belt or something.' It would be so that I would respond."

"Aggressively?"

"Well with my mouth or hands, not hitting him but doing it better. This is going to sound very strange. It's my old confusion, but like learning by its hurting. You know, no pain, no gain. But the exact opposite of this feeling of paralysis, of not knowing how to do it, of being powerless. I now think of the Jews and the lambs to the slaughter metaphor. In the fantasy, the spanking would increase my power. I would get better at blowing him. Giving him pleasure and release."

"Curing his grumpiness . . ." "Yeah, I feel very sad, and no, this is good. I think that it is the kind of sadness that means that I am really struggling with this, with what I have to give up, with what I want to change. I think that that is also why it feels good. When I was in West Hampton it was like being in a nightmare. This is quite the opposite, something like a dream as it is moving into the real and the fact that Rob and I are really friends, he would help me if I had to fight. He and I are, could I say this, learning how to do this together, learning *how* to do it rather than doing it. Does that make sense?"

"Yes," I respond.

In the ensuing hours, Michael continued to talk about the issue of doing it and learning how to do it. It became clear that something had been established between him and Rob that had to do with "How do you do it?" Each man helped the other to learn what one already knew more about and the other wanted to master. When Rob returned, Michael told him about the fantasy, and the two discussed it with interest, including the fact that Rob had had a number of sexual fantasies about Michael, too.

Sharing the grumpiness could occur in both directions, and the sharing was itself an accomplishment. Trying to quip, Michael said that one can bear what one can share, including grumpiness, a concept that seemed very interesting to him. He recognized in himself a similar self-state that he had long managed through his sexualization and his wife Anne's willingness to help him with their lovemaking. This, his characteristic way of dealing with grumpiness, seemed to fuel his fantasy initially. He noted that he loved Rob and that he loved Anne. Perhaps this love led to the sexual cure for grumpiness. But then he became increasingly interested in just what this grumpiness was and the multitudinous ways of thinking about it, bearing it, and understanding it. He thought about his persistent efforts to help his father. These were aimed both at alleviating his father's suffering, which was intense, and at trying to free up the little available energy within him for himself. This urge to help, too, had been mobilized in the feeling that he needed to do something for Rob in order to have Rob, that the self-state of grumpiness might preclude togetherness. Yet, when he was grumpy, he was propelled toward Anne and the sexual solution, a closeness, a togetherness with pleasure, release, and merger. This notion, too, seemed open to rethinking. Urgency in some sort of dialectic with continuity. Uncertainty dialoguing with certainty.

Michael regarded the friendship as a momentous achievement and attributed the ability to create such a bond with Rob to Rob's reaching out and availability—and to something that he had gained or refound in the analysis, something about being with another person.

"His being back is extraordinarily nice," Michael says in the first hour after his friend's return. "He is really here. By which I mean physically, intellectually, and spiritually. It's like the fantasy stands for a connection with him in his absence, but its power recedes as the real Rob, with the real Michael, assumes greater significance. Do you know what I mean? Like a part for the whole, but the whole is even better. I have wondered about this before. We have. What does it mean to have a whole relationship with someone? We do and don't. That's built into the analytic relationship. We really do even though the physical part, touching, et. is verbal only. Anne and I do and the kids and I do, I think. I hope, actually, I know.

"Here comes a thought, peculiar as usual. It's like you don't have to cop a feel, steal something, if there is a whole relationship, if all of the other person is really there. I mean, well, if you draw a circle around us, in this case Rob and me, he's willing, wants to be in the circle with me. I want to be in the circle within him, with him, in his head, I mean, in mine. This is sounding convoluted and in need of editing. But the ideas are sound, like doing the fantasy. Having to do it is akin to having to steal from the other because what you feel is not returned, is not even available. Rob is available to me and I am available to him. This is a help in managing grumpiness and all the rest of it. I think that this is what a father can provide, an available other who is like you, who likes you."

"And, even," I interjected, "Loves you and whom you love."

Michael then states clearly, "I didn't think that it would ever be possible for me to have this kind of real relationship with a man, because so much had been appended to the pain of my relationship with my father, the longing, trying to make it better with the sexual stuff—turning the coldness of indifference to the warming of spanking, I think you once said. But it has happened. Rob came to get me because I reached out to him. What we understood, understand together here, makes it possible for me to really connect with him, not to have to steal a feel. It seems too good to be true, but it is true. It's also strange. I need to do the analytic work with you in order to separate out the feel steal from the real and then I can have a real friend.

"I just had another thought, about liking his smell so much. It's the same as what I just said, I think. It's like the smell stands for what I actually have with him or what I thought that I could never have with him. Again, a part standing for the whole, synecdoche, I think that they call it as a figure of speech. You can steal a sniff, in a number of ways. You don't need to steal it if there is a real relationship;

then we both have the real thing. Essence of Rob and essence of Michael as friends, two men together. It's like the pressure to steal is pivotal; and that which is freely given, no, just actually there in the relationship, is, well you don't have to steal it. It's there, really there. It's genuine and therefore belongs to both of us. More like we can concentrate on how to do it, whatever it is at the moment, rather than feeling compelled to do it. The function is mobile rather than frozen.

"I have the thought that having to do it, sniff, blow, steal is in and of itself a robbery. It's like something much more than a physical act has been reduced to just that, a misuse of the body. Do you know what I mean? Restricting ways of being together when there are infinite possibilities of sharing, being with, symbolizing. Oh well, maybe this is just the philosopher talking again, but this is important, robbery of the body-self from the capacity of the self-to-be in dialogue. I mean, the body, wonderful as it is, here stands for a reduced rather than an expanded relationship. Body robbery means having to do it rather than how do you do it. What I was saying about Anne and me isn't quite right either. We make love and it usually helps, but we don't have to make love. We just like to."

I had previously written of two other men who suffered greatly from their father's unavailability, and I thought of them now. Each struggled with the having-to-do-it/how-do-you-do-it continuum. Each needed to do it in a more fixed mode than Michael and in a way that burdened the analytic process and prejudiced its outcome.

Andrew, one of the two men, had elaborated a two-pronged perversion that involved stealing a view of a woman and expecting that the enraged husband would punish him for this misdeed. Outside the analysis he actively engaged in both aspects of this concretized form of seeking his father. In the analysis, he pushed me to action when it became necessary to intervene on his child's behalf but was then dismayed when I could not remain in the *doing it* mode for all of our interactions and analytic work. His realization of the difference between us in the *having to do it* mode interfered with his being able to continue the analytic work. In brief, Andrew needed to *do it*, rather than learn to think about *how to do it*. And in analysis he likewise needed me to *do it*—to reprimand him, stop him, praise him, or encourage him as the occasion required. He could not tolerate it when I tried to look at this need of his rather than actually doing it.

The other man was Edward. Edward's father was a Holocaust survivor, in perpetual mourning for his murdered first family and almost silent during much of Edward's youth. Edward became a linguist in his efforts to find a language through which he could communicate with his father. He fantasized rousing a man by making love to him, literally bringing him back to life. He experienced these feelings in the transference with me and enacted them with a series of lovers, female and then male. He felt disappointed, as though my autonomy had been appropriated, perhaps by a consultant, when I interpreted rather than participated in his push to actualize these modes of recapture and revivification with me. This construction of his saved me from being seen as punitive or, worse, homophobic. But it proved insufficient ultimately, for we could not find a way for him to let go of the need for it actually to happen. What he felt he needed from me was a turning on, in the sense of arousing, which would restore the lost or never encountered father to him.

Let us consider the relationship between father hunger and the doing-it spectrum. Longing, needing, being, and doing, and the way in which each man pieces together the story of his manhood and its relationship to the man who made him are probably unique to each person. The fixedness of that story and the power it exerts is also likely to vary from person to person. In particular this quality of the man's inscape—which I am trying to convey with the terms doing it, having to do it, not feeling able to do it, and finding another to talk about and practice the how-do-you-do-it aspect—is crucial.

With a father who acknowledges that his son feels, thinks, and needs to manage self-states, impulses, drives, and sometimes disorganizing energies and conflicts, a developmental partnership is devised with the mother's active endorsement in which the question of how do you do it is the central motif. Intense affect modulation and organization and accommodative cognitive process are both strengthened and structuralized by a comrade-in-arms who is wired the way a boy himself is wired. That person interacts with the boy in play and with respectful seriousness. He knows what it takes both to sit on and to sit with an energized and at times overflowing inscape.

Sometimes the boy "asks for it," provoking or eliciting an outburst from the father as a way of matching or confirming the match in impulse and intensity between them and engaging the mode that is most arousing. In this way the boy attempts to elicit developmental help in not feeling overwhelmed. Thus a boy whose aggression is bubbling over may hit or hurt another, possibly the father, in order to elicit a limiting spank or sharp reprimand that has the sharp, sudden, and ragged curve of male aggression instantaneously released; by its very match with what he is experiencing, the father's response serves as a template for *self-with-help-from-a-similar-other* modulation, a comrade in arms. As with all other self–other interactions, the nature of the libidinal tie and the way in which each party feels about the other is crucial. A dismissive slap is totally different from a sudden eruption from a loving father in response to a startling and unacceptable aggressive outburst from the son.

The son who "asks for it" and evokes a response within a safe-enough range, or the son who "gets it" because there is a developmental alliance with his father within which they work together to help the son learn self-management by interactive experience with a like other, learns about his mind and about minding and begins to accrue self-experience and self-with-other experience in the realm of *how do you do it*. The reality of the relationship with the father—what actually happens between them in the intermediate male space composed of each's recognition of the maleness and mindedness of the other and of the generational difference that both unites and divides them—is represented as a schema of "he and I together can approach whatever comes in a *how do you do it* mode." This mode can be accessed under many and varied circumstances and lays the foundation for successive partnerships and friendships employing this orientation. It features overlap and separateness and difference and this feature I am calling tracking. Tracking is the immensely significant interaction in which each partner, in an emotional dialogue, thinks about the other and keeps track of the other's reality and of his own in such a fashion as to endorse and establish the reality of the mindedness, the mental life, and inscape of the other. In development and sometimes in analysis, this process is asymmetric, but to some degree in both processes it needs to be bidirectional, even if one party must show the way, sometimes even insistently.

The son whose father is not available, the boy who does not experience an answering male reality, both physical and affective, sets out to steal that which is not freely given or elicitable. Without a man's acknowledging his mind, tracking him, thinking about him, an array of problems in minding, mindedness, and employing the symbolic function ensues. These are all manifest in the doing-it constellation. Deformation in the direction of I don't know how, I lack the equipment, and I can never learn predisposes to stealing and flows into disturbances in having to do it. The how-do-you-do-it mode is almost always impaired and even superseded by valence from one or both of the other directions, I can't or I have to.

Perversion is a necessary concretization of the doing-it function, which does not permit of the learning mode and therefore lacks essential plasticity; it is a repetitive reminder of what has been stolen, the developmentally essential comrade-in-arms, whose absence is memorialized by the body's being coopted in the having-to-do-it mode and removed from the collaborative how-do-you-do-it mode. It is as if the mind's function were subverted to a necessary way of doing it with a fixed relationship to a restitutive or undoing fantasy that may well sport heterosexual garb and a heterosexual venue but that also depicts the essentially criminal nature of the self-with-other, same-sex self who might have been a comrade-in-arms.

In a sense, the collaborative how-do-you-do-it mode is the product of a man's love for his boy and the son's love for his father. It can be surmised that this love is represented by the object relationship of two who are alike figuring out in the action mode—and in other cognitions—the ways to go about sitting on, sitting with, standing (tolerating), and drawing the line. Thereby, the father fosters the boy's capacity to symbolize and thus to learn. Mutual tracking, even with developmental asymmetry, leads to valuing the thinking process in oneself and acknowledging and valuing its intricacies in the other. When reality has interfered with the establishment of this schema, and thus also with the ability to shift gears, then the resultant representation is of stealing and the stolen. The doing-it mode is concretized. And both self-love and other love are affected. Neither self-tracking nor thinking about the other is likely to occur. In the previous chapter, we saw this in statu nascendi as components both present in and absent from Bart's early development. We also saw the ways in which the analytic situation tried to provide him with a different template of mindedness and thus another potential mode of development.

Michael uses his analysis and his capacity to befriend and be befriended by Rob to play with the doing-it fantasy and to reencounter the how-do-you-do-it mode. Andrew and David, in the absence of this extant representation, struggle to find a way to use the analytic space. Likewise, they find a way to use concurrent reality to create it anew. The antithesis is between mindedness, which creates the possibility for interplay and thus new play, and the need to steal in an endless repetition of doing it because one does not know how to begin the how-do-you-do-it function. Embedded in the compulsion to do-it is an inability to share mindedness with a developmental helper who knows the predicament from the inside and who loves and is loved by the boy. The pressure for something real to happen, to be done, to be taken or forced is omnipresent and often inimical to the analytic process. The capacity to find a Rob is likewise hindered by the same pressure. Repair goes beyond the modes of have to or can not. It involves, too, the creation of minding and mindedness as the analyst's interest in the mind of the boy persists in spite of the boy's determined and persistent effort to convert this interest into something else. "Asking for it" evokes it but does not divert the analyst, now developmentally in the role of the father, from his primary interest in the mindedness and pressuredness of the boy who needs to be able to ask, "How do you do it?" rather than falling back into "I can't" or "I must." Either of these stances may also sculpt the transference and the analytic process.

Analytic neutrality always needs to be functional rather than absolute. Exploration must almost always be linked to support. The reality of his analysand's developmental and interactive history affects the position of neutrality that the analyst assumes so as to maximize his patient's experience of his own mindedness. It therefore also has an impact on the possibility of making a developmental alliance in which the analyst can serve as helper so that conflict can be both ascertained and addressed. Here, too, the question of how do you do it arises.

8 | MICHAEL: Looking for Father

WHAT DO WE LEARN FROM THIS EXPOSURE to aspects of Michael's analytic work, conducted in two pieces over six nonconsecutive years? How does this work contribute to our exploration of the role of the father in relation to conventional analytic concepts of trauma and derailment and to the function of play in the ongoing processes of restitution and repair? If we think of Michael as our guide, as I think we should, to what lands has he escorted us? First and foremost, a critical aspect of psychoanalytic data and theory is indisputably highlighted. Michael's story, his analysis, his torments, and his resolutions are distinctly his. The idiographic declares itself emphatically; the nomothetic is to be extracted with the utmost caution and concern.

Who is the Michael we learn about through the window of a therapeutic analysis later used—in this book—to exemplify something about trauma, play, and attempts at repair? Clinically, Michael is a man characterized by remarkable success in love and in work whose parents were affected by massive historical upheaval and whose caregiving featured not only unevenness but also the frank intrusion of unmodulated aggression and substantial injury to their son. Michael is also a man possessed of formidable intellectual and affective skills. He struggled against being beaten down and related that his own experience of reality was faulty. The architecture of his struggle has been both costly and creative. We can see both aspects of this process in the material I have reported.

Several aspects of Michael's ways of being are notable for their relevance for our journey—exploring the relationship of the father to traumatic process, play, resiliency, and repair. Michael continually tries to make sense of what impinges on him from inside and outside. On the positive side, this process involves his knowing that psychic reality, interactive reality, and external reality are in ongoing conversation. Yet there is more. Michael is burdened with a history in which time and meaning are confused. His parents' Holocaust history is very much present in his thinking, his imagery and symptomatology, and his push to succeed. He often stated to me and to others that he felt that he must contribute and produce to justify his birth and survival when so many Jewish children perished or were never born. "They might have been geniuses, like Einstein or Freud," he would say, "I must work as hard as I can to contribute anything of value." This position also reflects the plight of a little boy who was told by his father that he was not good enough within his family and extolled as wonderful by his mother when the father was not present. Always within him there is the tension between these two voices; each task he confronts is subject both to the belief that success should result and to the fear, often bordering on conviction, that whatever he produces will be flawed and reflect those negative qualities his father so frequently adumbrated.

There are many other examples of the impact of what might be labeled transmitted trauma, that is, the impact on Michael of his family's history and the horrors of the *Nazizeit*. In the first round of analytic work, he and I struggled to understand his great agitation when Anne became unexpectedly pregnant even with an IUD in place. The pregnancy was interrupted on medical recommendation, and Michael found himself feeling very disturbed. He tried very hard to support Anne, who was also troubled, but could not avoid feeling that the murder of Jewish children simply should not be. Long discussions in the analysis about fetuses and children revealed the impact of the murders of 1,000,000 Jewish children during the war and his own feelings of vulnerability, although we did not know the full extent of his father's physical brutality toward him at that time.

That Michael's father was away for two years during the war may have been decisive in favoring the emergence of *I can* as a concomitant to *I must*, rather than I can't and therefore I am not interested in the whole question of how to do it. Michael never thought of himself as a victim.

The absence of Michael's father until Michael was two years old may have been quite decisive. During this time, he not only consolidated a very close relationship with his mother, which had a number of sequellae both positive and otherwise for him, but he also constructed or began to construct the image of his father that has continued to play an important role. The image of his father as exciting, erotic, spanking, holding, helping, athletic, aggressive within acceptable bounds, and intellectually gifted appears to have borrowed from his mother's view of her man. This view probably characterized the way she experienced her husband in his absence and also seems to have borrowed from her view of her own father, a man of courage and accomplishment who was far less involved in sadism than was Michael's father. It was this amalgam, I suspect, that Michael's mother presented as *father* to her son during his father's absence. It is thus, in a sense, a transmitted representation that has a great deal in it of an adult man with his female lover, a good father with his daughter, an idealized and longed-for man. This image has, for Michael, always been conflated to a certain degree with the father–son relationship and with the male-male dialogue.

I am reminded of a time more than 15 years ago when a paper of mine on father hunger was being discussed by Dr. Evoleen Rexford, then a professor of child psychiatry at Boston University and the editor of the *Journal of the American Academy of Child Psychiatry*. To emphasize her point that a child's view of the father is heavily influenced by his mother's perceptions and her communication of them to her son, she told of a young boy whom she had treated during the war. Each day he would tell her what had transpired between him and his father: a series of exciting and pleasurable adventures. Dr. Rexford was quite startled when the social worker who met with the mother told her that the father had been in Europe in the army for the last three years. All her patient's stories reflected the mother's input and his own wishes and imagination. Each day he and his mother would speak of the father, often while regarding his photo. The mother had created and transmitted a great deal of her admiration, excitement, and longing to the boy. He had participated in this process, too.

Michael told me wistfully that he could remember just what life was like before his father returned. There were trips on the Greyhound bus with his mother and always the excitement when they saw a soldier. It was as if each man in uniform could be his father, at least from behind, before he and his mother saw his face. The *nicht Gesicht* Rilke reference that emerged in association to his dream about David's beating, with its interchangeability of face and buttocks and one of the determinants of his interest in rear views and bottoms, seemed to have a referent here.

This capacity to make up a father, growing out of a closeness with his mother and their mutual longing for a good-enough man, not only served as a template for a fertile imagination and creative ability in thinking and in work, but also fueled Michael's omnipresent father hunger and his derivative interest in men. Always there loomed the possibility that the way in which he and his mother desired a man might leave him in a more basically feminine position than in a masculine one. He felt overwhelmingly close to his son, David, with whom he carried on an active dialogue from conception onward. During Anne's second pregnancy, he felt certain that another son was en route and, although delighted with the arrival of Angel, he told me that he needed to actively mourn the nonarrival of Jonathan. It was a source of special meaningfulness to him that he could love each child equally and yet differently. In addition, the arrival of a daughter, with her extraordinary loveliness and feminineness, helped him as the relationship with Anne helped him further to strengthen and integrate what felt to him like his always somewhat shaky masculine identity.

His homoerotic interests seemed moored here, too. How to manage this hunger without its becoming, in a problematic way, desire? Together, we conjectured that his early anxiety about sports and physical activity had to do not only with his father's condemnation but also with the uneasiness that contact with other boys engendered. He never allowed himself to act on his uneasiness except with his friend Ezra, the son of friends of his parents from Vienna. This friendship somehow seemed harmless but never could get off the ground. Michael told me that he was as much of a "spaz" when fooling around with Ezra as he was on the basketball court, substantiating our hypothesis that these two domains were related.

In late adolescence, he began to think about spanking. This was not a feature of his family, but he had heard about it from some of his friends. These descriptions involved, to his ears, the father's being there in an intense and intimate way. With his usual verbal play, Michael said, "It caused me to *prick up* my ears." At college, he met some friends who spoke about it and about the excitement of initiation ceremonies that featured paddling. These activities made him too nervous for actual experimentation, but he was very interested. In high school he had begun dating and was generally popular with his classmates. In college, he had a number of girlfriends, became sexually active, and was bothered by noticing male buttocks and thoughts about corporal punishment. The topic remained exciting, but he remained inhibited and concerned. When a friend gave him a novel, *Mandingo*, to read and he found the whipping passages highly arousing, Michael felt really worried. He had a consultation with a university psychiatrist, who suggested that he try a benzodiazapam if these thoughts bothered him, or that Michael at least try it and see if he liked it. This consultation bothered Michael a good deal, and he chose not to try the medication. When he read the *Story of O*, he was also highly aroused and noticed that this book made him less anxious than *Mandingo*. He thought that this was because he could feel empathy for O and for the other women who were being whipped, whereas he had felt mostly excited by the whipping of the male slaves in the first novel and very little concern for their pain or humiliation.

As with everything else, he spoke with Anne about his preoccupation with spanking. She found it difficult to understand but was willing to play in a gentle fashion with his buttocks and to allow him to do the same with her. These spanking games were fun, Michael said, and they did not occasion massive anxiety. Their play, which occasionally was a part of lovemaking, bore only the faintest phenotypic resemblance to what had sparked his interest in *Mandingo*, Michael observed.

Michael and I thought that the spanking interest was related to the *nicht Gesicht* issue, the not-face of the sought-after father. Looking at backsides had been a highly cathected joint activity with his mother from very early in life—together, they were *looking for the father*. It seemed to us quite logical that this interest would become eroticized and aggressified after his father's return from the war and in conjunction with his displacement from the highly gratifying closeness with Michael's mother and massive disappointment in terms of his treatment by his father. His interest in spanking also seemed to contain an identification with his father's hyperaggressiveness, albeit toned down in Michael, as well as some repudiation of a wish to penetrate the father or any other man.

Michael talked with me about this aspect of his "fixation": "It's like hurting rather than killing or, more exactly, dealing with the surface rather than going inside." This, too, appeared to be a complicated equation in which hurling a child against the wall, as his father had done, causing Michael's original shoulder injury, was replaced through a long series of transformations by slapping the bottom. Similarly, themes of anal intercourse and injury, which had captured his interest in *Mandingo* and lay closer to the original traumas with the father, likewise were comingled in the imagery of slapping the bottom.

We also were interested in the persistence of his interest in how a man smelled between his cheeks. We wondered together if, in his search for the soldier father, he had ever walked right up and into a man from behind. At Michael's age and height at that time, his nose and the buttocks might have come into contact. No such memory could be recovered. Michael thought that smelling was a component of eating, something gustatory, but only one aspect of it. In this regard he brought up a troubling symptom that we had not hitherto discussed. Sometimes he would feel very troubled watching his wife and daughter eating. He had had a similar response to his sister's chewing when they were all at home together. The response was something like what he had described about Anne's need to do things before leaving the house. Now he had the thought, paraphrasing Shakespeare, that "something doesn't smell all right in Denmark."

This led to thoughts about Gertrude and Hamlet and back again to his mother and himself, both trying to get the scent of a man, to find the father. Again there seemed to me some effort at modulating an intense impulse, toning it down to make it more acceptable, here sniffing rather than biting into, a breathing in rather than the more total form of oral incorporation. We thought that both he and his mother must have been "starving" for a man as they waited out the war, alone and uncertain about what would transpire when his father returned.

Michael and I also thought that his intense interest in both smell and the view from behind had to do with the outside chance that he was really always looking for someone like his mother or at least that his image of the father was so maternally colored as to have an olfactory referent rather than the anatomically more precise visual one. This thought grew out of an extended period in which reminiscences of his mother's aroma figured prominently and were coupled with feelings about looking for either the same scent or something that smelled different. Here Michael returned to the notion that Anne and he smelled very different from each other and that this difference was a defining attribute of both femininity and masculinity. Michael considered that his interest in spanking was only a ruse constructed to access smell, but then he went on to say that this could not be entirely the case. There was also something very pressing in it about dominance and submission, about the control factor and the possibility that the boy being spanked would be pushed to a level of sensation that would exceed his capacity to retain control.

We spent a lot of time exploring this fantasy. It seemed to include the notion of being taken beyond one's limits by someone else. Two further aspects of this experience were that the other would guarantee a safe outcome; there would be a safe return from the beyond-one's-limits experience, and the other would want to insure this outcome. This paternal stand-in would be affectively involved and linked to the son by these endeavors. We wondered together about how being taken beyond one's limits was similar to or different from orgasm. Michael thought about this, first with some alarm. Then he had the sense that, of course, it seemed something like what a woman might feel with a skillful lover when she was sent by his stimulation to an infinitely pleasurable place. Here too the identification with his mother loomed. We also explored the sameness between intensely pleasurable sensation and intensely painful stimulation. Michael thought that it was the intensity that each had in common, intensity occasioned by the committed, affectively involved ministrations of the other, the man. He and I were able to see that this comingling of pain and pleasure under the rubric of intensity reflected his melded wishes (his and his mother's, libidinal and aggressive) for physical contact with and from his father and the brutal treatment he had, in fact, received. We wondered if this longing for intensity had begun in some still unremembered way even earlier than the shoulder episode. Had there been actual spanking or something more intense at the time of his father's return when Michael was two and a half? Had this incident involved his buttocks, or had it in some way featured smell? Such an experience would, then, have coincided with the time of his toilet training, the period of time when issues of anality and aggression often combine.

In all this sorting out and putting together, Michael has been showing us how he tries, both in the analysis and out of it, to make sense of what stirs inside him and how it is connected to what has been placed inside of him by his experience, his objects, and his interactions. We are in a realm in which the maternal and the paternal are conflated. Having identified with his mother's longings and desires, Michael creates a male–female amalgam that he must deconstruct and redifferentiate in order to keep his psychological house in order. Complicating this task, he has used women (mother, wife, daughter) as buffers against trauma, as ways of softening what is too hard, and even as means of anesthetizing his pain. His is a strange but understandable nurse indeed (as we saw in his dream in chapter 4). To use a multidetermined phrase, he whips up quite a frothy brew that combines identification, closeness with the mother, the search for the father, aggression and its modification, and some kind of statement about generational difference and the power attributes that attach to such difference. All these are colored or scented by the particulars of his endowment, his parents, their psyches and actions, and his process.

These interests and their closeness to consciousness and behavior were, of course, present in his choices of Hans, Erik, Rob, and me. Each of us was the right type, a good-enough man to be the ideal father. Also each of us qualified in the *a tergo* realm. Michael told me this latter fact with considerable embarrassment, although it had become quite obvious. We then set about discovering the relationship between feelings toward me and the intensity of his affection for Rob and both the course and weathering of that relationship.

Michael stressed how important it was to him that Rob could actually do things with him. Not only could he talk with him, but Rob talked to him about personal things, his past and his pain. This kind of transaction was totally different from what transpired between us. Rob could also go to the gym with him; they could drink and smoke together and go running. Michael hastened to reassure me that this was not to enumerate my insufficiencies, but to emphasize the difference between analyst and friend. And there was something else. Rob was looking for him just as he was looking for Rob. By this Michael meant that Rob wanted a closeness with a man, too, needed it for his own reasons just as Michael did. The same had been true with Hans and Erik. Michael did not know whether or not I needed a man the way he did, or what my status was in regard to father hunger. But he did know that I did not signal it as Rob or the others had. Perhaps this was because of our professional relationship; maybe it would have been different if we were colleagues or had a social relationship, but nevertheless it was a crucial factor in his feeling safe with me. "I would even go so far as to say that those guys presented their butts to me in some way and I to them. I don't mean grossly or literally, but some indication of availability and an overlap of interest. Maybe like what gay guys call gaydar, but here what we might call "fadar, father radar," he said. Together, he and I noted that fadar always involved straight men, preferably even married men, and that the "g" to "f" transformation involved complicated defenses as well as pressing developmental lacunae.

If he were to participate in fadar, Michael needed the other to signal a readiness to participate. His need for such participation was very great, and his inhibition and awareness of the dangers in such play well developed. I would have needed to be more actively seductive, perhaps even flirtatious with him, in order for these feelings to flower with me. Or perhaps even that stance on my part could not have occurred without my also needing to search for a man in the way Michael described.

The need to "do it" and the necessary attributes of the other as a defining quality of one's play-mode predilection is related to the question of how to do it. Each is an outgrowth of primary relationships in which questions of identification and shared range of competence are central. It is also an outgrowth of individual experience with the ego function of play and its developmental history. When the capacity to go on playing, that is, to make meaning under self-authorship and with built-in reversability and rearrangeability, is interrupted by either hyper- or hypostimulation and deficiencies of accompaniment, engagement, or understanding, then a "shift to the left" occurs. The result is a deformation of the play function.

Displacement as the predominant mode gives way to enactment or interactive enactment. Roughly speaking, enactment refers to having to do it; interactive enactment, to the fact that the other has to do a specific thing or be a specific way in order to maintain the ongoing thrust of the play. For instance, one child may play out a scene in which a truck spanks a naughty car; a second boy may spank the car himself or ask the therapist to spank the car; and a third may require that the analyst spank him. The last requirement may become absolute.

This sequence illustrates what I mean by a shift to the left, a term I have borrowed from hematology. With reference to the blood dyscrasias, the term means the ominous appearance of successively more immature stem cell forms; in my nomenclature, it means a reversal of the developmental trajectory by which play develops. First there is an actual doing it, often involving manipulation of the body itself; then there is the use of toys or other objects; and finally there is a symbolic process characterized by something standing for another process or person altogether. An added feature of the shift to the left as I use the phrase is that the most immature or "traumatized" form of play has the least flexibility and requires that the other perform a fixed or specified function; his role is fixed in order for the child to play at all. These play modes can be identified with adult patients as well, although instead of play with actual toys and trucks, the adult in health simply fantasizes. In other states, he seeks to enact these fantasies or requires that the analyst participate in a particular way.

Michael is a traumatized man with a deformation of play style. He is pushed to enact and even interactively enact. He combines this play-mode predilection with a compelled and well-developed capacity to formulate, differentiate, and distinguish between having to do it and a continuing concern for how to do it. The strength of his father hunger, as it has been seasoned by the particularities of his experience, his parents' behavior and unconscious fantasy, and the opportunities he has created and managed for enactment and interactive enactment, define the contours of his psychic reality and of his actual behavior. He does not have to enact a perversion, for example, spanking or some variant in actuality. He manages these urges in fantasy and fear and plays them out in highly modified form with his partner, Anne—a very felicitous choice. Yet, and importantly, the fantasy as an organizing and meaning-giving condensation remains vivid, even as his observing ego can observe its multiple determinants, its sustaining and diminishing attributes, and how and why it operates in the theater of his mind.

Michael oscillates between external and internal enactment, that is, between having to do it and struggling with the awareness that the internal dialogue contains much contradiction and dynamic between the representations of self-with-mother, self-with-father, and self-with-the-parental-couple. This oscillation is a reflection of his traumatization and his capacity to evolve and participate in a neurotic process. His father used to say to him, "Better an end with terror than a terror without end." Michael somewhat ruefully commented to me that he will always have to manage his terror, endlessly, and that one of his solutions has been to think about "terrorizing the end," meaning the rear end. "It has a certain very little-boy logic in it," he went on. "I keep it private, even when it comes to my work with Nietzsche. Well, you and I know that that is only partially true—and you have said that such partially true private–public separations may even be generally true."

All men need to participate in a relationship with a male parent who is loved by the female parent. It is in this matrix that issues of male selfness and problems of penetrance, fertility, disruptive attunement, aggressive modulation and nonfemaleness or nonmotherness are negotiated and worked on. Michael shows us how these issues are addressed in one man and how they persist in all men. His successive approximations in the search for a father, the management of intense longing in the absence of finding one, and his successive steps toward accepting what was not and its impact on his psychic structure (e.g., mourning) are nomothetic even though his content is idiographic. Michael does not develop a perversion as Jonah, who will be our guide in a later chapter, does. Within Michael's mind a perverse structure is constructed that he regards as both friend and foe but that is confined to the mental realm and not enacted. The analytic process in which he participates is rich, yet bounded. All is not possible within it. He needs and finds his Rob as well as his Anne. Yet, without the analysis, each of these bonds would be less fully examined and thus more open to rupture.

Each would be more subject to replay and less likely to constitute new play or genuine interplay.

Michael comments on the need to do it, actually: "Rob has pointed out to me, as have you, that I differentiate between words and deeds in a noteworthy manner. For me fucking is different from saying I love you. Of course, this is true for everyone, but in a way that is in my essence, I sometimes feel that it needs to be done to actually know, and feel that it is real. You and I think that we know why this is so, that what was done to me and how I struggled to know it and not know it is the reason. You said this a lot during the time that I was falling in love with Rob. Thank you for not interpreting that away, and thank you for continually saying that Rob's reality might not be the same as my fantasy. I felt so proud when I understood that Rob and I could be good friends without enacting my fantasies—without sniffing, spanking, or any other form of physical grumpiness reduction. I now see that that gain is against the backdrop of an ongoing tie to doing it, even as I want to know other ways that might accomplish in words, in spirit, the same thing. This is the hardest thing for me. It makes me sad. You know sometimes it feels that I have become hard wired in this way, that I have to do it to feel it, to really know it; sometimes it feels as though there is play in this system too—that I have to do it not quite so much and that I can, with help, inside and outside, figure out a new way."

As he and I listen to this statement of where things were and how he achieved them, his thoughts move still further. I ask him about the difference between the seeming fixity, with increasing mobility, of the fantasy and his take on the advice of the psychiatrist many years earlier that he just try it.

"I never have," Michael responds. "I have never really spanked anyone nor really been spanked. I feel almost as if doing it really would have nothing to do with the fantasy, sort of like ships passing each other in the night. Also, I would, I think, be immediately stopped by hurting the other."

We think and talk a lot about the relationship between the fantasy about doing it and how to do it and actually consider not doing it or having it done. Here the inaction mode both preserves the utility of the fantasy and contradicts Michael's belief that, around certain things, he had to do it. Michael thinks that this is another very important distinction. Pain persists and is remembered or otherwise preserved in fantasy, but there is a choice whether or not to repeat it in actuality, either incorporating transformed fantasy or in its original rendition.

Michael's sense of boundary is highly developed, even though he has known boundary violation in the most profound way. I respect these boundaries even as they inform my technique in a way that differs from that which might tutor another analysis. As Michael points out in his comments, my position in regard to his friendship with Rob takes cognizance of the way Michael is. The question of boundary maintenance in an individual whose boundaries have been violated is a highly interesting one.

Some years ago, I set out to examine this question by looking at 72 infants who had been brought to the emergency room for croup or vaginal or anal infection and in whom a subsequent diagnosis of sexual abuse or misuse was made. Careful inquiry was made into the nature of the sexual contact and by whom. A distinction was made between sexual activity that had occasioned severe pain and that which did not feature such intense dysphoric stimulation. Later the children were studied in play groups. There it was seen by blind raters that some of the children, labeled the "therapists," assisted other children in distress in a precocious fashion; whereas others, termed "abusers," seemed to fall on an injured or otherwise compromised child and thus inflict even greater burden. It turned out that the "therapists" were the abused children who had not suffered physical pain, and the "abusers" were the children who had been hurt the most seriously.

Subsequent play interviews with these children suggested that the "abusers" dissociated during the original abuse situation as though the pain were so intense as to interrupt the continuity of their processing. In such a situation, identification with the aggressor seemed to be the resultant patterning. When faced in the play group situation with a child in distress, they acted the part of aggressor and sought to inflict further distress on the victim. The other children, the "therapists," did not dissociate. They remembered. Their remembering appeared to function when another child was in distress and to inform their intervention.

Michael's situation is complex. He did and did not remember. He identified with the aggressor in dreams and in (spanking) fantasy, while vehemently eschewing such a stance in action. In his overt behavior, he did remember. Thus he was a father all his students and immensely concerned with how to be a good parent to his children. In his intense desire to be close to a man, he limited himself scrupulously and spared the other even the opportunity for extended participation. He continuously tried to prove his father wrong, while feeling certain that his father was, in fact, right. Eventually, but only by actually harming himself in the gym (beating himself as he struggled to beat the old representation) as he tried to make himself stronger, to work out and thereby work it out, did he recognize that both aspects of this dialogue were present in himself in a powerful and not-to-be-silenced fashion. This realization occurred in the context of his having allowed himself a more complex loving relationship with a man in reality, with Rob, and his having dared to readdress the old issue of his physical self, his inhibition, and his interest in how to do it.

"I wonder," said Michael, "what it means that the waning of the spanking fantasy, whether it returns again or not, accompanies the understanding of the 'beating' meaning of having pressed so much weight to make myself a man. Actually I, we, understand it. I need to employ the mode, like seeing the MRI, in some form, in order to really break through, really get all the layers of what I do, what I did, what happened, and what I made of it. In the end, it's all about making a man of myself and bearing the pain that was involved for me. It's an ongoing struggle, but why should it be any other way? I am what I am and what I am not. With you, I have been able to look at that. You know, I had a fabulous workout today at the gym. I really pushed myself, which I love, but I remembered and protected my shoulder and my hip. I can still play, even knowing my limits and my wishes. In a way, I am unchanged, and yet I am also much changed, by knowing, by our work, by your knowing me. I just had the thought that I also factor in your position about my working out. Do you remember when I worried that you were opposed to my going to the gym? Well, what I take there with me now is knowing that you feel that I can, but that I must know my vulnerabilities, my age, my past, and my baggage. To the best of my ability and it is a constant struggle, I do. Thank you."

For Michael, as for many with his kind of developmental history, some form of doing it is necessary if fuller remembering is to take place and if there is to be an impetus toward the continuous effort to effect a genuine shift from the doing-it mode to the how-to-do-it mode. When possible this shift is often advantageous in that it allows greater flexibility and less constriction of options. Such a shift requires accompaniment, engagement, and understanding. It leads to mourning, reequillibrium, and the capability for continued psychological growth.

> The way up is the way down,
> The way through is the way back
>
> —Heraclitus

> In my beginning is my end. In succession
> Houses rise and fall, crumble, are extended,
> Are removed, destroyed, restored, or in their place
> Is in an open field, or a factory, or a by-pass.
> Old stone to new building, old timber to new fires,
> Old fires to ashes and ashes to earth.
> Which is already flesh, fur, and faeces,
> Bone of man and beast, cornstalk and leaf.
> Houses live and die: there is a time for building
> And a time for living and for generation.
>
> —T. S. Eliot, "East Coker"

9 | ALI: The Mother Tongue

THIS CHAPTER ADDRESSES THE ISSUE OF HOW development and derailment inform the nature of the dialogue between analysand and analyst in the opening phases of an analytic relationship. Ways of being together, which instruct and construct the *who* with the *whom*, emerge as a function of the analysand's history and the analyst's receptivity. The play mode selected by the analysand—perhaps it would be better to say used by the analysand—may be displacement, enactment, or interactive enactment. This predilection for the play mode is both a component of and distinct from the compelling issue of how to be together and toward what ends. Developmental experience, challenge, and compromise inform ways of being with as well as play mode use. This is probably true for both players in the analytic *Spielraum*. Increasingly, the child analyst comes to appreciate the necessity to accommodate to his analysand's relational particularities and developmental necessities as well as to ascertain her play-mode constraints and the developmental *Anlagen* of each. I have selected the opening phase from work that was originally conceptualized to be a "summer vacation support" but later developed into a four-year analytic venture.

Before I begin, a few words about what I call the "mother tongue" (Herzog, 1991). I define the mother tongue as a language characterizing the earliest dialogue between mother and child and reflecting the ways in which the mother was able to attune to and engage with her infant. This behavior clearly reflected her own attachment history and, one hopes, included cognizance of the actuality of her child. Learning the mother tongue, then, became the child's initial challenge, for the mother tongue is embedded as it was in the very fabric of the evolving affective-linguistic relationship between the child and her mother. This learning, however, is developmental, by which I mean it is a coconstructed learning in which the style of the mother, the temperament of the child, and the "maternal preoccupation" (Winnicott, 1968) of the female caregiver all converge to create an *Umwelt* that becomes an integral part of the child's psychic apparatus. The mother's actual relationship with the child's father is, of course, part of this, too. I have hypothesized that the female child in particular is adept at teaching the mother tongue to her father and to subsequent significant others in her emotional life. The analyst must be interested in learning this singular language if he hopes to evolve an alliance with his patient and embark on a meaningful engagement with her.

Ali was referred to me when she came to Boston to attend summer school. She was 14, and it was her first extended period away from home. Her family supported this opportunity for her to participate in a university-sponsored program for exceptional secondary-school students. In her home town, she had been seeing a senior woman analyst in psychotherapy for about three years. Together, they had been working on her struggles with her parents and pervasive feelings that she was a boy trapped in a girl's body. This body was pubescent and distinctly female in its physical contours, although highly athletic and "refusing" to participate in the menstrual process. An endocrinological workup had yielded no clues to the basis for this phenomenon. Ali also had a kind of eating disorder. For several weeks of each month, she had complete control over her dietary intake and was nutritionally conscious, and what she ate was no problem at all. About every 28 days, she was overtaken by what she and her analyst had labeled a "feeding frenzy." For the subsequent three or four days, she would gorge herself on junk foods and then would feel repulsed by her behavior and gain between two and six pounds. During these days, she would also be dysphoric and have difficulty concentrating. Both she and her analyst appreciated the possibility that this cycling might be some form of menstrual equivalent. A psychopharm workup had also been undertaken, and both attention deficit disorder and an affective disorder had been considered but were not thought to be prominent enough to merit drug treatment.

This chapter presents some material from the first summer of our work together. Later, we were to embark on an analysis when Ali decided to attend university in the Boston area. My focus here is on the process between us and the reasons that it emerged as it did.

In the first hour presented here, Ali arrives with her guitar. She is wearing cut-off blue jeans, and her hair is braided. She sits down across the room from me and begins to sing and play. There are songs by Dylan and Joan Baez. The time seems to be the 60s. I listen, recognizing all the music, which is, in fact, from my adolescence. I ponder the meaning of this overlap and wonder if Ali is trying to engage me as peer rather than as parent. At a certain point, she asks me if I would like to sing along with her. I note to myself that I am singing along with her. I wonder to what extent she can hear me and say out loud, "Yes, but may I do so silently so that I may also listen?" She smiles at me somewhat quizzically and plays on.

Her next song is "Here's to you my rambling boy, may all your rambling bring you joy." I am stirred by this song. I contemplate how it is a response to what I have just said. There seems to be something about my attunement, separateness, attentiveness, and capacity to go elsewhere. After she has finished the song, I say that music sung can be very powerful. Ali puts down her guitar and starts to talk with me about her summer schedule, and we discuss when we can meet. As the hour ends, I am struck by how much has been evoked in me by this concert. It has, in fact, seemed to be a "together," "in concert" experience. I am reminded of an earlier treatment in which I was involved with an autistic girl. The medium of our exchange was song, never the spoken word. I, of course, do not think that Ali is autistic, but I contemplate, somewhat unclearly, that we shall learn together about state sharing and tuning and ways of being apart, that the self in relationship and self-containing relationships will be our text. After Ali leaves, I continue to sing, to myself, for a time.

Ali begins the next hour by telling me about the courses she is selecting. (I mentally note an initial disappointment that she did not again bring her guitar and a subsequent kind of self-righting as I begin to listen to her words.) One of them is Spanish. She says that she had a dream last night. She seems to be eyeing the couch, and I ask her if it would be more comfortable for her to lie down. "Oh, you want me to?" she asks.

"Whatever would work better for you," I reply, conscious that she has shifted it to me and that I am not taking up this maneuver.

Within myself, I reflect on the "singing together, listening while she sings" exchange of the previous hour.

"I'll try it then," she says. She gets up out of her chair and literally dives onto the couch. "It's no trampoline," she says. "I didn't bounce at all."

I elect not to explore this comment, but note that it has occurred.

"The dream was weird. My father was talking with a very young woman from Colombia. She was the maid. Someone showed me a book called *Spanking the Maid*. She didn't speak any English, so I guess that he must have been speaking Spanish. When I was 12, I spent a summer in Spain with my family. I learned Spanish very quickly. I'm very good at languages. Your road is very bumpy. The taxi bounced on it as I was coming here. I could feel every bump. How come you've not had it paved. It seems like it's a foreign country, not like the States." [The dirt road to my office is, in fact, unpaved.]

"Like which foreign country?" I ask.

"I don't know, does it matter? Why did you interrupt me?"

"What were you thinking?" I ask.

"Something about love, they were talking about love, or loving the language, I think he said that Spanish is the loving tongue. That's a folk song that Joan Baez sings. Do you know it?"

"I have heard it," I reply. I was still thinking about having interrupted her, like a bumpy road, like the bumps of either spanking or lovemaking. Now I noticed that I answered her question directly.

"I like Joan Baez a lot," she continues, "especially that her hair is short and that she looks like a man. Her voice is so powerful, and, when she sings, I can really feel what she is feeling. I like it better when she sings her own songs than when she sings someone else's."

Thinking that this must have to do with our music as it reflected "the music of what happens," as Seamus Heaney calls it, in her inscape, I say, "It is important to be able to sing one's own song and to have it be heard by another if you want it to be heard."

"My father doesn't speak any Spanish," she goes on, "He is completely amusical."

"He doesn't sing, or he can't hear another's song?" I ask.

"They go together. He scowls a lot, my father. It, it's actually a little funny because his hairpiece wiggles when he does." [I note the it-it's, and the wiggles and I associate to a little girl's view of a dangling penis or of a little penis.] "When I was little, I thought that he must be scowling because he heard yucky music in his head. It sounds nice in here. I can hear a bird singing. Is that a phoebe? I think so. It's like being out in the country here."

"You mentioned earlier that it was like a foreign country and now that it's like out in the country. Is it right that it seems quite different here from somewhere else?" I ask.

"Yeah, I can see how you came to that conclusion. This is good, I can follow how you think. Can you follow how I work. Probably not yet. But you haven't said anything yet that makes me feel like it's hopeless. Dr. B. [her analyst in the other city] said that you can hear. Not everyone can, you know. Also you look like a man. Are you an athlete? You don't look like a geek. I like your hair. It looks real. How come it's white? How old are you anyway? Joan Baez is 50. Are you, too? She used to sing at Harvard, at the coffee houses. Now that I am at summer school here . . ." She pauses.

I wait a couple of seconds and then ask, "What are you thinking?"

"Well, it's strange. I was going to say something about singing this summer, and then I had the image of your singing, maybe with Joan Baez, anyway with some girl."

"So, if I understand, your first thought was of your singing and then it shifted to an image of my singing with someone."

"Yeah, that's right," she says. "It makes me feel embarrassed. Would it be all right if I use the couch all of the time? I don't use it with Dr. B. but I think that I would like to use it here."

Ali is determining how she can most comfortably and profitably use her time here this summer. I do not return to singing, Spanish, the loving or the spanking tongue. I do not mention my association to the wiggling. I do note the movement between one and two, her song and another's, and the problem of bumpiness and interruption. I feel invited into and engaged with Ali's inscape, that she and I are beginning to explore the "music of what happens." It seems to me that she is particularly interested in whether or not I can appreciate the existence of her inner process, that there is a song from within which might be heard by the other.

At the very end of the hour, feeling somewhat hesitant to make this connection since she hadn't, I mention that she sang old songs yesterday and spoke of song today. She, in turn, tells me that it is easier for her to understand my comment about it's seeming strange here, a foreign country, than this connection. She says that she is not at all clear about how yesterday and today are connected, if they are at all. I remember that my comment was accompanied by a feeling of hesitation, and now I have the thought that how to connect content and how we might be connected so that Ali can feel self-connection is as yet to be determined. I think about the way in which self-caring is at its root an object relation and that there might well be a representation of self with mother that is inimical to the possibility that Ali's relationship to ingestion and ovulation could proceed in a felicitous fashion. Somehow, we are to approach this by how I listen and how we connect rather than by how I connect one song of hers to another.

The next hour is from six weeks later. Ali is to return home in two weeks. We have been meeting four times a week during her summer-school stay. Ali has had a pleasant time in Boston, made a number of friends, and enjoyed her studies. A boy called Mark has befriended her, and they have studied together and kissed each other. In this hour, she begins by telling me that, since I know all about her feelings, I seem, like a spy, to be spying on her. "Perhaps, I want you to," she goes on, "But it seems quite strange."

She has told me a lot about Mark. Today she returns to a now favorite subject: how straight his back is, he has wonderful posture and stands so tall. I can visualize this 16-year-old Adonis, and I wonder to myself why I am always being told about how he looks from behind. Is Ali reluctant to look at his front or at least to have me see her seeing this part of Mark? This thought may seem strange, but I have continued to feel that our work involves both deepening content and a process that centers on my seeing that Ali is sentient, that she feels, sees, anticipates, thinks, has intentionality, and feels conflict. We seem to be confirming the existence of her mind by my acknowledging that it is here in the room for us to experience. Through successive mishaps, I have mastered the notion that it is not helpful for me to share my associations, that is, to connect by virtue of what I think goes together, but rather to attend to her process and await an invitation to remind her of my cognitive process. Learning this restraint so that Ali may exercise her own mental functions seems to me to be the very essence of our undertaking.

Ali talks about her parents. They called last night; in fact, they call every night. Their calls are regarded as a nuisance by my patient. Today she has more to say. "They hound me. I feel as though I am under house arrest," she complains. "I get all these questions. What did you eat? When did you sleep? Whom did you see? No matter how I answer, my mother has a criticism or a suggestion. She always knows best. I feel like saying lay off, go away, actually, drop dead. That's a little strong—just leave me alone. I am supposed to be able to breathe on my own, aren't I? And you know what I hate the most? She always is asking me about my period. Something strange. No, maybe something normal, I didn't tell her that I got it here. I know that this is very mean, but I just didn't tell her. It's none of her fucking business."

I remain quiet and make no mention of her period. It has not, in fact, been mentioned to me either, and the hour has begun with Ali's feeling that I am spying on her.

Ali returns to Mark and how straight his back is. She says that she wonders about how he does it.

"Does what?" I wonder.

"Stands up so straight," she responds. "He stands as though he has the ability to hold himself up all by himself."

"Yes?" I say.

"How does he do that? I just thought, is there a safety net underneath him in case he falls," she goes on, "How does he know that he will bounce back up?"

"I remember that you were talking about the road being bumpy here and bouncing or not bouncing on the couch, I think you said that it was not a trampoline," I say.

"Funny," she continues, "when I said bounce, I thought about this couch and the trampoline. I was wrong, it is like a trampoline. It does let you sort of bounce, I mean instead of crumbling. It has something to do with us, right, with your listening to me, and not controlling me or what I say. It is being released from house arrest, being free to be me. I used to sing that song. It's from 'Sesame Street' maybe, 'free to be you and me.' I told Mark about getting my period. He thought it was neat. I thought it was even better than that, because he was interested in it because it was happening to me, a part of me, not because it was his. That's what my parents feel, that my period is theirs. That's why I have had it here with you, not at home with them." She begins to cry. "It's like I can have my own body here with you. You aren't the spy, I have my own . . . spine."

"In order to be able to stand up straight," I say.

"Yes, something like that. I am feeling very embarrassed. I said that I had my period here with you, and that is right. I got it here lying on this couch; I want to say bouncing here. It was when we were talking yesterday about that dream I told you about in the beginning, about my father and the maid. And yesterday you were asking me about whom my father loved, and I started to cry and told you that I had asked him once about him and my mother and he had shouted at me. Well, just then, I felt wet and something else, and I thought to myself: I'm getting my period. I didn't mention it, and I know that I am supposed to say whatever comes to mind, but it felt, well, private."

"Yes," I say.

"See, that's what we are doing here. Your not spying is helping me find my spine." She pronounces spine, spy-in.

I say "I think that you are saying that you feel able to see yourself here without having to feel that that function is like being under surveillance by your parents; and that you are then better able to feel that what holds you up, lets you bounce, is a part of you, not vested in them."

"Yes exactly," she says. "My spine is in me rather than outside of me, inside of them, stolen, misplaced, not a part of me . . . I just had the thought that I have not been seeing an analyst but rather an orthopedic surgeon. I regret very much that I am here only for the summer. I have learned a lot of Spanish in school, but I think that I have learned the . . ." Here her voice becomes very low, almost inaudible. ". . . the loving tongue here. Thanks for staying quiet just then. I almost couldn't say that out loud, but I wanted to."

I have been pondering what made it all right for me to comment about bouncing, the couch, and the trampoline. This remark was not accompanied by the hesitancy I have mentioned in regard to my earlier comment linking the first and second hours. I felt, rather, as though Ali had taught me to hear her song and listen to it simultaneously. It was as though my first comment to her, when she was singing in the first hour, had become actualized in a process whereby

I was ever more aware of her mind and mental process. By being so aware, it became possible for her to function, mentally and physically, and not to feel totally derailed or taken over by my observations, associations, or exercising of the analytic function.

Ali and I had traversed a developmental course in which she allowed me to function as an orthopedic/analytic helper. The job was to effect a "spy-on" to "spine" transformation inside her. This must also be a normative developmental process in which the endoskeleton of the psyche is constructed from the process by which the parents *see* the child rather than *see into* the child. In our work, the medium was singing, listening, and singing with.

I accompanied Ali by learning that my mode of connecting content needed to be placed in a secondary position to Ali's need to have her song heard. The two processes can be one and the same, but they are not always so. If there was to be new play and the possibility of interplay, I had to be a "rambling boy," who could hear Ali's song before I could be the analyst who would comment on replay and that which incapacitated by virtue of its unharmonious cacophony. In part I rambled with my own joy, perhaps especially in seeing the "minded" Ali, that Ali had her own mind and mental processes. Ali, too, was the rambling boy. In her later analysis, we were to take this up in considerably greater detail and explore the ways in which her spine had originally moved from within her to outside of her. The concept of the spine as something hard and of spy-on as something visible turned out to have phallic connotations and an elaborate unconscious fantasy involving theft by the mother of what had previously been her, Ali's, beloved penis. This work, which many would consider to be *the analysis*, could be undertaken only after the work of finding a way to be together in which Ali could sing had been undertaken. Of course, this complicated way of being together also featured the imprint of the unconscious fantasy about the stolen spine/phallus as well as the actual contours of the earliest interactive experiences and their initial representations.

I am inclined to think that in many analyses something of this paradox exists. Whatever is fundamentally derailing appears initially in the form of how analysand and analyst are together, how the initial interaction proceeds. By focusing not only on the song but also, and primarily, on the singer and on her definition of what she needs from the listener, that which is most painful in the child's past can be ascertained. A way of listening then evolves that permits the child to play in her own way and enables the play function to serve its inherent role of sorting out, meaning making, and meaning revising, and ultimately allows the play function itself to be returned to optimal performance. Child analysts are blessed with patients who are quite insistent about this necessity. These analysts are often, therefore, at an advantage when it comes to hearing their adult patients who may be more reticent in this regard or more socialized to comply with either established technique or diagnostic nosology.

Ali needed me to hear the words of her songs, the content of her dreams, and the multiple levels of her dysfunction and strength. First and foremost, however, she needed another player in our *Spielraum* who knew that she must inform me of her own rhythmicity, melody, and orchestration. Even though, as she played songs from my adolescence, I might sing along accompanied by fantasies about me from that time, I would need to establish a place where she could feel herself heard before we could sing a duet. At the beginning of this chapter, I mentioned the little girl's developmental need to teach her father the mother tongue. Ali needs to teach her father the mother tongue. But, in an important way, she herself has not quite learned to speak it. Here I want to note something about the way in which the mother tongue is learned, taught, and becomes internally viable. This phenomenon is closely related to Winnicott's (1958) seminal postulation that the ability to be alone is closely related to the experience of being with the mother and thus to the ways in which the mother tongue is evolved and represented. The spine, being inside, is first observed by the parents as a separate, intentioned being rather than being spied on by them.

The next several hours were devoted to anger at her parents, her increasing interest in Mark, talking about my posture and hers, and wondering about continuing to see me versus going back to Dr. B. "I know that I am going back to Dr. B.," Ali said, "I want to tell her about all of this and about us and bouncing. I shall miss you very much. I think that Dr. B. will be very happy about the improvement in my posture. I look more like Mark than I did before I came up here, but it's not really from being with him. It's from being here with you. That is what has made it possible for me to even think about

being with him. Let me say that a little differently. I look more like
Mark, but what I really mean is that your seeing me has helped me
to see what I look like. Both are true I think. And when I come back
to Harvard, I would like to see you again. I need to do more of this,
your looking at me so that I can see myself; your hearing me so that
I can hear myself."

10 | ALI: Opa and the Man Goose

ALI HAS RETURNED TO HARVARD. SHE IS A FRESHMAN. She has begun analysis. In this chapter I present two sessions from the beginning of this analysis, then two from the middle phase, a year later. In the opening phase, she appears to be doing a two-generation reconnaissance on the subject of fathers. I have said that girls need to teach their fathers the mother tongue. But girls also learn from their mothers what to expect from their fathers. And this means a girl learns from her mother how the mother went about teaching the father the mother tongue, that is, if she were able. As we discover, in Ali's family, unspeakable terror interfered with this teaching, and that legacy has been passed down.

"You seem tired this morning. It looked to me like there were circles under your eyes. Do you know Joni Mitchell's song 'The Circle Game?' I used to love to play that. 'And the seasons, they go round and round' . . ." Her voice trails off, "I thought you were so handsome when I saw you the summer before last, almost as handsome as Mark. He was incredible, especially his back. Did I ever tell you that he had a perfect butt. I wish so much that I had gotten to see it, I mean him without either his pants or underpants."

"When you said it, what were you referring to?" I ask.

"His butt. It was chiseled like a sculpture, like Michelangelo's *David*. I like guys' butts. My brothers are both athletes, and their butts are so taut. I hate that mine is rounded. I know that it is feminine and that I am muscular and trim enough for a girl but I'd rather look the way Mark did. I used to just stare at him, especially from behind. Once when he bent over, I thought that I would faint. His muscles there were so beautiful, so perfect. I could see these two tight globes and then the gap between them, perfectly defined. Like Scylla and Charybidis and a narrow strait between them, leading to somewhere divine."

"I don't quite understand. You call Mark's cheeks Scylla and Charybidis?" I ask.

"I just wanted to see if you were really awake. I think those are the twin peaks of trouble, and Mark's butt looked like anything but trouble. I really miss him so much. He's at Yale, I think. I often fantasy about looking him up. I think that means looking up between the twin peaks, dark, rich, moist." I elect not to explore this fecund imagery or why it is attached to Mark's posterior.

"There's this guy Jeremy in my Sanskrit class. He's got a perfect butt, too. I've been making eye contact with him, and, he returns my gaze. I don't know if I dare pursue it."

"What is your thought?" I ask.

"I thought that he might be rough or scream at me. Like Michelangelo's *David* goes beserk. Now I thought again about how tired you looked. Were you up doing it all night?"

"What?"

"Don't play dumb with me," she says, "You know what I mean, doing it, with the little lady. I've seen her here. She is very pretty. I think that she looks a lot younger than you. I wonder if she is your second or your third wife. I can see why you attract them. You're not bad looking you know. You're in shape, and your butt is O.K."

"Really?" I say with perhaps more interest than I realize.

"Oh that really gets you, doesn't it? Guys are so vain about their butts. Even Opa is. He's got Alzheimer's and lives at Ridgecrest, but when I go there and dance with him, he sticks out his butt as though I'm supposed to admire it. He's 88 years old. He was at Bergen Belsen and then Auschwitz, and he is vain about his butt.

"I'm remembering a dream from last night. But first I should tell you that I had a blow-up with Mom last night. She called to ask me about my studying for the chemistry exam. She is bound and determined that I should go to medical school. She's such a jerk. She said to me that I can be a surgeon or a gynecologist. First I told her that I was going to be a proctologist if I went to med school. She said that that was disgusting. I said that that was why I said it. Then she told me that I should write to Opa. I should have just been quiet, but I couldn't keep from saying to her that he can't read anymore. Then she told me that I was rude and I told her to get off my case and I hung up."

"Was that difficult?" I ask.

"It's getting to be remarkably easy, but I think that it bothered me, either the comment about Opa or hanging up on her. It sort of gnawed at me. Anyway, the dream. It was about a weasel, or maybe a mongoose, some kind of animal that looked a little like a rodent. It was my roommate. I didn't seem to find that strange. Anyway, he said something about a fight or struggle. He was telling me about it. Then I got distracted and started to look away or do my work or something, and he stopped talking to me. In the dream I felt like I had failed him, you know, that he needed my attention in order to tell his story and I got distracted.

"That's the dream. That's all there is folks."

"Why did you say that?" I ask.

"I heard it, too. It sounded funny like something in a Bugs Bunny cartoon."

"Bugs Bunny?"

"I had the thought when you repeated that 'bugger cunny,' I think that bugger means fucking butt, but cunny means cunt doesn't it?"

"It can," I say.

"Well that's what I'm thinking about now, fucking butt meaning fucking cunt. You know that I don't talk this way to my mother, just to you."

"Oh?"

"Well what I mean is I am saying everything that I think, trying not to worry that you will think that it's rude or disgusting," she says.

"Your mother did say something about that last night, you said," I respond.

"What is a mongoose exactly?" she asks. "I have an image of something biting the head off a snake. That's what it is, isn't it, an animal that fights with snakes? Riki Tiki Tavi. I have an eerie feeling, and I just thought that mongoose sounds like goosing a man. In the dream, it was like I couldn't listen to what he was saying."

"Why was that?"

"It was too terrible," she answers, "I just couldn't listen. It was like I couldn't bear it. I feel like crying. Now it occurs to me that this animal, man-goose had a beautiful butt, sculpted, a lot like Mark's."

"Were you saying that there was something in the dream that you just couldn't bear, to which you just couldn't listen?"

"The man-goose's butt was just perfect," Ali says, "Twin peaks of perfection."

"You know," I say, "We have learned together that whatever you speak about has meaning, often many layers of meaning, and that it behooves us to explore these. I am certain that your thinking about Mark's butt now is an example of this. Yet I also wonder if this thought takes you away from what is too terrible to listen to, which you cannot bear," I venture.

"I feel like you are interrupting me. I can only do this the way I can do this." She begins to cry. "When this happens, I feel like I'm losing you, like you go off on your own, like being interested in how my mind works, rather than in me. Dr. B was very interested in defenses and resistance. I called her Dr. Dr—you know, Dr. DR Dr. Defense Resistance. I hate it when you do that. It's like you become the cobra, almost a threat. I could go on a roll about this. I don't know why, but it feels when you do this, like you are a snake, or worse, a snake charmer, I mean a fake. I have just had an image of how strong you look from behind. You are quite an Adonis, too, you know, but when your eyes look so tired, then I feel like I can't trust you, that you will become technical like Dr. B rather than flesh and blood, like you were when we first met, a real person, a man. I just thought again about the man-goose, and that I couldn't listen to him, well this is the reverse, it's like you can't listen to me."

"You said that I was like a cobra," I remind her.

"You know that sounds like co-bra, like you become a part of me instead of our being separate," she says.

"Is that something like spy on and spine?" I ask.

"I think so, but I feel quite confused. This isn't very logical and I also have the feeling that you won't like me if I'm like this," Ali says.

"Where does that come from?"

"Now I want to sing 'Waltzing Matilda'—I think to say that it doesn't come from Australia," she says.

"I wonder, would it be all right for me to wonder if you are saying both that these feelings are not from Australia and that they may have something to do with down under?" I ask.

"Now I feel a little more with you, I was hoping that we wouldn't have to stop with my feeling like you are an asshole rather than a guy with a good butt. Or maybe that I feel like an asshole when I get so grumpy with you. I hate that feeling. I never had it in the beginning. Now it comes quite regularly."

"Yes." I say, "We shall see where it is tomorrow."

The next day Ali begins again: "You look better today, like you are tighter and not so saggy."

"What do you mean?" I ask.

"You don't have those circles under your eyes. I feel like singing where have you gone my blue eyed son, where have you gone, my darling young one."

"You sang that the first day that you came here," I say.

"I know. I thought that you were incredibly handsome, a blond, blue-eyed, six-foot-two-inch German."

I feel somewhat flattered by the description, I noted, wondering why. I had thoughts of Lord Byron. Also I notice the distortions. I used to be blond, but Ali herself had commented on my white hair. I was curious about the German allusion, in particular with yesterday's reference to her Opa and to Bergen Belsen and Auschwitz.

"Germans have the best butts, you know. Mark is German. When I was in Spain there were all these German guys, I loved the way they looked. When I competed at Sun Valley and then the winter I went to Davos, it was like Deutschland, Deutschland *über Alles*," she says.

"What do you mean?" I ask.

"Do you know the work of Leni Riefenstahl? She was a German filmmaker who made movies for Hitler. She shows all these beautiful young men. Their faces are like angels, and their buns are like buns of steel. I just had a horrible feeling. It's again like there is something unbearable. Wasn't I talking about that yesterday?" Ali asks.

"I think you had that feeling in regard to the dream."

"Oh yeah," she says. "About turning away, about not be able to listen to the man goose. I always thought that my face was quite masculine, but that my butt is a dead giveaway. It's a girl's butt."

"A dead giveaway," I say.

"Yeah, I couldn't pass with my butt. You take one look at it, and you know that I am female."

"And that is a dead giveaway?" I ask.

"Come on, it's a figure of speech. It means it shows."

"What shows?"

"That I am a girl."

"I hope that this will be all right," I say, "But are you saying that if someone sees that you are a girl, that it will be curtains for you?"

"I'm trying to be interested, but I can feel that I am getting grumpy again. Just let me talk," she says.

"Do you think that there is a way that we could manage your grumpiness together?" I ask.

"Why bother? Just let me talk. Well, maybe. What you said was sort of interesting, I started to think of the Nazis, how unspeakably terrible they were and that, if I had been in Europe then, they would have killed me just like they tried to kill Opa and did murder his wife and their three daughters."

"There were three girls?" I ask.

"Yeah, I used to know their names. One was Manya, I think. Or maybe Tanya, I don't know. The others had harder to remember names. I think Rachael and—yes, Ruth," she says.

"Those are harder to remember?"

"That's what I said, I, I don't know why. Manya I remembered. Manya Goosen was her name."

"Man ya Goose en," I repeat, separating the syllables somewhat artificially. Ali starts squirming and her voice gets seemingly deeper.

"You say it so that it sounds like Mann goose, like in the dream. She was an athlete, I think, Opa said like a tomboy, and she took care of them when they fled to the forest rather than going into the ghetto. She even joined the partisans, but they turned her in when they discovered that she was a girl."

"A dead giveaway," I say.

"This feels awful and eerie. Can we please change the subject? I'm just thinking now about their having nothing to eat in the forest and that Opa almost starved to death when he was in the camps." I think that Ali is telling me about the Holocaust influences on both her gender dysphoria and her eating difficulties, but I elect to remain quiet.

"Opa told me the most terrible story when I was a little girl. My father was furious with him because I had nightmares for a long time. He hated Opa. He said that he made me even more difficult than I already was. It was about Miriam. She was the daughter of some wealthy people, bankers, I think, from Warsaw. They went to New York and left her behind. She was in Bergen Belsen with him, and Opa tried to take care of her. She reminded him of his Manya when she was very little. He tried to feed her and protect her. She had some special status like a Spanish passport. That couldn't be right, but he said something like that. Maybe her parents were trying to help from New York. None of this makes sense, right? Anyway she got thinner and thinner. Opa said that in the end she looked like a boy. She had no shape, no butt, he said, and she died." Ali is beginning to cry.

"It's the most terrible story that I have ever heard. I can hardly listen to myself now as I tell it. I used to cry myself to sleep, and I would say, no butt. In the end, she had no butt. You couldn't tell what she was, just that she had starved. When Opa told me about Miriam, he cried. My father hates everything about the Holocaust. He says that people who dwell on it are simply excusing what they can't do now by blaming it on the past. That's what he thinks about this analysis, too. He says that it will make you rich and keep me from what I really need to do. Right now I feel as though I hate him and my mother too and my Opa is disappearing before my eyes with this Alzheimer thing. David and Matthew aren't interested in our family's past. And my mother, how she can be Opa's daughter is incomprehensible to me."

"Are you really German?" Ali asks.

"What does that mean?" I ask in reply.

"One of them, one of the people who kills, little girls, everyone. I don't know why I even ask that. I know that you aren't a killer. At least for me you have been mostly a listener and a helper, except when you make me grumpy. Grumpy sounds a little just now like rumpy. Your butt is a German butt."

"I think you said that those are the kind of butts you especially admire," I say.

"Can I help it that I am crazy? Please help me to figure this out."

"That's what we are trying to do."

"When I sang 'Here's to you my rambling boy,'" [She begins to

ALI: OPA AND THE MAN GOOSE | 111

sing, loudly and beautifully.] "It was because you looked to me like the person whom I could sing with. I thought that you would let me ramble and that you were the boy who could help me. Now I think that you are like my Opa, only with your head still working."

Ali is crying. I notice that I feel like crying, and I am not so sure that my head is working. I say, "I think that you are right when you say that I shouldn't interrupt and that you don't need me to be a Dr. D.R., defense and resistance, but rather that you ask me to accompany you as you sing and as we ramble through a very painful foreign country, which has now taken up residence within you."

"Do you remember that I said that this place seemed like a foreign country, very bumpy?" she asks.

"Yes."

"It's not good to be all alone in a terrifying place, but if your parents have left you, then you are. I get very frightened, especially when I get grumpy. I think it means when it is very bumpy and I am afraid that I am alone." I think about saying something about Miriam and Opa but remain quiet. Ali again sings loudly and beautifully, "Here's to you my rambling boy, may all your rambling bring you joy."

I want almost desperately to sing along, too, but I remain silent. Ali has finished singing now and says to me, "I could hear you singing too, but silently so that you could also listen."

The next segment comes from a year and a half later. Ali's search for a father has moved from two generations ago closer to the present. Opa is still on her mind, but, in what she talks about, themes of fathers, and their potential for brutality, come closer and closer. The same themes also emerge in the transference, in her dealings with me. We are shifting to a kind of enactive play, but it is also new play. Here are two sessions from this phase.

"You are a mean and nasty man, the way you spoke to that little boy was despicable. He's so vulnerable, obviously Jewish, dark and fragile. You are an Aryan brute. Why don't you pick on someone your own size. I feel like I want to vomit. At least some people have the decency to perform their fetishistic activities behind closed doors. I know that you have this dark side, this utter contempt and disregard for the feelings of others, I would not have thought that it would emerge in such a blatant way—and with a child. I am certain that you could be prosecuted for child abuse."

We were just interrupted by Ned, a 16-year-old atypical child who has been in treatment with me since he was four. This week Ned has been appearing at my office frequently at unscheduled times. When he arrived, he began banging on the door between the waiting room and the office and I excused myself and went into the waiting room to greet him and tell him that I could not talk then as I was with someone. I reminded him that we would be meeting together tomorrow and told him that he could stay in the waiting room if he liked. He left rather cheerily. This conversation with Ned was conducted in the waiting room and with double doors closed between that room and my consulting room.

"You saw the person in the waiting room?" I ask.

"Of course, I did, asshole. How else would I know what he looked like? You were terrible to him, just terrible, shouting, carrying on like a lunatic. You had absolutely no regard for his feelings or for how humiliated he would feel knowing that I could hear every syllable of abuse you were heaping upon him. Don't you feel ashamed and penitent?" I elect to just listen. In this phase of our work, Ali has been increasingly hostile to me and feels that I am unreliable and sadistic.

"He was so helpless," she continues. "Just cowering and half your size. You know he never had a chance in the presence of an ogre like you. It's like David and Goliath, but in your crazy and disturbed world, Goliath always wins."

"You found me to be not only not helpful but harmful to the person in the waiting room?" I say. The door to the waiting room had been closed, and I am reasonably certain that this scenario was being brought forward by Ali for reasons that would afford us an opportunity to learn more. I do not feel the need to refute her allegations or to reality-test them—although my initial question about her seeing Ned must have been somewhat influenced by such a concern.

"Where do you get off getting up and going to see him in the first place?" Ali now continues, "Don't I count for anything?" This seems more to the point, although I wonder to myself if it is more comfortable for me to be thinking about sibling rivalry than about the demolition of a helpless little Jewish boy.

Ali goes on: "I've been thinking lately that I must be a complete idiot to come here five days a week, not to mention coming back to

Harvard to see you rather than going to Yale. Everybody at my school thought that Yale was better, but no, I wanted to come back here and do an analysis with you. Stupid me. I thought that you were attentive and gentle and a beautiful man that first summer. I need to have my head examined. I could have been with Mark for two years before he came up here. What kind of an asshole would choose you over Mark? He's gorgeous back there and in front, too, and you, you are some kind of repulsive toad, not a man at all but some kind of subhuman. You should be exterminated. You're like vermin. I feel so angry that I could scream. You are an abusive, ugly man. Your German butt is hideous, not like Mark's. I hate that I have come to see you at all and especially that you have misled me so. I feel that I can see you much more clearly now as you screamed at that poor little Jewish boy, but I have been becoming increasingly suspicious for some time. You're the kind of coward who picks on children because you are afraid to take on people your own size."

"Why do you think that is?" I ask.

"Professor P was talking to us about the Russian campaign in Afghanistan," Ali replied. "He told us how terrified the young Russian soldiers were that they would have their throats cut if they were captured. Apparently that is how the Mujahdin rebels kill their captives. He showed us a video of a group of Russian boys trembling with fear. They were going to get their throats cut. Some people looked away, but I watched. It ended just before the actual cutting. I wanted to see what it looked like."

"What did you think that you would see?"

"Terror, blood spurting, screams, and then death; I saw this movie about a British couple in Venice and a crazy man who stalked them because he wanted to kill the man. It was connected to his having been abused by his father. He cut the man's throat in the end, and the woman had to watch. She was drugged and could not look away. I think that it was called *The Kindness of Strangers*. I just thought about what it's like to go to the operating room with my mother. I would always look away, and she would bark at me. I told you last week about going to Mass General with Mark, and we went into the operating room together, It was interesting to watch the herniography. Almost no blood."

"It matters whom you are with," I say.

Ali is silent for a few minutes and then begins to speak. I am noticing in the interval that this feels very much like transference, but I am also wondering a little about my feeling of remove—why am I not more in the thick of it, feeling abusive or like a child molester? As Ali began to talk about the Mujahdin and then *The Kindness of Strangers*, I felt more engaged, a kind of agitation that I recognize as a convergence of her sharing and my sharing, which usually means that we are closer to the core of things.

"I was thinking again about *The Kindness of Strangers*. I think that it was a Harold Pinter film or at least that he wrote the script. The part that was so interesting was that this man had been targeted by this other guy the moment he arrived in Venice. There was a feeling that he could not escape. Venice seemed eerie and like a trap. There was a scene in which the older man punched the younger guy hard in the stomach during a pool game, it was a total departure from anything expectable between them. The younger guy was totally stunned. For a while the younger guy stayed away. During that part of the movie there were a lot of scenes of him and his girlfriend fucking and eating and all of the regular things of life. And then, just when escape was possible, he and his girlfriend went back to say good bye. It was then that his throat was cut. It makes me think of how it was in Europe in the late 30s. I once saw this film about some Jews vacationing at a resort, and then, when their holiday was over, there were the boxcars, waiting to take them to Treblinka or somewhere."

"You said that the film was called *The Kindness of Strangers*, not the one about the vacation place, but the one about Venice," I say.

"Miriam had to depend on the kindness of strangers after her parents left her in Warsaw. She was lucky that Opa took care of her in Bergen Belsen, but he couldn't keep her alive without food."

I am silent for a few seconds, as is she, and then I say, "So, even the kindness of strangers is not always enough." I am not sure why I am saying this. I think that I am speaking about its being both insufficient to maintain life under overwhelming circumstances and fatally devastating in circumstances like those featured in the movie she was describing.

"I have never heard a crueler or more heartless statement," Ali says, "How you can malign a caring, almost saintly man like my Opa is beyond me. I don't know whether I can stay here on this couch

ALI: OPA AND THE MAN GOOSE

any longer. I used to say that it bounced, but I think that it has just gone thud for the last time."

"Is that how it feels to you, that I was attacking your grandfather's goodness?" I ask.

"Yes, although, now that you ask, this doesn't seem reasonable. But yes, as though you are saying that he wasn't good to Miriam." Ali begins to cry. "I don't quite know why I am feeling these things. It's like I get on a roll and either cannot or don't want to get off it."

"Why do you have to?" I ask.

"I might really just walk out of here or tell you to drop dead."

"Drop dead," I repeat.

"Why do you repeat that?" Ali asks.

"I think you said that before, that you would tell someone to drop dead," I say.

"I remember. It was about my mother and her fucking inappropriate behavior about my period," she replies.

"You got angry today because I went into the waiting room," I say.

"I've been angry with you for months now," Ali replies.

"I know," I say. "But today it was about my leaving you and going in to the waiting room."

"I just thought that it's like with my brothers," Ali says very quietly.

The hour ends shortly thereafter with Ali saying, almost in a mumble, that she knows that I didn't shout at the boy. I respond by saying that her thoughts about me and the way I am deserve more exploration. "Sometimes you remind me of what I hate most in the world," Ali says, "It isn't so easy, then, to remember that I've known you for a lot of time and that I trust you."

"I remember that you feel a number of ways," I say, "It's all right to push what you feel." "What if it's true," Ali asks, "that you are a sadist and an asshole?"

"Well we can deal with that, too," I answer.

The next hour Ali continues. "I was astonished by how yesterday's hour ended," Ali begins, "You said, 'We can deal with that too,' with your being a sadist and an asshole. When I left, I started to laugh. He's too much, so stuck on himself that he thinks that I'll put up with all of his shit. I felt furious, world's #1 narcissist. He probably thinks I'll put up with his asshole because I told him that

I liked Mark's, its smell, everything. I got so mad, I felt that you were so low that you would use that intimate revelation to stick yourself in my face. I wondered if that isn't psychiatric malpractice. By the time I was back in Lowell House, I had calmed down, and it actually seemed that you were not saying I'm in your face and that's how it is. More like, our relationship can tolerate whatever strain either of us bring to it. Is that what you meant? Don't answer. Actually, that is, I think that's what you meant, but just now I felt very uneasy again.

"I didn't tell you the whole truth yesterday. The video in Professor P.'s class didn't end where I told you. The guys did get their throats cut, and I did look away. Almost everybody did. It was not a pretty sight. The course is about the Holocaust, and we're now talking about why people do these things to other people and how a person gets to be able to do it. Professor P has been talking about what is happening in Afghanistan as a way of illustrating that this is not just about Germans or Poles or Ukrainians, but a more pervasive phenomenon. At the end of the video, the Afghani boys—that's really what they were—were sort of grinning and talking about how much blood was on their knives, one of them even licked the blood off. It was repulsive. The Russian boys were dead, lying in pools of their own blood, someone said like a stuck pig that has bled out. Beverly began to sob. She is from Cambodia, I think, and her family was involved in something terrible. I felt very sympathetic toward her.

"I looked over toward Ray. He's from Ireland, he was sort of grinning. I've notice Ray a lot, good butt and he's really cute. I thought, is this a guy thing, liking to do it so much that you forget about what it's like for the poor bastard who is getting cut? Ray is on the soccer team and he invited me to come and watch him at practice and then have a beer with him. I told him that I had a boyfriend. He grinned, that same grin as when he watched the video and he said to me, 'Don't tell, let's just do it. I think that you are really hot.' I got excited, because he's really hot, too. I wanted to, but I said, thanks but no thanks, I'm really serious about my boyfriend. Ray was still grinning. He said, 'OK, but if you change your mind just come over.' He touched his crotch and said, 'Big Ray would always like to show you a good time.' He was really hot, I got wet when he said that.

"Mark has been telling me about his surgical rotation, how the guys joke in the O.R. I asked him about the girls, and he said that it seems different to him when there are female medical students in the room, a little more toned down. The nurses don't have this effect, but the women medical students do. I wonder what it will be like when I go to medical school and if I'll get into Harvard. Mark will be in his residency then, and I don't think that he wants to stay here, but I would want to stay if we're not done. In the movie, the Pinter movie, the man who eventually cut the young guy's throat kept saying, it was about my father, you see he beat me, and something about his father's hair and mustache. I believe that the point was that he repeated something with this English boy that was because of his father. Almost as if his wanting to kill his father because he hated him so was the cause of his cutting this boy's throat.

"I feel both distant from you and not. You haven't said anything. I just wondered if I have insulted you and that is why you are so quiet."

"Do you feel like insulting me?"

"I didn't. It was like I was feeling, before I commented on your quietness, that it was good that you were letting me figure this out, that you weren't interrupting me."

"That has always been important," I say.

"Yes, but then it shifted, and I felt, he does nothing except sit back there on his butt, takes my money, and probably thinks about his sex life."

"Is that the insult?" I ask.

"I can do better, your wife is an old woman. No wonder you can only think about it and probably coax your dick to squirt once a month or so. Mark can come four times in an evening, and I can, too."

"Is there more?" I ask.

"I don't think so," she says, "But I don't know. This is all quite surprising to me, especially the vehemence. Do you have any thoughts?"

"Well," I answer. "Yesterday, when you were concerned about my behavior toward the person in the waiting room, you commented that I was picking on someone younger and smaller than myself, and now you mention that I'm stuck with an old woman and have to satisfy myself alone and cerebrally and infrequently."

"I just thought of the kindness of strangers again, and of poor Miriam. I don't feel angry with you now. It's so odd; I'm thinking about how beautiful you looked to me when I first met you and you know this morning when you opened the door, I again thought, he is a very handsome man; I like his body and I like his face. More, I thought about how hot you are and then I had a thought about big Jimmy, I wonder if that is what you call your penis. Well, I guess the prick is out of the bag—it's what I call your penis. It's so strange. I was feeling turned on by you, which seemed a relief after feeling so angry yesterday during the hour and then that you were such an asshole and so stuck on yourself and your asshole on the way home."

"These thoughts are often connected to their opposites."

"You aren't going to turn into Dr. DR, are you?" Ali laughs.

"Not intentionally," I reply, "but something does seem to happen in which you notice ways I am O.K. and ways I am not."

"It was not all right for you to go out into the waiting room," Ali says, her voice beginning to rise, "Let that bastard be out there— you have to stay in here with me. I need you. I can't live without you."

Ali starts to cry. She takes a few minutes to compose herself and then says, "I feel this intensely."

"That I should neither come to the aid of nor otherwise treat a helpless Jewish boy when he appears during our time," I say.

"Yes," says Ali, "But I can't mean it. I feel like I'm turning into one of those Afghani boys or at least one of the girls—no, it feels like one of those boys. I don't understand this at all. I feel like I should though, almost as if I've been explaining it myself in this hour."

"You mean as you were thinking about *The Kindness of Strangers* and what each of the characters was doing."

"Yes, exactly. I feel excited. The older man was repeating something and so was, I imagine, the younger one, not fleeing, being drawn to his killer like a moth-er to the flame."

"Like what?" I ask.

"What did I say?" asks Ali.

"I think you said, moth-er."

"Yes, I meant to say moth, but also, I must have meant to say mother. This is about my mother, and Opa, I can't stand this. What is it, about my mother and Opa?" She is almost screaming. "Do you think so?"

"Yes," I say. "About your mother, and Opa, but perhaps also

about your mother and you."

"I just thought about cutting a throat again. My mother was always very critical about her father in this country. She said that he knew nothing about how to be cutthroat in business and that she and my father had to start from scratch, that she had to make my father be mean and aggressive, and that was why he got to be the chairman of his department and now the dean, that he never could have done it without her.

"You know, I've been at this analysis with you for a long time now, but it still seems unbelievable to me how these things develop. I think that this is about my mother and the way she cuts or something. And the way, oh, I don't know, and I don't like that I feel these things toward you. I feel angry again, like you should protect me from this, not have it be all right, but stop it, nip it in the bud. My friend Angela's father used to spank her, and he would sometimes do it before she really got into trouble; he would nip it in the bud."

"Is that what you are feeling now that I should do?"

"Yes, nip it in the bud—now it sounds like nip it in the butt. I feel ridiculous, but that's what I feel. Daddy take control, stop this from happening now, do whatever it takes to stop this from happening now."

"Why is that ridiculous?" I ask.

"It's like a three-ring circus. I shift from second to second, and it's all between you and me. Is that what is supposed to happen? How can you keep up with it?

"Miriam's parents both left her." Ali is crying again. "It is incomprehensible to me, how that could have happened, leaving one's daughter as the Nazis are invading your home, Just now I thought that I am gladly leaving my parents, but that's different, right?"

"I think that you said that you wouldn't leave here when it comes time to go to medical school unless we were finished with our work."

"I never said that," she says, "This is an example of your intolerable narcissism and your belief that your asshole is the cat's pajamas. You know, before, instead of saying let the cat out of the bag, I said, let your prick out of the bag. Now I wanted to say your prick's pajamas, I hate it when I have these sexual thoughts about you. I get excited, and then I can't think straight. I told Mark that that happens whenever I see him and that if he bends over or takes off his shirt or, worse yet, his pants, I'm a goner. He laughed and said that I wasn't a goner but a comer and that he finds my orgasms totally wonderful and more exciting for him than anything he could have imagined before we started to make love."

"So, when you have these thoughts . . ."

"They're not just thoughts; they're feelings," Ali interpolates, "It feels like I can't think straight. I just want to take you in. But I don't want you to be a Dr. D.R. I *can* think straight. What did you say, yes, that yesterday I did say that I wouldn't interrupt the analysis before it is over—not yesterday, but this morning, right?"

"Yes, you were saying that."

"Well, here it is again. I feel this about you. Can't leave, don't want to, can't stand that I feel this way, feel like I'm going to melt if I catch a glance of you. Miriam couldn't leave, even with her Guatemalan passport. They killed her. I wonder if she wanted to kill them."

"Who?" I ask.

"I don't know—her parents, the Nazis, even Opa for trying to help her." Ali begins to cry again.

"It's too confusing for me," she says, "And it's not this time about being so hot. I just can't sort it out. Now I just thought that when I saw the movie *Shoah* that they interviewed Polish peasants near Treblinka who laughed as they told about the Jews arriving there and made a gesture of drawing their fingers across their throats, cutting their throats to show them that they were doomed, that they were on their way to death."

"There is every reason that all these feelings about coming and going should feel so confusing and that we get to encounter all of them here," I say.

"You know a person would have to be crazy to do an analysis," Ali then says, "Well, let me amend that: she would have to be hurting like hell or want to become a psychoanalyst. I guess both were and are true about me.

"I think that I get what you are saying, but it's all like through a haze, that I hate you and have killing feelings and that these are related to things about my mother and me and to things about Miriam and Opa."

"And that you have loving feelings, too," I say.

"Not toward her, I was about to say, but then I had the thought that that man in the movie who slit the younger guy's throat, he probably loved his father, too. I think that I once read that Hitler hated the Jews because a Jewish doctor had saved his mother's life, talk about ambivalence, I think he was supposed to have loved his mother very much. I find me almost incomprehensible. But you know what, the fact that you are interested in what goes on within me makes it possible for me to be interested, too. I think I can say it better, in spite of everything I say and feel toward you, I know that you are my friend. That's all, that you are my friend. You have been since I was 14 years old, right?"

"Right," I answer, feeling that she was right on.

She goes on: "I was told a story that I can't get out of my mind. It was in Prof. P's class. I came in late, and it was already in process. I don't want to cry. I just want to tell you. I think it isn't published yet, but I may have that wrong. I asked Beverly after class, and she said something about a Polish Jewish writer. Anyway, it was about this boy who hid during a roundup in his village and all the other boys got marched off by the Nazis. He was overtaken by the thought that he was missing something and rushed out to join them. The Nazis were taking them out to shoot them, and the next day they found this boy, I think his name was Schmuel, dead, but up a tree— he was trying to climb away. All his friends were dead on the ground. I don't know why it came to mind, but it is something about being able to get away and then choosing not to, like the young guy in Venice, something about choosing to participate in one's own destruction. This is what I think frightens me the most, like when I had those eating binges and didn't want to be a girl and have a period. I think that I am shaking. I could have never felt what it is like to have Mark inside of me, to feel the power of his coming, and to answer with the joy of mine." Ali is crying very hard. "I feel that my being like Miriam, although I didn't know it, could have kept me from loving Mark. I can't stand it. Without coming here, I might have been shot climbing up the tree or not been able to leave Venice. Does that mean that I have to stay with you in order to know me? I know that that isn't so, but it frightens me."

I was told the story of the Polish Jewish boy and the tree earlier in the week by another patient, who had found a totally different meaning in this terrible tale. I remain silent now, sorting out these two evocations. Ali then says, "Again, when you are quiet it makes me feel that I can and do do this work on my own. I'm glad, because I have the feeling, too, that, if you were to talk, I would fight with you, even that I would want to kill you."

The work with Ali continued for another two years.

11 | THE T FAMILY

PLAY IN CHILD ANALYSIS (AND IN ADULT ANALYSIS) is a complex and changing phenomenon. It may involve displacement, enactment, or direct interaction with the analyst. It may feature only one mode of activity, an unvarying, identifiable series, or a collection of activities under the sway of differing developmental and dynamic pressures. Techniques may shift and stages vary within the same child.

This chapter presents material from several related child analyses—they are of siblings—to illustrate the ways in which play modes vary or remain stable. By doing so, I hope to document an important variable in this critical human ego function, "the capacity to play," and to demonstrate its vicissitudes, both idiographic and nomothetic, within the analytic situation. I believe that the principles derived from a careful study of children's play in the analytic situation are pertinent to analytic work with adults as well. I present a brief vignette from an adult analysis to explicate this hypothesis.

I conceptualize play as the action language of doing, redoing, and undoing. It is a mode for representing, communicating, and trying on, both within the evolving self-system and between the self and others. The exercise of play involves taking oneself and one's agenda—cognitive, affective, and putative—seriously enough to be playful. The capacity for play appears to be innate, but, as with almost every other human ego function, the *Umwelt* must provide a suitable haven for and response to the inchoate capacity. Just as there is no vision without stimulation by light, so does play not fully develop without an adult's taking it seriously. Developmentally, the task of endorsing the child's play is performed by both parents, each with a somewhat characteristic mode of play interaction.

Some of the play material presented here derives from the evaluation of an extraordinarily distressed family with three preschool children. As these children were later seen in an analytic situation, it is possible to advance certain hypotheses about the origins and variability of what Ritvo (personal communication) called "play signatures"—in this case, familial as well as individual.

A DISTRESSED FAMILY

Every evening at around 11, Jack gets up from his bed. He cries a few unintelligible sounds and heads for the window. His parents say that his behavior is like clockwork. His younger sister, Kerry, is like a whirling dervish. Her mother says Kerry is tough, nasty, and, at 23 months of age, the most difficult of her three children. Robby, who at 43 months is the oldest of the family's children, clings to his father. He literally will not let go except to clobber Jack, who is 33 months old.

At the Clinic for the Development of Young Children and Parents at Children's Hospital, we were asked to evaluate and assist this young family. The referring social worker told us that the father, who is 24, has a hereditary cardiac condition. He has already suffered several heart attacks and is a virtual invalid. He cannot work. Moreover, the family has been reported for child abuse, and our evaluation is to be part of the social service agency's assessment of this issue. Interestingly, the initial referral made no mention of the mother. The family's first appointment was almost canceled. The problem has been solved, we were told, because Jack has not awakened for two nights in a row. Tactfully, we suggest to the parents that it might be useful for us to meet anyway. Twenty years old, Mrs. T agreed and added that maybe we could help her, too. Her mother, she told us, insists that she is retarded. Can we give her some tests? Then she'll show her mother a thing or two.

In our initial meeting with the T family, we were impressed by how thin, ill, and wan Mr. T was. He smiled and told us that his illness was nothing. His mother had it, and so did his son Jack. He was not afraid of dying. "When your time comes, your time comes," he said with a smile. Although he was 24 years old, his manner and appearance suggested a 14-year-old, while something else in him suggested a very old man.

He illustrated his attitude about mortality and something of his cognitive style and capacities by telling us that his mother had "died" on the table during a cardiac catheterization, but, as it was not her time yet, she came back to life and was now fine. Mrs. T did not appear to listen as her husband talked. She wanted to speak only about her mother. She was quite adamant. What does it mean to be retarded? Could we tell whether or not she was? She was not much concerned about her husband's health but did say that it took him longer than any of the three children to climb to their third floor apartment. In contrast to her husband, who seemed affectively attuned and present, Mrs. T had a preoccupied and absent quality. Her face seemed blank and without emotion. For example, when Mr. T told us that there was no heat in their apartment, that they were cold, and that it was nice to be in the clinic because it was warm, Mrs. T merely shrugged her shoulders and grinned.

As we spoke with the parents, the behavior of the children was most noteworthy. They were absolutely and totally silent. Jack and Robby clung to their father, one on each leg; Kerry sat on his lap. It was almost impossible to see Mr. T, who was completely covered with children, but it was possible to hear him. He spoke about how difficult the children were. They were always naughty, he said, and he had to use the belt on them a lot, especially on Jack. He didn't like to do it—children were to be loved not hit—but what could you do? It was strange, he said, that there was much more trouble since he was home full time after his last heart attack. He didn't know what got into the kids, what made them so difficult. Again, Mrs. T did not pay much attention. From time to time, she muttered about her mother, who was called Angel, even though she was "hell on wheels." When Mrs. T was a child and her mother became angry with her, the mother would burn her with matches. Maybe, Mrs. T wondered, she should burn Robby and Jack and Kerry. Her husband burst in: "We don't want to do that. That's why we are here. We love our children and don't want to hurt them." Throughout all this, the children were frozen to their father and watched him like a hawk. When at one point Mr. T coughed and put his hand on his chest, an expression of concern appeared on Robby's face and then on Jack's and even on Kerry's. Mrs. T appeared not to notice.

As is our protocol in the clinic, we then observed the family interacting behind a one-way mirror. Mr. and Mrs. T conversed very little. The subject was Angel and her cruelty to Mrs. T. Mr. T seemed sympathetic. As his wife's anger grew, so did his own excitement. Mrs. T began to cry as she described her mother's threats against her; Mr. T became so upset that he said that he would strangle Angel. The emotion was apparently too much for him. He clutched his chest and became silent and pale. The children, who had been playing on the floor, immediately stopped and stared intently at their father. Robby said, "Ma, stop," but Mrs. T continued what had now become a monologue about her mother. Concerned about Mr. T, we interrupted the observation at this point. He said it was nothing; it happened often (which his cardiologist confirmed), and he took some propranalol. The children's watchful wariness and the mother's obliviousness were particularly noteworthy to us.

After we left the room and the observation recommenced, little Kerry launched into action. She got the boys to join her, and they all began first to throw things and ultimately to fight with one another. Jack, after much provocation, pulled Kerry's hair. At this point, Mr. T, who was again looking very upset, threatened Jack with his belt. We once again intervened as Mrs. T told Jack he was going to "get it" and grabbed him while Mr. T took off his belt and prepared to strike his son. As we entered the room for the second time, it was clear that in some way Mr. T's gesture had decreased the tension rather than increased it. All the children, including Jack, the would-be victim, now seemed relaxed. Robby smiled, as did Jack, and little Kerry sang, "Daddy here, Daddy here."

In this segment of the observation, the interaction between the children and their parents had markedly increased. Kerry had initiated the "naughty" activity about which the parents had complained and had elicited a response from Jack that led to their father's taking physical action. We hypothesized that her triumphant singing, "Daddy here, Daddy here" represented her reassuring herself that her father could still respond—that he was "still alive." Although the concept of alive or not alive is in many ways beyond a 23-month-old's comprehension, her later play seemed to substantiate the notion that her father's reactivity was a central concern. Her two brothers were equally concerned with this issue.

Each of the children was seen in an individual play interview.

Kerry, nearly two years old, played with some teddy bears of differing sizes. She made the little teddy bear poke the big teddy. The big teddy was still and did not react. She repeated this sequence several times. I brought in another big teddy and asked, "Who is this?" "Mommy," said Kerry. The little teddy kept poking the first big teddy. "What will Mommy do?" I asked. "Lone, alone," said Kerry. After what seemed like interminable poking, the first big teddy (Daddy?) made a loud noise and started to hit the little teddy. Kerry smiled. "Good, good," she said.

Jack, nearly three years old, the child who would awaken like "clockwork" at 11 at night, played at a more advanced level. He created a doll family with puppets. A truck hit a big doll. He was badly hurt and could not move. Jack thought that the truck had hit his legs. The doll mother would not or could not talk. Jack thought that the truck had maybe hit her, too. Maybe it had hit her mouth. The little boy in Jack's made-up family didn't know what to do. He couldn't go to bed. What if a robber came? His father couldn't do anything; his mother couldn't say anything. The little boy puppet got up and stood by the window. Eventually, I persuaded the puppet to go back to bed. I taught Jack a lullaby and we sang the puppet to sleep. Jack turned to me and said, "Move, move, talk, talk." (I wondered if I was being asked to be both mother and father.) Finally the little boy puppet fell asleep. I took out a pen, my "dream machine," which allowed us to look into the puppet's head. I showed Jack how to place it on the sleeping toy. Jack announced that the little boy was dreaming of a monster. The monster had a big mouth. It would tear up, eat up the little boy. I asked how the boy felt.

"Scared," was the reply.

"Let's get help," I suggested, "Shall I get a daddy?"

"Daddy can't. He's hurt," said Jack.

"I'll get a mommy," I suggested.

"Mommy can't," said Jack.

"Why?" I asked.

"Mommy can't," Jack repeated.

Then Jack had the little boy awaken, go over to another puppet, and hit him. The daddy moved his arm to hit the boy. "Is the boy still scared?" I asked.

"No," beamed Jack, "Daddy better."

Robby, almost four years old, played on the most advanced level. His was also a family scene. Robby's puppet family had a lot of trouble. The parents were both sick. Robby told me that the mothers were to blame. Mother's mother had hit her on the head and made her sick; father's mother had fed him something bad that had made him sick. The mother's ailment rendered her incapable of doing anything. The father's condition was even more serious. Because of the parents' illnesses, the children had to be very quiet and do all the work in the household. The affective tone of the play was very grim.

I introduced a television reporter from "Sesame Street." He had come to do a report on this unusual family where the children took care of the parents and had to be quiet all the time. Robby told me that he had seen "Sesame Street" at a friend's house. The T family did not have a television set. Robby said it would be nice if they had one, because his dad, who must rest, would like to watch it. When the play resumed, Robby had one of the little children begin to cry. A bigger child went over to comfort his sister. "Daddy, Daddy," Robby had her wail. "You know Daddy is sick," the bigger boy told her, "I will take care of you. Don't be sad."

Then Robby made the little girl hit her brother. He started to laugh and told me he could see all the children smile. "They are saying, 'good,'" he told me. I expressed surprise. "Is it good to hit?" I asked. Robby grinned at me and said, "When we hit, then Dad hits us. Then we have a daddy." "And the rest of the time?" I asked Robby. The little boy stared at the floor. He looked very sad indeed.

This play material is, of course, not analytic. It was elaborated in a diagnostic format designed primarily to elicit information regarding the children's safety and, secondarily, to foster the development of a plan to aid the entire family. Nevertheless, each child's play does tell us much about his or her most pressing individual conflicts. The play scenarios seem closely related to reality concerns as they might be conceptualized by an outside observer. The variation from one child to the next is more in the realm of causation, of theory making, than in the basic predicament depicted. Moreover, in our very cursory diagnostic examination, the children were neither invited, nor did they attempt, to evolve the play beyond their most pressing real-life concerns.

Following our initial interventions, which were aimed at assisting the T family, decreasing the beatings, and simultaneously arranging in-home care for all five family members, each of the T children entered an individual treatment situation. Mr. T died six months after our plan went into effect; and, despite serious consideration by the responsible authorities of the recommendation that the children remain together, they were separated and each went to a different new home. Their individual treatments continued for about six months following the relocations and then they ceased. The boys' therapists, who were not child analysts, reported that the two boys, seen separately, played out age-appropriate "cops-and-robbers" scenarios and seemed to be concerned with aggressive themes and matters of right and wrong. Kerry's therapist stated that the little girl displayed the disturbing symptom of pinching herself, with resultant ecchymoses. In contrast to her play facility during the diagnostic workup, she did not play and was often withdrawn and difficult to reach in the therapeutic situation.

I was able to monitor the ongoing experiences of the T children, albeit distantly, through the good offices of the Department of Social Services, which held their guardianship. It was through this same channel that Kerry came to me at age six, adopted by a concerned family. Similarly, I was able to assist the two boys, Jack and Robby, in finding child analytic placement.

Kerry's new parents introduced her to me by stating that she was a great success in school but seemed miserable at home. She pinched herself frequently, was quiet and withdrawn, and did not seem to want to have anything to do with their two older children, a boy and a girl, both also adopted, who kept reaching out to their new sister. The parents also complained about her extreme politeness. "If only she would have a tantrum or just cry," her adopted mother said. "They love her in school because she is so good and compliant, but we see this as a liability, not a strength."

Kerry did not appear to recognize me when we met. She was indeed a picture of great sadness, with many visible black and blue marks, and of doll-like obedience and compliance. She waited for directions before taking any action and then repeated what had been said to make sure that she got it right. After five or six meetings with me, she began to explore my play cupboard. She took out some teddy bears, not the same ones that she had used at the hospital some four years earlier, and initiated an interaction between two of the bears. One bear did something to the other. The second bear screamed. The first bear laughed. Kerry had a hard-to-decipher look on her face and played on. The two bears were given names: Abra and Kadabra. It was established that they were both girls. In the second week of the analysis, I was asked to "Do it to Kadabra." In response to the query, "Do what?" Kerry tried to take my foot and smash it down on Kadabra. I attempted, probably unwisely, to explore this scenario rather than to enact it. Why should Abra do this? What was Kadabra thinking, feeling, wanting, and so on? Kerry continued, "Do it!" and substituted Abra as the doer when I did not comply with her request.

The play did not seem to move forward; the sequences were repeated without any deepening of insight or understanding; and my attempts to question their meaning were not productive. Eventually Kerry began to look ever grimmer and to pinch herself during the hours. While this behavior alarmed me, it seemed to calm her in much the same way as the father's beatings or threats of beatings had a calming effect during the diagnostic interviews. The child then wondered if I would pinch her. I declined and asked if I should "Do it to Kadabra." "Yes, yes," Kerry responded. "But what is 'doing it'?" was my next question. Kerry proceeded to stomp on Kadabra, causing the teddy to scream, just as had occurred in the initial analytic play sequence. She then touched (gently) my foot, clearly guiding it into stomping position. I allowed my foot to be so guided. Kadabra was stomped on and once again screamed. Over the next several months, the syntactical play expanded significantly. It appeared that the partially displaced mutual enactment was required before further elaboration was possible. It is important to note that Kerry moved from the request that I do it to Kadabra, to allowing Abra to do it, to doing it to herself, to asking me to do it to her, to redoing it to Kadabra, and then to requesting again, by physical gestures, that I do it to the bear.

What was happening and what kind of play was this? The child allowed me to do what needed to be done to the bear rather than to her; but she insisted that I actually "do it." Could I have forestalled this event by an interpretation? Should it have been forestalled? I think that the answer to the first question is probably yes; and the answer to the second question is probably no.

It is possible that I could have posed questions or offered possible meanings of the request and attendant play that would have interrupted the ongoing process. If my thoughts about the origins of enactment in the play process and their interactive component are valid, then my acquiescence facilitated the subsequent playing out of material, not only deepening it but also elaborating the modes by which it could be expressed and thus become accessible to consciousness and to analysis. I realize that, for ethical and technical reasons, as the analyst, I must abstain from most forms of requested gratification. I am positing, however, that this kind of pressure for mutual enactment represents a frequently encountered and repetitively experienced aspect of some children's play repertoire. It is always imperative to explore the meanings of the request, although it does not disappear by interpretation alone. Its origins, as in the case of the T children, are often tragically apparent. Yet it is sometimes necessary to decline outright, as in requests to touch or hurt. But it is also often possible to accede, to enact in displacement, to "do it," and thereby allow the material to flow and the process of exploration to continue.

Material from the separate analyses of Jack and Robby came to me in a more indirect fashion. Jack's analysis began when he was seven and half; it lasted for three years. His female analyst communicated with me only after the treatment had been completed. She described an active, affable boy who suffered from nightmares and who exhibited provocative behavior toward male classmates at school.

In the analytic situation, he had elaborated syntactical play that the analyst understood to be primarily oedipal. In a variety of forms its focus had revolved around overcoming the father, winning the mother, and then fearing castrative retribution. Interpretation of this dynamic constellation and subsequent working through had proven ameliorative, according to the analyst. I wondered if there had been much enactment or press for particular interactive participation in the analysis. Jack's therapist reported that the play and discussion would occasionally be interrupted by an upsurge of tremendous depressive affect. Attempts to explore or to interpret these occurrences produced neither clarification nor resolution. On one such occasion, while in the grips of this "awful feeling," Jack had come over to hug his therapist. Somewhat to her surprise, but eventually with comfort, the analyst returned the hug. Following the introduction of this "parameter," as Eisler (1953) termed any fruitful deviation from a purely interpretive stance, Jack's behavior in school improved dramatically.

With appropriate reserve reflecting my distance from the primary analytic data, I speculate that the analyst is describing a press for interactive enactment (mutual enactment) emanating from Jack and eliciting a "necessary response" from her. Jack does not "insist" that his analyst do something in displacement. Rather, a recurrent, refractory, affective state is eventually discharged in action, and the analyst "finds herself going along with it." Apparently, the important play that took place within the analysis did not lead to a deepening of the exploratory and reconstructive processes (although it may have happened and was just not shared in the postanalytic communication), but there was a dramatic and decisive change in Jack's behavior nonetheless.

Robby entered analysis at age ten. Like his brother, he lived in a city different from the one where he had grown up. His difficulties seemed to be primarily in learning; he had particular troubles in maintaining a narrative. He apparently experienced a kind of blackout or absence that led to his being worked up for petit mal and then receiving the diagnosis of attention deficit disorder and being started on Ritalin. Failure to improve after a trial of pharmacotherapy led to referral to a child analyst and to a subsequent four-year treatment. Robby's analyst contacted me during the treatment, but, to the best of my knowledge, I did not influence the analytic process while it was underway.

Robby complained bitterly to his analyst about his "blackouts," and the two of them set out to understand them, beginning with play involving some shenanigans of Big Bird and Mr. Hooper. The Sesame Street motif had reappeared, but now in the play of a ten year old. Robby asked his analyst to play the role of Mr. Hooper, who was portrayed as warm, loving, and supportive. He never became upset with Big Bird. The shenanigans appeared to be quasi-aggressive, quasi-sexual attacks or forays that always "knocked the wind out of Mr. Hooper." These scenes were played over and over again. Mr. Hooper survived, in contrast to events on the actual television program. The analyst participated in his assigned role while trying to learn more about the shenanigans.

During the play Robby often asked questions such as what time it was. When the analyst answered either by exploring the meaning of the question or by answering it forthrightly, Robby "blacked out." He would not or could not or did not hear the analyst's reply. In the second year of their work, Robby began to observe that the blackouts occurred only when he and the analyst conversed, not while they were "playing." "It has to be with you," he stated. "Aren't we together when we are playing?" the analyst inquired. "It's not the same," was the boy's reply.

In the third year of the analysis, Robby asked the analyst to call out, "I'm here, I'm here," when the blackouts occurred. This request was explored for a long time. Various substitutions were attempted, and eventually the analyst complied. There was no symptomatic relief, but Robby was "very happy."

The Sesame Street play was resumed after a long hiatus, and it was learned that Big Bird was enraged at Mr. Hooper for smoking cigarettes, which was bad for a bird's breathing. In his direct interaction with the analyst, Robby now began to ask for a new behavior: Would the analyst take his hand if he reached out to him during a blackout? Once again the request was explored and attempts were made to displace and to understand. The analyst even suggested that Robby was longing for someone who was no longer there and that the blackouts were, quite literally, blocking or blacking out a very sad feeling, the feeling of loss. Just as before, Robby could not hear. His blackouts increased in frequency and duration, and he began reaching out to the analyst. One day (notwithstanding Patrick Casement's 1982 paper recommending that one not do this), the analyst took Robby's extended hand and held it. In the next hour the play reverted to displacement, and Mr. Hooper died. The analysis concluded the following year. The blackouts had been understood and no longer occurred either at school or in the treatment hours. It was necessary that the analyst and Robby physically connect, as Robby and his father had done much earlier. There were no further "presses" for interactive enactment.

Kerry's analysis lasted for three years and featured subsequent requests for me to "do it." At first these were all in the displacement mode, that I stomp on a play character, but then they overflowed into real life. Kerry wanted me to stomp on a classmate who was annoying her. Together analyst and analysand learned about the offending Samantha. I was assigned the role of Herlock Homes; the name was less suggestive of "Sherlock" than of being "locked out of her home." During this time, Kerry's agitation and distress were very great. She berated me for my unwillingness to stomp on Samantha. She clearly recalled the episodes with Abra and Kadabra but made no connection. She felt miserable.

Eventually, to the accompaniment of several self-attacks and a few swipes at me, she changed my name first to Furrock Homes and then to Kick-out Kid. Kick-out Kid was asked to kick Sam, another classmate, in the pants, again and again. Kick-out Kid, now represented by a doll, did this to another doll, named Sam, and it became clear that the kicking both delighted and terrified Sam. The play led to the analysis of a number of sexual and aggressive fantasies that appeared to be linked to the original "sadomasochistic" sibling play in the T family and to our understanding why Sam had been incorporated into the analysis. At the conclusion of this phase of the analysis, it appeared that the capacities to tolerate painful affect and to explore earlier formulations in displacement were developing.

THE DEFORMATION OF PLAY

The depth of material available from these three cases varies greatly. In each, however, the emergence and handling of the press for interactive enactment (mutual enactment) as one form of play can be detected. What is this press? What are its origins? How ubiquitous is it in children, in children in analysis? Is there an analogue in analytic work with adults? What are the implications for understanding it and handling it technically within the child analytic situation, within the adult analytic *Spielraum*?

The T family illumines the presence of mutual, or interactive, enactment in each of the children's analyses because of the unique opportunity afforded by prior contact with this family and an ongoing opportunity to track each child's analysis. It appears that some aspect of each child's experience or of their shared experience might be involved in the genesis of, maintenance of, or necessity for the mutual enactment mode in their analytic play.

Much has been written about the role of trauma in psychological development (Furman, 1986; Kennedy, 1986; Yorke, 1986). For the purposes of this discussion, I suggest that trauma occurs when what actually happens or does not happen overwhelms the ego's capacity to play, that is, to try on, take off, orchestrate, and reorchestrate, changing both key and meter at will. Ordinarily, a child plays flexibly with the objects at his disposal, with dolls, trucks, toy animals, and the like, and invests them with life. Technically, his play involves "displacement"; that is, he is taking themes inside his own head and displacing them onto the toys and letting the toys play out various permutations and combinations. This is the ordinary form of play—"symbolic play," as it is called by developmental psychologists. The presence of trauma, then, can be seen either retrospectively or pari passu to coopt the play function, as in the case of the T children, in the early diagnostic interviews—or to deform the play function as in a "shift to the left," namely, from displacement to enactment to an obligatory mutual enactment. This shift to the left may be conceptualized as a regression in an ego function that is the reciprocal of the original developmental sequence. Ordinarily, a child moves from action, to action with another, to displacement in which the action happens between characters in the play; trauma seems to make the sequence go in reverse.

It is immediately obvious that the pervasiveness of play interruption and the overwhelming of the play function in the three T children were not totally apparent from observing their initial play styles or capacities. Nor is the pervasiveness of the disruption solely a function of their individual developmental positions before and during the loss of their father and the breakup of the sibship. More information about the nature of the trauma for each emerges in the analytic situation; but here, too, it can be seen that what is learned is deeply affected by the combination of what comes from the child and how it is regarded, understood, and responded to by the analyst.

In what is often called the widening scope of analysis, it might also be noted that Jack's treatment did not seem to focus much on his earlier life experiences, whereas the work with Robby and Kerry could not steer clear of their early experiences even if the analysts had been so inclined. With our adult patients, too, these questions about etiology arise. The *pressure to do* may remain in the *Wortspiel* (word play), or it may extend beyond it. Often matters of fee and schedule arise, as do questions of extra contact be it by telephone or at analytic institutes. One senses the quality that Jeremy Bentham has called deep play (see Geertz, 1973), in which the stakes are so high that it feels like a life-or-death matter.

By deep play Bentham means play in which the stakes are so high that it is, from his utilitarian point of view, irrational for men to engage in it at all. Bentham has in mind circumstances in which one risks personal or financial ruin or a tear in the very fabric of society. Clifford Geertz (1973), the anthropologist, uses a Balinese cockfight to expand this concept to a describe the way in which what happens in such a culturally sanctioned event allows a society to imagine and to feel tumultuous internal and interactive themata that are otherwise unavailable. The point is that in an otherwise peaceful society like Bali, where fighting is totally taboo, an institution has been created in which unbridled violence can be expressed and vicariously experienced in a bounded and sanctioned setting. Great sums are wagered on these cockfights, which are savage enough in themselves, ensuring the visceral participation of the onlookers.

I use the concept of deep play to convey something about what transpires in the analytic situation when both analysand and analyst risk, are able to risk, are *compelled* to risk, in order to understand more fully. By so doing, they attempt to gain not only greater clarity regarding past traumata but also some opportunity to effect mimetic mobility, to alter the inscape, and to allow development to proceed.

Dr. G, a 45-year-old pharmacologist, said, around a proposed change in hour in the fifth year of her analysis, "I cannot come at all unless it is in my time. I might as well stop if you don't care enough to keep that time for me." She meant it too. I needed "to not change the hour" because to do so would not be distinguishable from the traumatic past for this woman, who had been sexually and physically abused by her psychotic father. He did these things "for him, not for me," she reminded me. There were, in fact, many things about how her analysis was arranged that were, like the hour, obligatory and non-negotiable. Meeting these requirements was the only way her analysis could continue for her. Only after I acknowledged that the proposed schedule change felt exactly that way—"for me, not for her"—could Dr. G recognize that this was a kind of replay. Still, she maintained that she could not stay if the hour was actually changed. Recognition of the repetition did not change her stance. She was interested in this feeling of conviction—that is, why she had it—but insisted that it had to be so. We worked on this feeling for many weeks and understood much of what it represented, but the feeling did not change. "You cannot change the hour, because I cannot change the hour," Dr. G finally said. She and I had a history together of finding out what happened when actions I could not take were unavoidable and what transpired when I was guided by her instruction. We had learned that Dr. G was commenting on a reality in her play repertoire.

Is this not an example of an interactive enactment? The analyst can accept his patient's insistence that she must have the hour, or he may be equally insistent that she cannot have it. Either stance, of course, is assumed to be accompanied by the usual mode of inquiry and examination. But, in either case, the analyst's response is an entity linked with the patient's operative play mode. He must do or not do something. He can comply or resist and always try to understand, but the play demand usually includes the necessity for action or inaction. I recognize that the material in this brief vignette does not compare with that of the T children and is open to innumerable interpretations and technical responses other than that which I suggest. I should also tell you that I knew before proposing the schedule change that Dr. G might experience it as she did. We had weathered and tried to understand previous occurrences that had elicited this same feeling and absolute transcending of the rest of the analytic process. I brought up the possibility of the change not as a provocation but because it was absolutely necessary. The feeling that this play mode supersedes the alliance or, more accurately, necessitates a "widening" of it can be quite striking. The countertransferential components are always highlighted and require close scrutiny. The analyst is likely to feel constrained, and he is; and he may feel uncertain about the viability of the undertaking. I hope that this example conveys something of the flavor of interactive enactment in adult analysis.

I felt that this enactment was a kind of deep play because Dr. G needed to impose on me conditions that corresponded to Bentham's original definition. Matters of time, money, and meaning were not negotiable as they reverberated with earlier profound traumatic experience. Only by recognizing that this scenario constituted play and that I needed to be controlled and muzzled at that time could I accede to these conditions. Thus I extended the definition of deep play to her and the clinical situation in order to be able to begin and sustain the process of accompaniment, engagement, and true exploration.

Ten years later, as her analysis was about to end, Dr. G and I discussed another change in our schedule. "You know that this is difficult for me," she began, " but not the way it used to be. All the reasons come up about why I can't and why you mustn't. That hasn't changed. Next, however, comes something new. I know about all those feelings and how much I need, maybe even have to have you take my point of view. Now, though, I also know that I can survive changing this hour, even if it hurts. This is because of our work. I am very glad." I believe that Dr. G was able to change her play mode as a result of our joint play. By my joining her where she was, which I *had* to do, it became possible for our interplay to allow her access to new play; and thus she could move from exclusive utilization of interactive enactment to play that featured a larger repertoire.

In chapter 4, I considered maternal and paternal play styles with infants and toddlers in the second year of life as possibly pertinent to evolving modes of experiencing affect, sensation, and interaction. To recapitulate, fathers tend to attune disruptively, with or without mother's collaboration to set limits. I am inclined to wonder further about the father's role: his particular use of disruptively attuned, non-matching play to provide gear-shifting and intense-affect experiences in the construction of a part of the ego's capacity to roll with the punches, specifically, to resist the overwhelming, interrupting, traumatizing intrusion of actual hyperstimulation or actual hypostimulation on the play function. Might the paternal rough-and-tumble play mode also allow experience with disruption against a maternally provided background safe enough to prevent the experience of what Winnicott (1974) called an "interruption of its going on being"? That the father's mode of interacting in play with his child might help to construct a protective shield against traumatogenesis is a way of stating this proposition. Successive approximations in the aggressive realm, when conducted in the safety afforded by a good-enough father–child relationship and of necessity a good-enough mother–child relationship (and a good-enough mother–father relationship), allow actual play to be the substrate for both resiliency and strength in the face of actual onslaught. In this regard, good-enough actual play inoculates against those very circumstances which otherwise foment the necessity for "deep play."

Just this kind of inoculation is what was poignantly lacking in the besieged T family. Mr. T's ability to participate in rough-and-tumble play with his children was severely constrained and sometimes nonexistent. He could not provide experience with the intense-affect paradigm, with gear shifting, and with the experience of asking his children to match his style rather than his matching theirs. When he was roused to interaction with them, it was to strike them with his belt, an experience that must have elicited a wide range of responses in both the somatosensory and associational (meaning) areas of both brain and mind. The children were thus deprived not only of the normal paternal contribution through play of affect modulation and perspective shifting, but also of the establishment of a zone of comfort with disruption and derailment, which is posited to act as a protection against trauma.

Mrs. T's contribution is equally pertinent. Her lack of "homeostatically attuned" (Herzog, 1984) maternal interaction deprived the children of the "background of safety" (Sandler, 1960) against which the father's more active and disrupting play style could be profitably juxtaposed.

I hypothesize that these factors—maternal deficiency, lack of "disruptively attuned paternal play," and desired but painful repetitive beating by the father—combined to lead to the occurrence of trauma, namely, the overwhelming and disrupting of the play function, and then to its subsequent deformation, the shift to the left and the press for mutual enactment. Similar historical factors obtained in Dr. G's anamnesis. Pathogenesis and play deformation can be seen to develop as two sides of the same coin.

12 | DR. C: Trauma and Character

DR. C'S STORY IS AN EXAMPLE OF HOW TRAUMA becomes transmitted from one generation to the next, how it becomes entombed in fantasy, and how that fantasy and its entombment can become embedded in erotic play. Historical calamity is seen to impinge on a boy's fantasy life in a way that is revealed disturbingly some 50 years later. The psychoanalytic situation offers access to the underlying unconscious fantasies, both the initial attempts at the formulation of a coherent narrative and the secondary elaboration of what I call a facultative or play enabling fantasy, and to their subsequent detoxification. Such therapeutic intervention allows for a restoration of the hitherto deformed play function, of the capacity to remember what could not be recalled, and of a greater ability to appreciate meaning and mean what one appreciates.

Two points before I begin: The first has to do with the transmission of trauma. In studies of survivors of the Holocaust and their families, it has become increasingly apparent that the overwhelming and devastating experiences of parents are passed on in varying ways to their children (Bergmann and Jocovi, 1982). This transfer appears to occur through deformations in parenting practices and style and takes place both in situations in which the parents are open about their wartime travails and in those where the entire subject is barred from family discussion. Recent research in the area of attachment (Hesse and Main, 2000) has revealed that subtle interruptions in coherent narrative and discourse characterize the speech of adults with unresolved traumatic histories and that these lapses shape a disorganized attachment picture in the child even in situations in which the child is otherwise securely attached. This empirical research suggests a causal mode for the transmission of trauma.

The second point concerns how trauma can be embedded in a character structure. Dr. C is an example of what one could call "a traumatic character." A traumatic character is not the same as someone suffering posttraumatic stress. Indeed, it is almost the inverse; a traumatic character is someone who is not suffering posttaumatic stress, because he or she has found a way of sealing off a trauma which allows for the untraumatized part of the person to go forth creatively in life. It is often the case, however, that in the areas of play, and perhaps most especially erotic play, we find in the traumatic character a tendency toward enactment, constriction, and a prescribed text that silently reflects the trauma but also keeps it sealed off and thus again allows for creative self-expression. In Dr. C's case, this all broke down under the weight of new stress—and the original trauma returned in a way that temporarily wrecked his ability to play in a meaningful way.

Dr. C, 51, entered analysis because of a dilemma involving his marriage. His wife of 23 years had been diagnosed with a malignancy, and he was disturbed that, rather than feeling concerned and empathic, he found himself experiencing disgust, rage, and a recurring wish that she would simply die and get it over with. His wife, a mental health professional, although currently in remission, found it difficult to tolerate her husband's attitude toward her illness. It did not seem clear to her, nor for that matter to him, whether Dr. C did not choose to keep his negative feelings to himself or whether he was totally unable to suppress them.

Dr. C found himself becoming increasingly agitated and distressed. It became harder for him to concentrate, and his temper became ever-shorter. The precipitating event for his choosing to consult me was the unprecedented occurrence of his making a derogatory comment to a female associate and then attempting to punch her in the mouth. He told her that her mouth was like a sewer and then swung at her. He then mumbled something of a sexual nature to her. Both she and he recognized that he was unwell and that this behavior was most uncharacteristic of him.

In his work as a hematologist, Dr. C was renowned for his ability to relate to ill patients and to provide them with hope. Often he was asked to provide a second opinion, when the primary physician thought that the patient would be particularly helped psycholgically by a consultation that realistically but optimistically evaluated the course of the illness and the prognostic options and probabilities. Dr. C himself recognized the discrepancy between these features of his professional demeanor and what was evolving in him regarding his wife and her illness. He was terrified by his outburst with his colleague, which had occurred while they were in the cafeteria at the hospital having lunch. He had become fixated on her mouth as she ate and in particular on the rate of speed with which her fork approached the open mouth. He felt that he could not suppress his comment. He said that it felt as though he might have Gilles de la Tourette's syndrome, except that his anger pointed to something else.

He was referred to me by a psychiatric colleague on the consultation-liaison service at his hospital in part because this colleague knew of my immersion in the study of the effects of the Holocaust on children of survivors. After an evaluation that lasted about three weeks, in which together we ruled out an organic illness and decided that this was a psychological reaction that could and should be further understood, Dr. C pressed to embark on psychoanalytic treatment, and we began to meet five times a week. This decision was influenced, I believe, by Dr. C's increasing distress about his feelings toward his wife, which were now accompanied by a dread that he would continue indefinitely to behave toward her in an uncharitable, if not overtly hostile, manner. He expressed the concern that this urge felt almost irresistible at the same time as it was repugnant to him. It was his wish that we meet five times a week rather than four. "I am really quite afraid," he said, "And maybe we can understand and cure this faster if we increase the dose by 20% from the beginning." The decision was also influenced by a feeling within Dr. C that "somehow, things I have managed to sit on all these years are finally getting out of control."

Dr. C was the first-born child in a family of European origin who had emigrated to this country in 1941, just before the U.S. entered World War II. The family had lived in Berlin, where father was a prominent surgeon and mother an actress. After the rise of the Nazis, they were unable to continue with their careers, although each continued to work in increasingly constricted settings: father in the Jewish hospital and mother at a Jewish theater. In 1940, father was arrested and transported to a concentration camp. Mother moved heaven and earth to effect his release, and, immediately after he recovered from his injuries and malnourished state, they fled first to North Africa and from there to the United States. As father often said, during Dr. C's childhood, he and David's mother had to "call in all their chips" in order to get out of Germany and be admitted to the United States.

This feeling of having *no more chips* made a great impression on Dr. C, particularly as his early life seemed to feature an abundance of "personal chips." He was athletic and academically gifted, graduated first in his class, and went on to an Ivy League college and a premier medical school. He had never previously sought psychiatric assistance, although he had consulted with a friend who was a psychiatrist some 12 years earlier when he had been threatened with a malpractice suit and had become extremely anxious. His friend had thought that benzodiazepam would help, and David referred to his 2 mg. Valium prescription as "my friend in need." When I asked him what he meant by that, he told me that he had never taken any of the Valium but felt comforted by the prescription: "I know that there is something I could take if circumstances became desperate." I noted that his current state had not prompted him to try to activate the more than a decade-old prescription but that it had pushed him to seek a different kind of help. He mentioned further that the Valium prescription felt like a visa to a safe house. I asked him to explain this reference, and he associated to his parents 'first refuge in Casablanca, the only safe place where they could wait for their American visa. He thought that his mother had arranged this somehow, too.

He had considered his marriage solid until this recent upheaval. He had met his wife while in medical school, and they had married after she completed her Ph.D. She wanted to be self-sufficient and not need to depend on David for financial support. He thought that this was a fine idea. As he told me about Elizabeth's independence, he contrasted her situation with his mother's. His mother had not worked after the emigration and had, in fact, been chronically depressed. She had really cashed in all her chips, David said. Elizabeth came from a Yankee family, was kind to his parents, a good mother, a competent professional, and "great in bed," David told me. "Who could ask for anything more?" he said. I noted to myself that he expounded significantly on the importance and delightfulness of their sexual life together. He seemed to emphasize Elizabeth's lack of inhibition and her persistent interest in him and his body. He led me to understand that she had been his only lover and that he could not have asked for anyone more ardent. I was surprised when he told me that he had had some sexual troubles but that she was the perfect therapist. Her mouth could cure anything, he said. I thought out the intimacy of his revelation and also that there might be transference implications. I also noted that, just as his mother had saved his father, David's wife had continually "saved" him.

Everything had been perfect until she got sick. Now he said that everything was terrible. There had been a complete reversal. He was terrified, enraged, and preoccupied with the prospect of a dreadful outcome, which he hoped would happen quickly. "Better an end with terror than a terror without end," he stated, quoting his father. Recall that this phrase was also used in Michael's family, and I surmise it may be a part of the familial vocabulary in a number of Holocaust-involved families. Shortly thereafter he made some reference to his mother's "just going on and on" in her depressed state, and this remark strengthened my hunch that his reaction to his wife's illness was connected to his mother and perhaps to his parents' Holocaust history and its effect on him.

As the analysis began, David became more and more anxious. He told me a great deal about his childhood in a midwestern city and about his mother's depression and his father's paranoia. The theme of having to cash in all of one's chips gave way to a more pervasive conviction that a person could withstand anything and everything as long as the person who loved him most was at his side. This was how his father had survived. His mother had literally extricated him from Dachau, from hell itself. True, she was never the same again, but she had done very good work, incredible work in effecting his father's release. David appeared to believe that his mother had completely exhausted herself in the rescue and could never recover from the effort.

As he spoke further, he invoked the image of a tremendous oxygen debt, one that could never be rebalanced and thus was tantamount to death. I wondered about this theory of maximal exertion, when had he formulated it, how did he understand it, was it a metaphor? David appeared to believe that some forms of lifesaving, the kind his mother had, in fact, performed, were lethal to the rescuer. Only one player in such a drama could survive. I thought that this quite puzzling theory of life and death might be relevant to his ego-dystonic reaction to his wife's illness. The theory seemed to have two components: one can survive anything if accompanied; and the accompanier is depleted beyond the limits of viability. Again I thought, as in the "end with terror" versus "terror without end" comment, that he was approaching a more conscious link-up of the two women in his life.

It is not at all unusual for analytic treatment to be the locus for encounters with thoughts, fantasies, and convictions that are not apparent in the daily function and behavior of the analysand. Nor is it unusual for such mental processes to be directly linked with a disturbing symptom. David and I set about the business of deepening our understanding of his theory of accompaniment and lethality. Not surprisingly, these issues had an impact on the transference. David liked the idea that I would listen to his thoughts and associations and that this was his analysis, that he was the main actor, and that I was an accompanying person. He thought of us as being like the Cisco Kid and Pancho, characters in a TV program he had watched as a child, or like the Lone Ranger and Tonto. He began to call me Pancho. This had a humorous quality, but also something of a bite. Just in "jest" David would say things like "how are the employment opportunities for Hispanics, Pancho?" or "I bet life was slower and therefore easier for you to comprehend south of the border, Pancho." I tried to explore the multiple dimensions of our relationship that were contained in this humor and how they might be related to his marital problem and his theory about his mother and father. I, of course, noted that these dynamic duos were male–male dyads and that they in a sense involved a top man and a bottom one. I wondered if they might be a much toned-down rendition of a dialogue between a Nazi and a Jew, perhaps in Berlin, or even Dachau, in 1940.

In the third month of the analysis, following a particularly successful grand rounds presentation in which his topic had been the role of empathy in the treatment of myeloproliferative disorders, David brought his first dream to our work:

"I think that I was in the Pergamon museum. It's in the eastern part of Berlin, you know. I was talking to someone about eating lung. I just thought of the iron lung and polio. I think that they were returning priceless Egyptian art that had been taken to the West for safekeeping when Berlin fell. I think that one of the pictures showed six Jews who had been strangled. That's the dream. It doesn't make any sense. The Pergamon wouldn't have such a picture. That's not even art. Besides which, it wasn't six but 6,000,000, and they weren't strangled but gassed. I just had a very unpleasant thought. I was looking at a lung engorged by lymphocytes at a post yesterday. There seems to be an upsurge in non-Hodgkin's lymphomas, and some of them grow so rapidly that they kill even before you can get in there and bring your big guns to bear."

"What is the unpleasant thought?" I asked.

"Eating that lung, all engorged with those anaplastic cells," David responded, "I am vaguely remembering my mother talking about eating lung as a girl. I can't remember whether it was a delicacy or if she was eating it because of the first world war and there being no other food. I would gag if I had to put that into my mouth. I feel foolish saying all of these things that come into my mind. Besides which, dreams only represent unorganized neural discharge during the altered state of sleep. Let's drop this."

"Does it feel uncomfortable for us to follow your thoughts, wherever they lead?" I asked.

"Deadly," was David's somewhat surprising response, "I think that gassed lungs might look rather similar, a very fast catastrophic response to the assault. This makes me feel sick. I can't stand Elizabeth's cough. It seems to announce her impending death. I wonder if you could hear the coughing in the gas chambers or just the screams and sobs. Someone once told me that you could hear people crying Mutti. That's German for mother."

"Is that what you called your mother?" I asked.

"No," David responded quietly, "but sometimes my father calls my mother that now. You know both his parents and my mother's were gassed."

Our work on this first dream proceeded by fits and starts, and

David alternated between poking fun at Pancho, me, for my lack of insight and being repulsed by the image of the engorged, malignant lung. I wondered about the repeated references to engorgement and also noted that the illness that had produced the postmortem specimen was the same as the one that afflicted his wife. David reported that he was no longer so bothered by negative thoughts about her and that he could now empathize with her suffering. He proposed that his previous antipathy and indifference had been an aberration and posited a viral etiology. He berated me for having missed an organic pathology in him after all. I pointed out that we seemed to have learned something about the connection between his wife's respiratory symptoms, which bothered him so much, and the catastrophe that had engulfed his grandparents in Germany.

Simultaneously, the idea began to develop in his mind that I was a chain smoker and that I had a carcinoma of the lung that was clearly the result of my irresponsible smoking. Although this idea seemed implausible to David at its inception, he became more and more convinced of its veracity. He would express derision that I, a stupid Pancho, had done this to myself and add that he wouldn't be foolish enough to stay with me given that I had brought this irreversible misfortune upon myself. He suggested that smokers should not be treated if they developed either pulmonary or cardiovascular illness, as "the punishment fits the crime." It seemed clear that the feelings that had brought him into the analysis in the first place now informed the transference. David could acknowledge this parallel but could not dislodge the underlying notion that I was a goner and that he hated sick and dying types. He then added that he was glad that he could talk about this with me, because it wouldn't fit in very well with his papers on empathy.

"I think that they were bringing back the head of Nefertiti, in that dream about the Pergamon, that just came to my mind. It makes me think of losing her head and now, this is strange, of giving head."

"I wonder how that is related to the picture of the six strangled Jews," was my response. I was also thinking of his having told me of Elizabeth's skill in treating his sexual dysfunction.

"I had forgotten that one, but now that you mention it, I think that it goes something like this. Nefertiti is a beautiful, beautiful women, a beautiful head. That makes me feel embarrassed saying that, you know, like giving head. I both like and dislike that phrase. Actually it turns me on. But Nefertiti's head is severed from her body. Either she lost her head, didn't think, or did it to herself somehow. This no longer feels sexual, like giving head, but morbid and disgusting, like the guillotine or something, mass slaughter, no, more like suicide, I think."

"Do you mean she or the six strangled Jews caused their own misfortune?" I asked.

"Yes, although it sounds somewhat crazy, they brought it upon themselves."

"Is this similar to the carcinoma of the lung that you feel I have?" I asked.

"Yes and to Elizabeth's lymphoma. She put stuff into her too."

"Who else put stuff into her," I asked. I was thinking of David's description of Elizabeth's lovemaking and its oral feature and was not prepared for his response, which revealed that he had associated in a different direction to my query.

"My mother," David literally screamed, "How else do you think she got him out of there. It was said that she had the most beautiful mouth on the German stage, and she used it. She blew the fucking Nazi. That's how she saved my fucking father, by being a fucking whore. He refused to get out when it would have been possible. He thought that he was too famous for them to touch. He brought Dachau on himself." He was sobbing and writhing in pain on the couch.

David was astonished by his outburst and its content. He began to think that the six strangled Jews represented the six inches of the Nazi penis that had been blown. He then had the thought that his penis was six inches when erect. He felt quite uncertain about the authenticity of any of these thoughts about his mother, although they had a strangely familiar feel. We both thought that they represented, at the least, a childhood fantasy that had caused him great pain and that now was resurrected in the light of his wife's illness. "It feels like déjà vu, only more so," he said, "I don't think that that is what Yogi Bear said. This feels amazing."

He began to tell me of his delight in oral sex with his wife and that she had often told him in happier days that he had "six of the best." He now associated to this being an expression sometimes used for caning, but previously knew it to be about his penis and his wife's love of it. "This association to caning is important," he said, and we explored together how enraged and "beating" he had come to feel toward his wife. A huge reservoir of rage toward his mother began to emerge. It took us a long time to unravel that the fantasy about fellatio seemed to have its origins in viewing his father rage at his mother when he was very young and hearing the word *Mund*, mouth, which he could only barely understand. We recovered a memory of the father shouting at the mother in German and striking her. He thought that his weeping mother had cried out, "If only you had been willing to leave earlier, then I wouldn't have had to do it." Then came memories of his father beating him and screaming *Schweinehund*. He knew that the Germans screamed this at the Jews. He thought that this particular beating had occurred after he had been caught by his father drinking a bottle of beer, maybe when he was six. He had sneaked it from the refrigerator. His father said something about his looking disgusting with that big thing in his mouth. Then his father seemed to loose it entirely and began pummeling Dr. C.

Together we reconstructed the young David's formulation that his father had decompensated around the image of David's having something huge in his mouth—"Engorged," David said—and that this traumatic experience had been linked to the earlier scenes of pain between mother and father and the word *Mund*. Now David thought that he could remember his father calling his mother a whore, too, a mouth-whore, and saying that he would rather have been gassed than have his mother suck the Nazi. He could recall his father saying that it made him want to vomit, and then he told me that his mother suffered from recurrent bouts of vomiting. A first symptom of his wife's illness had been nausea and vomiting and a disinclination to make love, and for them this meant that his "six of the best" was neglected.

David was overwhelmingly interested in what we encountered in the psychoanalytic process and in the power of his unconscious fantasy and earlier attempts at understanding what transpired between his parents and what emerged in their interactions with him at moments of great intensity. As we learned more and more, he not only began to feel better but was more able to help his wife and empathize with his aging parents. The transmission of trauma, as activated by the exigency of his wife's illness, had triggered a reactivation of an old and repressed fantasy that could be detoxified by psychoanalytic exploration. We began to see how the previously unconscious fantasy about his mother and her "cashing in her chips" had become activated by the illness. We encountered impaired lungs, self-occasioned irreversible oxygen debts, engorgement and malignancy, biting or eating, and the return of something hidden in Berlin. All this was embedded in a theory of accompaniment and lethality. The analysis needed to explore many more issues, connections, fantasies, and conflicts and these were, in fact, addressed. The uncovering of the pathogenic Holocaust-related fantasies afforded Dr. C great relief and acted as a kind of encouragement for him to do the rest of the analytic work.

Trauma and traumatic experience, including its aftermath, are variously conceptualized, according to whether or not one's focus is the phenomenological or the intrapsychic. Often a concurrence occurs among schools of thought in situations, either personal or historical, in which the impact of reality or real events is conspicuous and the response of the affected individuals is visible. I have thought about trauma, psychologically, in terms of the impact of certain kinds of hyperstimulation and hypostimulation on the child's or the adult's capacity to continue playing.

I define play as the ego function that is involved with trying on, revising, and making meaning without primary attention to external reality constraints. Its primary feature is the undisputed authorship of the self and its reversibility and permissible multiple-draft quality. Trauma is defined as an impact on this function that interrupts its ongoing status and often results in what I have called a "shift to the left," a term I have borrowed from hematology. Such a shift to the left features a change in play mode from displacement and symbolic equivalent to enactment and then, further, to interactive enactment, a state in which the prescribed and preprogrammed participation of the other is both required and demanded. This shift is thought to constitute a regression that parallels inversely the developmental sequence by which the play function develops and matures.

I wish to discuss Dr. C's seemingly curious attitude toward his wife's illness, the interruption of their preferred and perhaps mandatory sexual relating, his eruption toward the female colleague, and the uncovering of the fantasy or perhaps fact of his parents' Holocaust history within this framework. The issue of posttraumatic behavior is addressed obliquely as an aspect of its etiology and intrapsychic significance.

Exemplary adaptation is a not uncommon posttraumatic state in which that which has disrupted the play function, and as such is traumatic, is both perpetuated and disguised. It seems that this state occurs most regularly in circumstances in which the trauma is both directly inflicted—when something is done to the child that interrupts his ability to go on playing—and transmitted indirectly from the parents to the child, when something that is unmetabolizable for them becomes a part of the child's experience, transmitted, as it were, with one's daily bread. This bifurcated posttraumatic pattern, featuring as it does both highly adaptive functioning that often includes disguised elements of the original derailment and the emergence of a symptom picture that appears to bear no connection with past history or function, can be clinically quite confusing. Traumatic character is a concept I have advanced as a way of describing a set of adaptations, defenses, and accommodations that encompass both the traumatic stimulus and the resultant narrative and facultative fantasies that are the unconscious underpinnings of its memorialization and management.

Dr. C is a highly accomplished man both personally and professionally. His adaptation can be seen to utilize both his extraordinary endowment and that which he needs to manage. Thus, renowned for his empathy as well as his clinical acumen, he accompanies those who are ill and dying, his patients, in an exemplary way. He attempts to rescue the damned from their hell of illness in a way that can be seen to contain elements both of identification with his surgeon father and the heroic act of his mother. In his sexual life, a primary arena in adulthood for play and for repair, he is helped by his wife, whom he calls his therapist. "Her mouth can cure anything." He has chosen his lover, playmate, well. She loves him and is not put off by his need to have her repeat a specific script in order for the sexual play to do its job and thus for the sexual "problems" to be overcome. The material provided does not allow us to conclude that Mrs. C's capacity to be what her husband needs and thus to help him is any less developed in other play areas.

Dr. C breaks down when his wife's illness precludes her continuing as his playmate. This is most apparent in the sexual realm when she is coughing and nauseated and thus not able to use her mouth therapeutically. She is also, of course, less independent, less able to rescue, and more in need of care than has previously been the case. We learn through the analytic work that there are multiple determinants of this play.

Mrs. C must do exactly what the mother did in her husband's compelling but unconscious fantasy about the way in which his father's life was spared (spare the rod, mouth the rod). By performing her role exactly, she allows her husband to maintain "a desperate dialogue with a receptive you," to quote the poet Paul Celan. I would call this sexual play interactive enactment. For the play to continue, the other must perform a preassigned and often invariant role. How aware either of them is of the desperation involved or managed in their sexual play is not made clear.

This analytic material allows a beginning appreciation of the way Dr. C, as a little boy, strove to make sense of what had happened between his mother and father and the way each of them was, alone and in interaction with him. We hear of his mother's depression, the recurrent metaphor of "cashing in one's chips," of his attending to the appellation *Mund*, and of outbursts of violence from the father directed to both mother and son. In the dream material, the relationship between engorgement as a sexual event and as a catastrophic reaction in the lung becomes clear again, underscoring the Holocaust history and the individual body and sexual meaning making.

The relationship between the unconscious fantasy about his mother's sexual behavior in the rescue of her husband and Dr. C's need for his wife to perform fellatio appears to have been completely unknown to him, although he was aware that his penis "wouldn't work" without his wife's mouthing. In a sense, one might say that Dr. C's sexual dysfunction signaled the underlying trauma's continuing hold on him and that what he and his wife had worked out was both symptomatic and enabling. It allowed him to keep the fantasy–reality knowledge of his parents' history, including the mother's extraordinary but denigrated heroism, unconscious, that is, repressed. It perpetuated a dysfunction in the sexual area, in play, which simultaneously memorialized the original assault as transmitted from the parents and fantasized by the young Dr. C as he strove to make sense of the domestic ambience, and the pain and sadness and rage that he both detected and experienced.

The unraveling of the meaning and origins of posttraumatic fantasies that have generated facultative fantasies can occur without an external disruption and symptom eruption as occurred for Dr. C. Often, however, it is exactly this situation, when external reality interferes with the ongoing interactive enactment, that the underlying fantasy and its action determinants are revealed. As in the case of Dr. C, such revelation is often shocking and ego dystonic. Analytic inquiry often succeeds in helping the patient to understand the origin and meaning of his adaptations and their unraveling. Mourning and acceptance can then be facilitated and a new accommodation effected. Greater freedom in play and a reversal in the play mode deformation, that is, a return to displacement and a lesser need for obligatory participation and behavior from the partner, can be achieved. Dr. C's work and play, not to mention his love, are likely to become less constricted and more open to his multiple talents and proclivities. A safe-enough space for a fuller play function can emerge as the need for safe words and safe houses is understood to reside in the past and as this need is sufficiently understood to permit its reintroduction into consciousness and integration into ongoing accessed memory.

13 | ETTA: Something Is Happening

It has to be on that stage
And, like an insatiable actor, slowly and
With meditation, speak words that in the ear,
In the delicatest ear of the mind, repeat,
Exactly, that which it wants to hear, at the sound
Of which, an invisible audience listens,
Not to the play, but to itself, expressed
In an emotion as of two people, as of two
Emotions becoming one.
     —Wallace Stevens, *On Modern Poetry*

IT IS DIFFICULT TO DATE THE ONSET OF DEVELOPMENT; it is impossible to specify the beginning of meaning. The self develops as a self-seeking entity. Process and being are in a sense the same. This interactive contingency means that the caregivers must have available selves with whom the emerging self of the child interacts in vitalizing and development maintaining ways. In both development and in analysis, such a meeting, an I–Thou encounter, can occur; something can happen. In both settings, tragically or seemingly inevitably, the obverse can and does occur. Developmentally this often results in deformation or at least in restitutive alteration of the self. In treatment such a nonmeeting often leads to clarification of previous derailment but may also feature a loss of hope or the repetition of the very sort of mimetic occlusion that is conceptualized to reside at the core of the "pathology." Interpretation itself, then, may constitute an enactment, a painful repetition; understanding may seem ironic rather than growth enabling.

What is the phenomenon I call "something is happening"? What does it look like developmentally and therapeutically? What are the essential conditions for its occurrence, and what, if any, are the safeguards against its abuse? When does it not occur, and then, in its absence, what transpires? I try to address these issues by presenting analytic experience as it has evolved in my work. Of necessity these encounters are of two: the analysand and the analyst, the you and the me. To enhance explicative clarity, here is such a happening from the analysis of a child.

Etta is now 11. She has been in analysis with me for three years. Her divorcing parents sought a referral from their pediatrician, who pronounced them "the most difficult caregivers I have ever encountered." Etta's parents are both nonproductive artists; Etta, in a sense, is their only creation. Earlier, they "shared" an analyst. Following this disaster, they became ever more furious with each other. They are now estranged, although occupying adjoining primary and vacation residences "for the sake of Etta." Neither works, and each is enmeshed with the daughter. Mother and she share a bed; father and she exchange flirtatious explorations that are grossly overstimulating. Father has accepted a referral to an analytic colleague. He often wonders if Etta should not see her also and is troubled by recurrent concerns about a sexual relationship between his daughter and me. Mother refuses to see anyone, although she is quite interested in father's analyst and me. She states that she cannot afford treatment, which does not seem to be primarily a financial statement.

I meet with both parents approximately every three months to assess their concerns and to try to respond to their queries. Most of these meetings end up focusing on their battle, and I have referred the couple to yet another analyst who is available to discuss "coparenting" issues with them. In addition, there are relatively frequent telephone conversations with the father when his agitation about either his daughter or her analyst reaches a point requiring immediate reality testing. His analyst fully supports this contact with me. Etta and I meet four times a week.

In my responses to both Etta and her parents you will hear a combination of my transferences, impressions, irritations, and the limits on my availability. Etta is beleaguered and imperious. She is physically quite attractive, tall, blond, and blue-eyed. Her play favors the mode that I have called interactive enactment. I have previously posited that this mode, representing a regressive "shift to the left" in the ego function of play is often encountered posttraumatically (Herzog, 1992). She demands that I do certain things, which vary according to the scenario of the day or week, but this feature is quite persistent. She is constantly preoccupied with self-regulation, which she delegates to me. The quality of this delegation is usually unpleasant; I feel put upon rather than as if I am a partner in a developmental dialogue designed to build a self-regulating inner structure. Stated somewhat differently, the feel of this interaction is of a transferential repetition rather than of a developmentally nutritive request. Yet I cannot easily determine whether the repetition is of passive or active experience. What is being repeated is unclear; why it is being repeated in actual interaction with me is, likewise, not understood.

Concomitantly, her libido and aggression are much in evidence. Displaced play, when it occurs, features iterative clashes that are highly eroticized and often culminate in severe spankings. Considerable affect, mostly of excitement, accompanies this kind of play. Although usually assigned a role at such times, I feel peripheral, even though the scenario features seemingly intense action. Despite my inherent interest in both domestic loving and hurting, in intercourse and in spanking, I occasionally drift off during these interludes. This behavior is quite noteworthy for me. After considerable self-investigation, I have tentatively concluded that it is because I am not really a part of this play. It is occurring in my presence but, in a sense, without me. I could perhaps force my way into it but, doing this does not seem to me as though it would make analytic sense.

I feel that I need to be alert and attentive at all times. Not only will Etta notice my inattentiveness, for which I am rebuked, but she is quite likely to take a swipe at me if I am not "on guard." I am very alert during our interactive enactments, less so when the play is displaced. I regard this phenomenon with great interest as the displaced material is inherently and, in terms of my own psychology, much more interesting than is the interactive enactment. I consider that I am "checking out" defensively, but this does not feel right. It seems more likely to me that the interactive enactment is the scene of the action. At the moment, this mode and the material in displacement are divergent rather than convergent. My attunement and nonattunement are informative and related to the nature of the self–self dialogue which is being conducted.

The parents elicit strong feelings in me as well. Mother's anger is never far from the surface and her dissatisfaction with the course of the analysis quite clear. She does not want Etta to leave her bed and resents my counsel that this constitutes a goal. I seldom feel that she and I are on the same wave length but appreciate her contention that she must protect Etta from her father's overwhelming intrusiveness. The father is a flamboyant and unusual man. He seems to use almost no repression and expresses interested astonishment in such observations as, "Even though Etta says she would like to examine your penis, it might be prudent to think about the meaning of her request before acceding to it." My response to the father is often that I cannot quite believe his naiveté, or at least that I do not fully understand his thought processes. He is always polite to me, even when voicing his concerns about my morality. In nontechnical language, I find the father to be bumbling and inappropriate, usually responsive to suggestion, and not frightening.

Etta's mother seems more frightening, misguided in her methods, but understandable in her cognitive design. I feel that I have compassion for Etta's daily interactive struggle, for the complexities, cacophony, and impingement on her *Umwelt*, and that she and I have established, albeit with difficulty, an analytic *Spielraum* in which the contours of her inner world can be divined and, perhaps, addressed. I am both with her and at a greater remove than I am with many a patient. I like her, wish to be available, feel put off, do not fully understand the relationship of the play modes she employs, and feel that there is more to come. This last seems crucially important. I feel neither demoralized nor that the pace of our work has become asymptotic. Furthermore, Etta seems still to be productively at work.

The following therapeutic dysjunction—its unfolding, resolution, and the impact of these events on both participants, analyst and analysand—is a "something is happening" encounter. It suggests what is involved in aporia, mimetic openness, and subsequent intrapsychic refiguration.

Etta has been playing out a somewhat complicated scenario in which she and I are detectives. We are investigating the murder of a woman in a "random act of violence." The murder was particularly gory, involving beheading. Etta is insistent that this was accidental. The murderer only intended to kill the woman, not remove her head. I am assigned the role of coinvestigator, but clearly as a bumbling assistant. I suspect that I am being cast as the father and the beheaded woman is the mother. In the play, we continually are looking for clues. Etta suggests that the deceased had three children. They might have something to offer. I am dispatched to consult the "register of children of murdered mothers." (There is some interesting exchange as I profess ignorance of the register, while Etta harangues my stupidity. I immediately note to myself that I feel very much involved, alert, interested, and totally there.) This imaginary computer document indeed proves valuable. There is a special section devoted to beheaded mothers, which allows us to construct most of the details of the victim's life and even of the events surrounding her death. We definitely seem to be on to something. Often at such moments in the past and now again, the syntactical play is interrupted by Etta's suggestion that we play a game of cards called Spit. I have repeatedly observed this "interruption of the action" aloud, wondering why it occurs. Etta scoffs and reprimands me for "playing analyst." This transition from displacement to interactive enactment is, of course, very familiar. Usually, I experience it as "now the action is really beginning" and wish that the action were in displacement. Today, however, the action is in displacement. We are both really there, or at least, I, the analyst, am really there. I note that I am really there in both play modes and that I wish that the displaced play had not been interrupted.

We play Spit. As often happens in the game, Etta is dissatisfied with the outcome and grabs the cards out of my hand or pushes me aside with considerable force as I try to be the first to put my remaining cards down on one of the piles. He who puts his cards down first is the winner.

On this occasion, I not only protest, but say that we have agreed that she will not do this. I, in fact, have injured my shoulder in another activity, and Etta's assault was quite painful. Etta expresses surprise and then apologizes. She promises me that it will not happen again. When I do not seem totally mollified, she raises the ante. She will give me her vacation home in Tuscany if I will resume the game. Moreover, the Ferrari, too, if she doesn't keep her promise and should inadvertently strike me again. The hour ends on this note. Etta appears convinced that we will resume tomorrow. In fact, we keep the cards out in the exact disarray that our interaction produced. I feel engaged. I look forward to the next hour and feel as though we are in the middle of something important.

The next day, the play begins with a return to the murder. We learn more about the register of children of murdered mothers. There is a special section, very small, of mothers murdered by fathers. By far the largest volume is occupied by mothers murdered by their own mothers. This section is entitled: "Killing in the Family; Children and Mothers." I note the ambiguous title wondering how it is connected to the fact that most mothers are killed by their mothers. Etta screams at me to be quiet. We are on a case, she says. My questions get in the way rather than forwarding our investigation. "Don't you know, stupid, that sometimes mothers and children look the same," she screams, "Don't you have a brain in your head? Have I beheaded you?" As the play progresses, we try to learn if the child of the beheaded mother had a father. "What is a father," Etta has this imaginary child say, "I've never heard of that, of a father."

I think that the play is moving in a very interesting direction. Dimly, I comprehend that both play modes now reflect the same questions: "What is a father? Where is he?" At that precise moment, Etta turns to the cards and announces that we are going to play Spit. I ask about her question, "What is a father?" "Never mind that. Come here and play," Etta responds. I comply, and moments later there is a repeat of the "assault" of the previous day.

I remind Etta of our agreement. She is annoyed but remembers. Several more promises are made. I say that I can see that she wants very much to continue to play Spit, but that I am unwilling. I shall not play Spit again. "Forever," Etta asks in great agitation. "Not for awhile," I respond. Etta begins to cry. She is very shaken. The hour ends with Etta in evident distress, but very engaged in the analytic process. I feel similarly engaged, no longer put off or put out. The intensity of my feeling that I am being asked to be a part of critical action, that I need to be, and that I want to be is very striking.

The next day, we resume play. We spend the entire hour reconstructing events in the life of the murdered mother's child. She, it turns out, is a girl who was forced to hear her mother's dreams every night in bed and could not stand anymore what was in her mother's head. She did not really wish to kill her mother, rather just to "dedream and demouth" her, behead her. Furthermore, there is a rethinking of the paternal absence in the evolving story. The child reveals that she knew what a father was all along. She states that a father is a person who says yes by saying no; come in, by saying stay out. Etta does not suggest that we play Spit. She gazes toward the cards a few times and then resumes play. For the next several weeks, we continue with this scenario. Deeper and deeper levels evolve. My role has changed. I am not disparaged so frequently. When I ask a question about motivation or meaning, it seems to be heard and is sometimes even responded to.

Etta notes that it is easier to come to her analytic hour than it used to be. Her father tells me that his fears about what is going on between his daughter and me have ebbed. Furthermore, he shares that Etta has asked that he read her bedtime story downstairs before she changes into her bedclothes, rather than when she is already in bed as had been their practice. He is "mystified" by this request but interested in my counsel. I support his "interpretation" that Etta may need a "room of her own"—after Virginia Woolf. Mother reports that my waiting room is chilly and that the lighting seems to have deteriorated. It is no longer comfortable for reading, so she will drop Etta off and do her grocery shopping during the analytic hours. Etta does not object to this change. I now think I understand what has transpired and that the changes in each parent or for each parent seem good to me. Has "something happened"?

Something has indeed happened. For both analyst and analysand, a shift has occurred. Feeling and doing have conjoined on both the levels of displaced play and interactive enactment. The father has been found in the saying of no; the repetition compulsion has been confronted, aporia introduced, and the possibility for refiguration advanced.

Etta's analysis featured from its inception the complexities of multiple personae and multiple transferential dramas. This is often the case in child analysis and perhaps also in the analysis of adults.

In both situations, adult and child work, the analyst needs to consider the ways in which content, interaction, and the analytic relationship reveal parallel, convergent, or divergent processes. We often comment on the reality for the child of his relationship in the present with parents or others and of the analyst's capacity or propensity to be a real object and to have a transferential relationship with the significant others in his patient's life. We are, perhaps, less aware of similar process with our adult analysands, particularly if we or they exclude their "nonneurotic" issues and self-constituents from the analytic playroom.

It is a reality for child analysands that life, average expectable and otherwise, prohibits them from excluding the "nonneurotic." It is a privilege for child analysts to have such experience, which can be a profound influence on their openness to such work with their older, that is, adult, analysands.

I propose that the "something that has happened" involves the accessibility of Etta's inner world to the influence of the analytic encounter and to me, the analyst. Conversely, that my availability is neither static nor to be taken as a given. For "something to happen," there must be an overlap between availabilities: the analysand's representational world must be enterable to be alterable; the analyst must be able to participate in this process. It is in the service of explicating this later condition that I have tried to share what was going on within me while I was with Etta. It goes without saying that biographical and conflictual issues within the analyst, subjected to analytic illumination, are at constant play as a factor in determining his availability. Here, however, I try to highlight those emanating from the analysand.

There were many previous times when I felt the need to prohibit in the direct interaction with Etta. Most of these occurred when I felt uncomfortable with what she was doing to me and concerned about her inability to modulate her own impulses. This time, it seemed different. I needed to protect my shoulder, but I sensed as well a self–self encounter that was fueled by the displaced scenario, a reflection of Etta's unconscious fantasy life and mounting drive pressure that could not be contained, and some developmental need for help. Etta could not stop the combined oral, anal, and genital compulsion for us to "spit and tussle" without the presence of a paternal introject that said yes to her separateness and competence (including the competence to elaborate the scenario in displacement) by saying no to her disregard for the well-being of the other. Beheading and heading, that is, structure building, intrapsychically were condensed in the question of a register—what will register and how?

It felt to me as though a new attachment was occurring between us. Etta regarded me differently, with a new "essentiality," with a kind of awe. I felt this shift. I was being asked to be a no-sayer, in Chasseguet-Smirgel's (1985) terms, to stand for reality as a paternal principle in order to effect a further differentiation of self and other in the object relations world, on the representational stage (in this case between Etta and her mother). I felt both a pull toward returning to the displaced play, which seemed increasingly important, and a rising sense of indignation and conviction both about limiting the assault on me and about Etta's inability to do this on her own.

I want to emphasize that this sense of "rightness" about the intervention, including specifically my saying that we would not play Spit again for quite awhile, seemed loving to me. I also felt somewhat stern, a self-state I had not previously experienced with Etta. It was almost as if I were thinking to myself (which I was not), "This is not good for Etta and therefore I shall prohibit it, no matter what." I say that I was not thinking this, and that is true, but I was feeling it, strongly. This feeling was a component of an even stronger feeling that we were really at work. This was a core issue for Etta and that the play modes had converged because she and I were now in a position to get it, work with it, and do something about it. In this context, the stern feeling was particularly noteworthy. I do not usually feel stern, with or without Etta. Now it not only felt right, but part of a larger picture. It is important to note that I would not call this a corrective emotional experience, after Alexander (1954). This feeling was not contrived. It was my, our experience in the play.

Often—perhaps always—such a strong feeling on the part of the analyst is the occasion for self-analysis, consultation, or, at the least, a deep breath. We are accustomed to thinking about this sort of "enactment" with concern if not derision. It is also, however, one way, perhaps a critical way, in which "something happens." The convergence of material in displacement and in interactive enactment signals a readiness for mimetic mobility, for a self-seeking–another-self encounter to occur. The analysand's representational world is now open. If there is room on the representational stage (template), then a new internalization can occur. The interaction between analyst and analysand may be represented. The analyst must be affectively present, involved, and willing. His feeling state is of critical importance here. Often the analyst cannot or will not let himself be so used. He does not love the analysand; he does not understand the meaning of the converged play modes, displacement, and enactment; the match is not good.

I have often wondered if the representational world can be entered only if the match is "good enough." Is there a protective shield available to the inscape so that it is sealed against intrusion unless the overlap is appropriate? Is the result of a mismatch simply a stalemate, no remodeling but also no injury—or do catastrophes of enormous significance regularly occur when mimetic openness is achieved in the absence of a facilitating overlap? Often, in relational dialogue, the external and the interactive are recapitulated primarily in terms of memory and representation. It is an example from the terminology of our age of CD-ROM, read-only memory. The role of the repetition compulsion in this arrangement is particularly germane, and the concept of transference fully applicable. It is, however, possible in intimate relationship to achieve circumstances in which the reprogramming mode is usable. Such openness to mimetic mobility necessitates a series of conditions that developmentally might be labeled as "primary maternal preoccupation," or love, overlap of agendas with a trusted other, an asymmetry in the relationship so that the needs of one party are placed in conspicuous prominence while the needs of the other are not disregarded (Cooper, 1992).

In the analytic playroom, the reprogramming mode can be activated. Often such an opportunity is signaled by the convergence of the displacement and the interactive enactment mode. The openness of the analysand must be matched by the availability of the analyst. The analyst must feel, speak, play. The interaction is then represented. Once admitted to the relational inscape, its effect is determined, at least in part by what else is there, by the company it keeps. With children, development is our ally, and we are temporally closer to the last "open period" of programming, of representational ground laying. It often seems that new representations, specifically of the analyst–analysand dialogue, are more easily and expectably introduced into a "less cluttered" space. With older analysands, the repetitions and iterations may be—usually are—considerably more formidable, but the opportunity still exists, and with this opportunity a reemergence of hope, a respite from despair.

"Something happens" when a particular overlap or particular forms of overlap occur. Analysand and analyst together create a new poem (recall Wallace Stevens at the beginning of this chapter). Aporia, the poet's openness to new experience, replaces certainty. The repetition compulsion is challenged. Mimetic openness is possible and new representations facilitated. A self seeking an encounter with another self finds someone home. There is an encounter, the representational door reopens, and intrapsychic change is possible.

> Soon it is supper time. In the kitchen they feed
> and talk, while I, invisible as I was
> in high-chair days, silently sit on Sears,
> wearing the weight of my big and bigger ears.
> "Well, you'll never guess what your crazy kid did
> today—if that wasn't the limit!" The story swells
> into ache in my stomach, then Dad's laughter and hers
> slice and tear like knives and forks and a worse
> hurt is opening in my middle; in familiar
> smells and muddle of voices, mashed potatoes,
> dimming light, hamburger, thick creamed corn,
> the milk-white chill, a self is being born.
>
> —Mona Van Duyn, "The Delivery"

14 | NATALIA AND THE BACON FACTORY

ANALYSIS INVOLVES AN INTENSE INTIMATE DIALOGUE in which the analyst uses himself to find the most painful and most conflictual parts of the analysand and to establish a means by which it is safe enough for a play process to be initiated between both parties which takes cognizance of extraordinary vulnerabilities and sensitivities. This chapter describes analytic work with a little girl who was subject to interactive assault and internal challenge. It begins with my first meeting with Natalia, an hour in the third year of our work together and concludes with material from our final year of work together, by which time Natalia was almost 10.

Natalia's parents first consulted me at the request of her nursery school teacher when the child was four years old. The school was concerned that Natalia was withdrawn, often seemed terrified, and did not manifest cognitive or affective readiness to go on to a scholastic environment. The parents expressed concern that Natalia was damaged, and the father advanced the notion that his four-year-old daughter might become a bag lady. Angrily he spoke of her low Apgar score and of how she lacked the prerequisite brain capacity to become a mathematician. Both parents reported that they tried to link feeding Natalia to her doing simple math problems at the table. The child would become either panicky or withdrawn and often end up not eating at all.

As further history was obtained, it became clear that the mother's capacity to attune to her daughter was highly impinged upon by her own history and by the demands her husband exerted. The father appeared not to understand at all that a child might have a mind or body of her own; rather, he seemed to believe that he could make her into anything he wanted her to be.

Natalia presented as a frightened and withdrawn child, immediately evoking in me a wish to protect her. I had already had this response when hearing from her parents, and it was amplified by her thinness, her look of fear, and the depth of her large, dark eyes. She did not look to her mother, who had brought Natalia to my office for solace, but made her way through the open door from the waiting room into what was to become our play space. She did not speak but seemed to monitor my whereabouts. In fact, it felt as if she noted my every move with a kind of watchful wariness that Fraiberg (1975) had identified as being the hallmark of abused infants or toddlers. I greeted Natalia by name, smiled, and waited. As the silence grew, I tried to decide whether it would be better to remain with her in it or to speak. After about five minutes, in response to feeling that she was becoming more anxious, I asked, "Natalia, would you like to see the toys?"

She nodded and followed me in the direction of my toy chest. She sat down next to it but did not examine any of the chest's contents. After another silent interval, in which I found myself contemplating the extent of what felt like an almost complete inhibition of assertion or other aggressive capacity, I asked, "Would you like to take the toys out of the chest and see what is there?"

Again Natalia nodded, and now she began to examine the contents of the chest. She seemed to be particularly interested in a fire engine and a pig. I noted that I was initiating the action. I wondered why and was aware that the feeling of fear that seemed to accompany Natalia's silence was difficult for me. Natalia seemed to need my initiatory verbalization to combat a psychically induced, inhibitory apraxia.

As Natalia handled the two toys, I had a curious association. It was as if she were touching them tentatively, without a preconception of what they were or what they might do. I wanted to say but did not, "They are perfectly safe; they're toys. You may see a colossal danger resident in them, but it need not be there." My association was to a traveler arriving in a completely foreign culture and having no sense of either conventions or taboos. I also continued to have the feeling that we were in a realm of considerable danger, as yet to be defined, but palpably present. The whole mood in the room felt like a kind of global piloerector, literally hair-raising, response. Simultaneously, it felt to me that my verbal invitations had settled Natalia in a noticeable way and that I apparently wished to calm or protect her as well as to learn more about the dangers that threatened. As much as one can in a first hour, I recognized both the technical dilemmas resident in these two positions and the likelihood of transference–countertransference reverberations. Having asked two questions as the hour began, I now felt somewhat more comfortable waiting, not inclined to ask Natalia about herself or her understanding of being in my office.

Her tactile examination of the pig and the fire engine continued. From time to time Natalia would gaze in my direction. I smiled, and she seemed to note my expression. Perhaps 40 minutes into the hour, she looked directly at me and said, "Shalom." I responded by saying shalom to her. She then said something rapidly in Hebrew that I did not understand. I thought for a moment about what to say and then said, "Natalia, I don't understand. Will you tell me what you just said?" She smiled and said, "Do you speak Hebrew?" I answered that I did not. Natalia was silent. She looked at me as though she could not quite fathom what I had said or that I really did not speak Hebrew. I thought about asking her if she would teach me the language. I wondered if I should have regarded her question as more symbolic and not have immediately responded that I did not understand. After another silence, Natalia said, "I will teach you Hebrew."

Natalia's mother was Israeli, her father American, and I found myself thinking that this declarative statement must refer to her mother's language, the "mother tongue." As Natalia was leaving after the first hour, she smiled at me in a tentative fashion and said, "I watch you closely. You shrug your shoulders before you speak. You don't hit." Having previously written about the mother tongue (Herzog, 1991) and the ways in which children and adults must both learn this language and teach it to a would-be analyst, I thought that after this first hour Natalia would use her mother's language to initiate a dialogue or trialogue with me in which we could come to understand her experience. We were, however, to learn that Hebrew was not what I thought it was and that Natalia's linguistic burdens and skills were, indeed, to constitute our text. She was highly concerned about hitting-feelings and wanting-feelings, about piggishness, and about fires. The piloerector response I had noted and the aura of danger were unmistakable constituents of this *Hebrew* and of our joint linguistic venture.

The next hour is from the third year of the analysis. Natalia has been composing operas with me. We are working on the *Tel Aviv Tangle*. It is an enormously interesting libretto, and there is very serious music. (Natalia brings in a tape of the music from *Schindler's List*.) The story involves a pig who has come to Israel from somewhere in Russia. The pig, who is called Tod by Natalia, is always expecting to be slaughtered. Natalia pronounces "Tod" with a long "o"—making it the German word for death. Tod cannot get it through her head that in Tel Aviv pigs are not routinely consumed. The hour begins with Natalia's singing a song while working as the breakfast chef in the Hotel Blood and Milk. The song goes as follows: *Bacon and eggs are a perfect delight. Bacon and eggs at the end of the night. Hm, hm good, I want more. Bacon and eggs will settle the score.* The "chef" repeats this song with great relish, and Natalia asks me to join in. I sing a chorus of the song with her. Natalia acts as my coach and says, "Louder, harder, more feeling. Now softer. Do it this way." There is a decidedly sexual feeling to these incantations. I say, "You want me to do it so that you can really feel it."

"Yes, Dr. Hard," Natalia says. "That's how I want it."

After my instruction ceases, Natalia asks with mock concern, "Where is Tod?" We begin a search, although in the previous hour, it had seemed very clear that if there was to be bacon, Tod would need to make a very great sacrifice, or, rather, be sacrificed. We search, and I say, "There is probably a clue in what we have just sung as to Tod's whereabouts."

Natalia responds, "I can't understand what you are saying. It doesn't make sense. You are not speaking Hebrew. I think that you are talking pig talk. Shh, that's dangerous." She grins and breaks into a sotto voce chorus of bacon and eggs. Her words are followed by her picking up a toy knife and making a throat-cutting gesture. I feel, in this phase of the analysis, a familiar chill as I realize that I am not the father, but the pig in this play (or is Tod really Natalia?) and I say, "Bacon and eggs will settle the score," perhaps defensively becoming the commentator rather than accepting my assignment as the about-to-be-slaughtered swine.

Natalia tells me that I am lazy. She converts her knife into a whip and flicks it at me as though to say, "You won't get away with dawdling, Dr. Soft." "We need to visit the bacon-making plant, now," she says, "Maybe we will find Tod there."

I say, "Let's go and see." I am relieved to be a part of the search party rather than one of the "guests of honor" at the bacon-making plant.

In this phase of our work, I am particularly alert to those moments when she says "we" and when the work involves her being subject and my being the object. To be the object of this murderous slaughtering is terrifying and threatening to the sense of self in a pervasive way. I comment to Natalia on the atmosphere in the bacon-making factory. I feel it and I can only wonder at what it must be like for Tod. There has been much interpretive effort directed at Natalia's rage at pig fathers and its relationship to other feelings toward both pigs and fathers. These two themes—of fury and excitement and of fear and despair—are often echoed. I note that Natalia mobilizes her aggression in the slaughterhouse when she acts as the slaughterer. I wonder if she also experiences herself as the about-to-be-slaughtered Tod.

Before we began composing the *Tel Aviv Tangle*, we had spent a number of months during which Natalia played that she was a mommy pig and that she had three piglets. There was also a daddy pig in this play who was very busy at work and sorely missed by the three piglet daughters and their mother. Sometimes one of the piglets, called Natty, also played by Natalia, would be angry with the father pig for being so busy. She would want to pass gas when her father came home. The mother pig would then be very angry with her and say that Daddy couldn't help it, that's how daddies are. They have to do what they have to do, and that includes working.

In response to passing gas, Natalia would have the daddy pig angrily slap Natty. Often he would slap her repeatedly. As we immersed ourselves in this play, it became apparent that Natty was trying to direct her father's slap, and thus his hand, to her bottom, from which the gas was emitted. He insisted on slapping her face, which Natty said "just won't do."

During this phase of the work, we were able to observe together that Natty was both excited by and angry with her daddy and that mommy pig just didn't get it. I wondered how a girl could manage such intense feelings, and Natalia suggested that it would help Natty to see a pig-doctor. There had, in fact, been an interlude of pig doctoring play in which Natty had come to see me in my capacity as Dr. Pig-straightener-outer. Natty's complaints were all about the itchiness of her bottom, and all my attempts to understand the etiology of her distress were met with contempt. What was needed was for me to scratch her bottom or slap it. Only this would do. Natalia seemed genuinely saddened by my various maneuvers to displace this action. Eventually the play shifted with my commenting that she wanted something from me, whereas I thought that we had more to understand about Natty and her dilemma and that we could best approach this task by playing. "Why are you Dr. Soft when I need you to be Dr. Hard?" was Natalia's response.

During this play, Natalia often told me that I didn't understand much about her or for that matter about Natty. "Pigs," she said, "aren't interested in figuring out what things mean. A pig feels something strongly and then needs to have it done. Words don't matter to pigs, or pigs would speak. Pigs feel and need to feel it and it needs to be hard." Natty adumbrated a theory that, no matter what a pig felt, if what was done to the pig was hard enough it would feel good. This is why Natty wanted her father to slap her really, really hard; this is why she was angry when he stayed at work rather than attending to his fatherly duties at home. I commented that I thought that Natty might wish that intensity were the only variable in pig feeling, but that I suspected that she could tell the difference between pleasureable stimulation and attack.

Natalia told me that Natty had told her that she would need to see another pig physician because I clearly did not get it. I really did not understand fundamental truths about porcine psychology. Hard was how you knew that someone was there. I thought about the hardness of Natalia's early experience and the cruelty of her parents and said, "I imagine that a pig who has had a very hard early pighood comes to expect that life in the family means doing it very hard."

"Again you don't understand," said Natalia, "Hard is exciting."

I thought that we were seeing the intricate ways in which defense and adaptation make use of developing sexuality and threaten to appropriate its enlivening and connecting functions in the service of maintaining coherence in the face of incomprehensible assault.

To return to the hour and to our opera: Natalia and I were now in the bacon-making factory. Natalia began to squeal and scream. She said, "Isn't that a pleasant sound? The pigs are saying good-bye." She waved her knife excitedly. "We must find Tod," she said, "We have to make him into bacon."

Tod had always been female before, so I repeated, "Him?"

"Get Tod. Don't let Tod escape. Tod is going to be bacon," Natalia screeched. She continued to make squealing sounds and to scream. Suddenly she shouted, "Schweinehund, Schweinehund." "You understand that Hebrew, don't you?" she screamed, "You dumb pig." Again the roles had shifted and I was Tod.

I said, "Tod must be terrified to be here in the bacon-making factory. What score is being settled?"

Natalia looked at me cooly and said, "Killers get killed."

I thought that we were encountering some amalgam of her earlier experience of being murdered and a retaliatory killing feeling. I said, "It's better to eat bacon than to be bacon, to settle a score rather than to be able to do nothing."

"You do understand Hebrew," was Natalia's response. She then continued with the opera singing: "I'm the bacon maker. Ha, ha, ha, Good. Good. Good. Do it now, do it hard, do it fast. Bye-bye, Tod, ha, ha, ha. Do it hard. Do it fast. Bye-bye, Tod; hello, Bacon. Ooh, warm blood. Tastes good, ooh!"

This last aria was sung with a kind of blood lust that was palpable. Her oohing and aahing sounded sexual as well as faintly reminiscent of Sondheim's *Sweeney Todd*. I listened with interest and a certain degree of restraint. In a way that seemed to echo Natalia's familial Holocaust history, we were in a kind of Israeli-porcine Auschwitz that she called speaking Hebrew. It was true that Natalia needed to teach me this language, which seemed to be an amalgam of her mother's family history and her father's psychological and behavioral disturbance. I could recognize the meat eating—which puts her at the top of the food chain—and aggression-structuring aspects of Natalia's attempted resolution of her painful past and her raging drive endowment. I could also hear that there was a distinctively sexual component, albeit tinged with sadomasochistic overtones, to life in the bacon-making factory. I knew that Natalia realized on some level that it had been exciting for her parents to torment her together and there was a differential contribution from each of them to what had been done to and with her.

I said to Natalia that the making of Tod into bacon featured much excitement and a lot of action. Natalia looked at me intensely and said, "It's just an opera. There are too many books here. Professor Hard-Soft. Let's burn them. You would want to count all of them. [Her father is a professor of mathematics.] It doesn't matter how many, just that the flames burn really, really hot."

I said that this was about something very, very hot. I said that Natty pig really wanted her dad to slap her bottom hard.

"Yes, it itches so much. That would make it really burn, really be hot. It really needs something hard to deal with that itch."

I said, "It burns and itches and making bacon seems to help a lot. These feelings are really hard to handle by yourself. They come from within you and also from all that you have been through."

"You really do speak Hebrew," said Natalia.

"Hebrew is the language of having been hurt and wanting to hurt, of feeling excited and having a very big itch," I said.

"Tod becomes bacon, the books burn, and we settle the score," sang Natalia.

"This opera, the *Tel Aviv Tangle*, is very real," I said, "We may be singing, but this is about a terrible trouble and what you have tried to do to master it."

Natalia continued to scream and wave her knife. Tod's throat was cut again and again. Blood spurted, squeals were emitted, and then Tod died with a strangulated whimper and bacon was provided for the Hotel Blood and Milk.

The final portion of this chapter begins with Natalia's own words. She wrote this essay in the last year of our work, when she was nine. Its manifest content is about a younger brother born the year after the material you have just read.

Blood. Dark red blood issuing a warning to anyone near. It made me shiver just to think of it. I hated the sight of blood. My heart stopped. I would have screamed if I could have. But all I could let out was a squeak. It was a squeak of utmost terror. I stared down at the blood for a while. Richard hated blood too. Richard!!! What if he was playing with the knives? And he cut his fingers? What if that was his blood? No, I would have noticed. But I rushed to the silverware drawer just the same. Nope, the silverware was just as it had been five minutes ago. I calmly approached the situation at hand. I went to look through all the rooms in the house hoping to find him. I started going down the hall. There was a huge lump in my throat that just wouldn't go down. I walked through a couple rooms. No blood but no Richard either.

I was starting to calm down a little. I walked through a couple more rooms. Nothing there. Now I was starting to get scared again. As I turned every corner I expected to see Richard's body on a couch or hanging on a lamp. Then I walked a few spaces and stopped. I think I fainted. It sure felt like it. There on the wall were smudges of blood. Bright red blood echoing disaster, terror, fear. I turned pale at the sight of it. But my fear just made me more determined to find Richard, dead or alive. I continued searching. Then I saw a streak of dark red blood. I jumped like somebody had just jumped out at me. And then tears came to my eyes. I tried to hold them back but I just couldn't keep the tears in. I cried uncontrollably. I wanted to disappear or be someone else. I prayed my brother was safe. I wanted my parents to come home. I wanted them to make everything all right. And then I got angry. Who would do this to us and why? Who could be mad enough or mean enough to do this? Why was this happening to me?

After what seemed like an hour of crying, I felt a tug at my leg. I looked around expecting to find the murderer but I didn't see anybody. And then there was another tug, and I looked around to see Richard with his big blue eyes. I started crying long and hard, but it was a happy cry. The cry of joy. And I started asking about a billon questions. But all he would answer was "Natalia, I got a scrape. Natalia. I made a mess." And he held up his arm and there by his elbow was a little scrape. That's all it was—a scrape. It didn't make sense. There had to be more.

The rest of our work focused on the analysis of Natalia's story. We were able to tease out her memories of her father's blood-curdling attacks on her when she was a little girl and their series of transformations as we had encountered them in our pig operas, slaughters, erotic, itch-relieving, disciplinary scenarios involving little Miss Natty and other play. Now they were merged with her intense feelings about the arrival of Richard and a combined fear that her younger brother would be similarly abused and a wish that what had befallen her would also constitute Richard's fate. Natalia clearly remembered that her father had called her a pig when she at age three had said at the dinner table that she thought that apes were descended from people rather than specifying the correct evolutionary directionality. He had slapped her face so hard that she had fallen to the ground. It was during this time that Natalia also remembered that her father had called her a *Schweinehund*, a word she did not know but that had found its way into our bacon-making play. It was a crucial term in our Hebrew and a classic in Natalia's experience of "soul murder" (Shengold, 1989).

Natalia said that she could remember more because we played together for a long time and that she wrote the story for school, but really for our work. "It's like the operas," she said. "What we do with it here is different from what would happen in music class or in English class."

"Yes," I said. "Here we understand the parts that are in Hebrew."

"Isn't it funny?" Natalia said. "Our Hebrew is a language that only you and I know. It has nothing to do with what they speak in Israel. I thought that I would teach you the language. Now I think that we both taught it and learned it together."

I realized that my ability to speak Hebrew came from many sources. I drew upon my own Holocaust history and my own experiences with my traumatized parents. I felt intense rage at Natalia's father for his assaults and profound disappointment with her mother's lack of protection. When we were in the slaughterhouse, I was aware of my terror and of my interest. In the Natty play, particularly when Natalia would position her bottom for a whack, I felt invited and excited in the play. I was glad to be grounded in a stance that allowed me to observe and clarify as well as to participate and enact. All these feelings, experiences. and commentaries were a part of my growing ability to speak "Hebrew."

In fact, I came to understand that this language was some mas-culine, aggressive, sexualized lingo applied to and experienced by a little girl. He-brew. It was more than a child could metabolize or inte-grate. It was the product of a deformed parental alliance, one in which the sacrifice of a child took precedence over her protection and nurturance. The cumulative or strain trauma involved in such experience (Kris, 1956) fueled a hypersexualization of the play process, which alternated with a withdrawn retreating. In our play, there was an intense pull for interactive enactment, the play mode that ensues from traumatic deformation of the play function and "requires" the analyst to play in a specific and sometimes stereo-typed way (Herzog, 1993).

I found it both helpful and necessary to formulate what was tran-spiring by focusing on the ways in which Natalia's parents' conjoint pathology had reduced average expectable triadic reality (Herzog and Herzog, 1998) to a pathological dyadic reality in which their daughter was denied the balancing, titrating effects of having two parents and thus self-with-mother, self-with-father, and self-with-mother-and-father together representations. I could begin to appre-ciate that He-brew was different from He-and-She-brew. I could see that Natalia needed me to be both a better father and a better mother so that she could construct an interactional internal schema that would allow her to achieve neurotic functioning. I have previously defined this level of functioning as "freedom of interactive permu-tation and combination amongst good-enough self-with-mother, self-with-father and self-with-father-and-mother interactions (Herzog, 1995). In Natalia's lingo, it might be said that she needed to speak She-brew, He-brew, and She-brew-with-He-brew.

At about this time in our analytic work, Natalia's father became profoundly depressed. At his daughter's urging, he came to see me in consultation. I saw him once and then referred him. During our meet-ing he spoke about whipping himself with his belt until he bled and said that he thought that he should be hoisted and slaughtered by having his carotid artery opened. "Just the way a pig is stuck," he said. He expressed overwhelming guilt about slapping and whipping Natalia and about his verbal abusiveness toward her. I was very inter-ested in the confluence of his thinking, fantasy, and behavior with Natalia's opera and essay. I speculated privately on the ways in which this material, as well as the mother's Holocaust history, had been transmitted to my patient and tutored her processing of her own trauma and her restitutive formulative and creative fantasizing efforts.

I did not share her father's material with Natalia. She felt glad that I had seen her dad and was very worried about him. She told me that she did not want to know what was inside of him. I told her that it seemed as though she already knew a great deal about that and that her father had not always been able to contain what stormed within him. She smiled at me when I said this and replied that we had learned a lot together. When her father began to respond to medication, she expressed enormous relief. She asked me if I had a daughter and if I whacked her bottom. I said to her that her question reminded me of Natty's dilemma and of our play several years earlier. Natalia's eyes widened and she said, "You know that you are real for me. I have feelings about you that are like what Natty feels for her dad." I said that I knew that the work we had done together made us feel very close to each other. I also said that I thought that Natalia needed me to be like a dad, including one who might whack, but also like a mom, who could hold and protect and make certain that whacking did not get out of hand. I was interested in the fact that the learning and speaking of both He-brew and She-brew involved my being both disruptively attuned and homeostatically attuned, offering penetrating interpretations and more empathically attuned accompaniment and role assignment (Sandler, 1967; Herzog, 1993).

We were talking now about stopping our work, as Natalia was planning both to try out for her school play and to begin playing field hockey. "I wanted to really tell you about how I feel about you," she said, "I never could have written the operas with anyone else, even though they are about my childhood before I even met you. But that's not true. They are about you and me and what really happened between us even though they are about the past. Does that make sense? I remember because of us, even though it is about me and them."

I told Natalia that I thought that what she said was true. The operas were based on the past, but, because what we did together and felt together was true, they could be written only by both of us playing together. I said to her that we had to construct a He-She-brew together.

"I've never heard of such a language," Natalia said with a growing smile, "Where do they speak that? Here in Natalia- and Jim Herzog-land, right here in Newton Center. Shalom, Halom, both she and he. That's it, isn't it?"

"I'm too old to write operas now," continued Natalia, "but if I weren't I'd compose a love duet between Tod or Natty and Dr. Pig Understander, that is, between me and you. I was both Tod and Natty, I think, and you were the man who, well, with whom I wanted to do everything. This is embarrassing. I really am too old to write this opera." There was a poignant silence, and Natalia said, looking directly at me, "Actually I am just a little bit too young to sing the opera with you that I would really like to sing. I guess this is mostly about He-brew even though what we have said about He- and She-brew is surely also correct."

Natalia and I negotiated the issues of reality, trauma, the analytic situation, and her developmentally fueled interest in growing and changing in many ways. An exemplar situation involved her wish, expressed by Natty, that I whack her. This technical and theoretical issue was juxtaposed with our play in the bacon-making factory.

When Natalia, playing Natty, jutted out her bottom toward me and saucily requested a swat, I felt like complying. I did not wish to hit her really hard as she suggested, but it seemed as though a love pat would be just in order. I felt that I could do this and that it would continue the play. As the term love pat came to my mind, however, I knew that I could not do this quite so cavalierly, nor should I, as the conflation of aggressive and libidinal underpinnings was inseparable. This became even more apparent as the question of Natty's itch was elucidated and Natalia's sexual excitement grew. This feeling of being willing, but not being compelled, that there was therapeutic choice, came, I think, from Natalia, even as she implored me to "just do it" and had Natty declaim that a different porcine physician would surely need to be consulted. I could feel that parts of this play were traumatic, representing the actual assaults that had occurred and that parts of the play were eroticized elaborations in which the hyperaggressive had become amalgamated with more normative psychosexual conflicts and longings. I also wondered about how this interaction mirrored or elaborated still earlier aspects of Natalia's attachment history and showed us something of the ways in which she had dealt with the paradox of having a mother who was both a safe-enough refuge from anxiety and a potent cocreator of the same effect. I was aware of all these detriments of the "have to," actually optional, nature of Natalia's request. It was just this amalgam that allowed for some flexibility in my range of response.

I have my own range of permissible behaviors. These are determined by my own libidinal aggressive and narcissistic play availability with a particular other in a particular setting. They are also determined by my priority-taking commitments, my theoretical stance, and even the vagaries of my immediate psychological equilibrium. All of these factors prevail in the analytic encounter, with a different set of defining parameters for all intimate conversation. Something of this kind of sorting-out process is always operating in analytic work. It is probably most conspicuous in child work, where action and interaction are constant, but it surely also is constantly present in work with adults as well. The current intense interest in enactments in psychoanalysis (Renik, Spielman, and Afterman, 1978) attests to the omnipresence of this phenomenon.

Even as I tried words, with the freedom that Natalia's stance granted, I did not know that they would suffice. I wondered if Natalia would need an experience with a more controlled aggressive interaction, for example, a whack, to counteract her experience with her father's out-of-control attacks on her body and her spirit. Were this to be an actual requirement, how would the two of us negotiate it, and how would we disentangle such play from the concomitant sexualized itching and touching issue?

When we were in the bacon-making factory, I knew that we had to kill, albeit in displacement. It would not do to propose whacking Tod, the German (her mother's mother tongue) word for death, much less scratching her itch, rather than cutting his throat. That this act could be performed and repeated in displacement seemed clear. That the exact act needed to be approached, anticipated, and repeated was also pertinent. In this play, it felt mandatory to follow Natalia's script, to accept my role assignment, and to interpret or enact from within its confines, whereas, with the Natty and her Daddy play, I felt able respectfully to decline Natalia's directions and state what I thought the meaning of her request was. Always I tried to attend to the interface of her tolerance for my amending her play-mode prescription and my sense of where I was, what I would or would not do, and the way these variables would facilitate our work or occasion an impasse.

I felt that this dichotomy showed us something of the ways in which the libidinal and the aggressive components of Natalia's developmental interactions and subsequent representations with her parents allowed for some survival of herself and a relatively volitional use of play-mode selection. Both play mode and her history's impact shifted dramatically over the course of our work together. She could gain access to her aggression in the Tod bacon-factory play and use her hierarchical superiority in the food chain to gain some control over her terror when her father assaulted her. Claiming her own aggression allowed her to experience her terror and move beyond it. In the Natty play, we encountered the erotization of her terror and her father's loss of control alongside the need for a more normative experience with paternal limit setting and the use of discipline in this pursuit. Thus Natalia said about her father's face slapping, "This just won't do," instructing him about where and how to apply, even if very hard, a paternal whack rather than an assaultive blow. Here we can see the confluence of both developmental modulation and sexualized appropriation of the relationship. Natty's bottom is both a more appropriate site for a whack than is her face, but it has also begun to itch in a most insistent fashion.

I think that Natalia's use of both kinds of play, not to mention her later use of the essay, reflects the fact that her play function was restored to "full deck" capacity by the analytic work (O'Connell and Herzog, 1998). She did not need to rely solely on interactive enactment, the mode in which the other must do exactly what the self dictates in order for the play to continue. At the beginning of our work, there was something of this flavor, what Paul Celan (1972) called "a desperate dialogue with a receptive you," and I found myself anticipating her needs in the early hours and often verbalized when she was silent. Over time, she began to be able to use both enactment and displacement as I became a stable and reciprocally available playmate whose individuality she could appreciate and tolerate, too. I felt that I had earned a place on Natalia's internal representational stage and that she had taken me with her onto that stage because doing so worked for her and because she worked better with both of us on board.

At about the time we stopped, Natalia said to me, "You know

me better than almost anyone else does, and I know you better, too. I know how you do things. That is very important. I know how we do it together, how it goes between you and me. I know you so well that I even know how you smell. You know how I smell, too." I thought that she was right.

15 | EXPECTANT FATHERHOOD

MEN APPROACH FATHERHOOD BY DIFFERENT ROUTES. Each has constructed a kind of conceptual road map of what his life is to be. For some, family may figure predominantly; for others, life is organized differently, for example, primarily around career. A man experiences his wife's pregnancy largely in terms of his underlying views of his own life.

For men to whom caretaking is important, the development of this attitude is continuous, beginning with an early identification with their own mothers and undergoing character changes throughout childhood (Kestenberg, 1974; Ross, 1979). For other men, it is more difficult to trace their particular line of development. Fathering fantasies and preoccupations of earlier years are either blurred, buried, or negative, or perhaps they never occur at all. In such cases fatherhood seems accidental and is experienced as being neither an essential nor a complementary aspect of life.

This chapter discuses the study of a special variant of expectant and experienced fatherhood. The subjects were 103 men whose wives had given birth to premature infants. In each case, the prematurity was not expected. These were all first fatherhoods, or at least first fatherhoods within the present marriage. The children were born between 25 and 39 weeks' gestation, and the families were referred to the infant follow-up clinic that I administer. The technique used involved retrospective, analytically oriented interviewing of these fathers.

The initial interview was often at a severely stressful time in the life of the family. The newborn's life often hung in the balance. Subsequent interviews occurred over the next 24 months during regularly scheduled return visits of the children and parents to our clinic.

During this time, it was possible to form a unique relationship with the parents. The great stress around the premature birth imparted a certain transferential element to the relationship with me, the interviewer, and in many cases facilitated the revelation of deeply personal information that might otherwise have been expected to be available only in a well-established therapeutic alliance.

I set out to determine where each of the new fathers was in his particular expectant fatherhood, interrupted as it was anywhere from 26 to 39 weeks along its course, and I asked the new fathers to reconstruct what their earlier experiences during the pregnancy had been. Many of the new fathers considered this work important to them, both in dealing with the trauma of the moment and in consolidating the course on which they were embarking.

Studies have suggested that during pregnancy women experience a more or less orderly reworking of earlier issues involving intimacy, caretaking, and previous experience in the parent–child matrix. The character structure and style of the individual woman appears to play an important role in the intensity of this experience (Bibring et al., 1961). There also appears to be a rather close correlation between physiological changes and processes and psychological reworkings, regressions, and reintegrations (Benedek, 1970; Kestenberg, 1976).

Men's experiences of their wives' pregnancies have a somewhat different flavor from their wives' experiences (Gurwitt, 1976). Men can choose how much they will be involved in the process and thus to what degree they will respond psychologically to physiological changes in their wives. During this phase of the caretaking line of development in males, there appears to be more of a correlation between capacities for caretaking and intimacy in men than is necessarily the case for women. Men who have already tended to be intimate with their spouses are more likely to participate fully in the experience of anticipatory fatherhood than are those men not involved in such intimacy.

If one accepts the idea that a man need never know that a child has been conceived or can, even if he does have such knowledge, elect with greater or lesser success to ignore the fact, can one still say that there are inevitable patterns of expectant fatherhood that can be observed among groups of men as well as in individual men (Marcel, 1962)? The results of the present study support a tentative yes. In the interviews with the men in my sample, certain repetitive concerns, preoccupations, and general themes, which formed a relatively consistent pattern, emerged. These themes, feelings, and concerns were not equally felt by nor available to all the men. Rather, it soon became clear that the men could be divided into two distinct groups: those who were in touch with feelings and fantasies pertaining to the pregnancy, and those who were not.

An initial attempt to understand this dichotomy in terms of character type was not rewarding. It appeared, however, that a valuable discrimination was the nature of the marital relationship. Roughly speaking, men were cognizant of their own feelings about the impending arrival of their first child to the extent that they were empathic with and invested in their wives. It seemed, then, that fatherhood both qualitatively and quantitatively is related to the conjugal relationship. This was the first major finding of this research.

A second feature, however, should also be noted: the individual, even idiosyncratic, meaning of each pregnancy for each father. One hundred and three separate stories of gestation and birth seemed to be intricately linked to as many separate life histories. Bibring et al.'s (1961) interviews with expectant mothers also revealed tremendous diversity of meaning and processing of experience, but it was my sense that this diversity was much more pronounced in the men than in the women. Thus our second major finding was that prospective fatherhood is assimilated in terms of its meaning within the individual's life history—this to a far greater extent than in women. That men can be at least once removed from the actual events of pregnancy, childbirth, and childrearing may imply that their psychological participation in these events and experiences bears a clear imprint of their previous experience, conflicts, and conflict resolutions. In women, life experience and meaning may be clearly detectable, but there is a stronger psychological cast.

The material that follows focuses primarily on the approximately 35 fathers who were deeply involved in an empathic intimacy with their wives. For convenience, I have labeled this group the "most attuned" group. I divided the remaining fathers into "less well-attuned" and "least well-attuned" subgroups. I mention some highly suggestive aspects of these latter two groups, but principally for purposes of comparison and contrast. I have also omitted much of the more strictly individual or peculiar findings and report the elements that the 35 fathers in the "most attuned" group seemed to have basically in common.

I must emphasize that my conclusions are impressionistic and hypothetical inferences in need of corroboration by single cases studied in depth as well as the careful quantitative analysis of similar large samples.

THE GETTING READY PERIOD

There occurred a "getting ready period," to use Gurwitt's (1976) term. Among the 35 couples in the most attuned group, there seemed to be a distinct period in which both parties knew they would try to make a child soon. Husband and wife were sometimes on different timetables in this regard, and any discrepancy was worked out by the couple. The men reported that "having sex to make a baby" felt different from "just having sex." "This is procreation," one father said. Several men reported that they and their wives had discussed the difference between simply making a baby and being able to care for the baby. The distinctions between recreative, procreative, and "parentogenic" sex were explored and experienced.

This getting-ready phase was recalled as a more "rational and controlled" phase of the total pregnancy than were the phases that followed. Several men reported feeling that they were embarking on something new and very foreign. One recalled the sensation that this was much different from "going off to college or graduate school, or even getting married." Some reported a sense of entelechy, that fatherhood was the reason for their being. About half the men in the most attuned group were transiently concerned that they were sterile or would not have sufficient "stuff" to do it. Two men who had been involved in a prolonged getting-ready period related to reality constraints (e.g., financial and educational restraints) had felt an urgency "to get on with it before it was too late." Neither could recall what "too late" meant, but both, interestingly, noted that their wives were over 30 years old. In the less well-attuned group, several men reported that it was their feeling that "a kid would be OK sometime," but that there had been no particular plan to have one now. Some of the men thought of suggesting abortion, but this option was not elected by their wives. Three of the pregnancies in the least well-attuned group occurred during serious marital rifts and were the ostensible reason for the marriage's continuing rather than dissolving at that time.

STAGE OF CONCEPTION

The getting-ready period was followed in the most attuned fathers-to-be by the stage in which conception occurred and was medically confirmed (Gurwitt's, 1976, second phase). The affect characteristic of this phase was joy. "I jumped three feet in the air and shouted, 'Hurrah,'" one staid gentleman reported. "We felt an inner glow," another said. Several of the men described an initial surge in their feelings of manliness. A physicist reported thinking as he was about to give a seminar, "I've got the cock that made her pregnant. My seed is sown." He felt very aroused at that moment and created quite a stir in his classroom when he wrote on the blackboard, "My physics is sexy," and then hastily recovered himself and went on to speak about quantum mechanics. Most of the men reported a substantial improvement in their sex lives with their wives in the ensuing weeks, and, with this, the wish to love and be loved seemed to expand. Several indicated that they became "quite hyper." "Making the kid was a high," one man reported. Only a very small number of men betrayed their ambivalence. One man said, "I kept thinking, it is true what my mother said that every time you open one door another is closed. The thought made me kind of edgy, like you know you can't go home again. You know, I don't believe in abortion." In the less and least well-attuned groups, the news of the pregnancy elicited various responses. Seven women whose husbands were in the least well-attuned group elected not to tell their husbands that they were going to become fathers. One man said, "She probably just hoped it would go away, the dumb broad. By the time she did tell me it was too late. I had no choice but to go along with her."

END OF FIRST TRIMESTER

The initial mood began to change toward the end of the first trimester. The well-attuned fathers-to-be remarked on a perceptible change in their inner lives. Eight of the men remarked spontaneously, and the others concurred in response to directed inquiry, that they first became aware of this transformation by way of an increasing incidence of new and different fantasies during lovemaking. Contact with the themes and issues of expectant fatherhood was, in fact, most often achieved in the sexual realm, which suggests the possibility at least of a connection between sexual expression and the prospect of caretaking in men.

Fantasies often intruded on lovemaking and were of several sorts. A number of men reported fleeting images of themselves as huge bottles of milk or as a cow's udder, pumping necessary nutriments into their wives or into the fetuses. "I'm like that guy in the Philip Roth book," one man said, "I've become the Breast." The feeling of having to refertilize or nurture the pregnancy seemed to come to the fore (Bettelheim, 1954). "They need more and I've got it to give," one man recalled feeling. Another dreamed of the final scene from *Faust*, where Faust oversees the building of irrigation ditches. This same man, a psychiatrist, recalled the play's closing lines, *"Die ewige weibliche zieht uns hinan"* ("The eternal feminine draws us on").

For some of the men, this shift in their fantasy lives had an enriching or pleasing quality; others experienced it as distracting or irritating, with an obligatory or compulsive quality. Many of the fathers in the most attuned group revealed feelings on both sides. These fantasies, I conjecture, may reflect a reexperiencing of the earliest stage in a boy's caretaking line of development, his identification with the nursing mother, the furnisher of oral supplies. Of further interest was that some men described themselves as nurturing both the mother and the fetus, almost as one. The differentiations between parent and child, between mother and father, seemed to have become blurred. In this fantasy of feeding the fetus, the nurturing also appears to have become genitalized and heterosexual: equations between penis and breast, and semen and milk seemed to obtain.

In the other two groups, it was much more difficult to uncover these fantasies. In the least well-attuned group, an interesting variant occurred. Several men reported that they needed more sex than they were getting. "I'm hungry for it all the time," one man mentioned. Generally, these statements were couched in terms of the man's needs and deprivations rather than in terms of his spouse's.

The next characteristic to emerge among the most attuned men was an increasing preoccupation with their own insides. Several men reported a new quality to their ejaculatory experience, focusing on the sensations that just preceded climax. There was a new awareness of thrust and power. "It feels like a bull trying to get out, a volcano exploding; it hasn't been like this since I was 13 years old." One man recalled in vivid detail his first ejaculation as an early adolescent.

"I was rubbing myself on my pillow. I was thinking of my girl— that we were in a swimming pool together, there was water all around—I was very close to her. Then I felt waves like the water was in me. The waves were coming stronger. I wanted to scream. I could feel it inside like it was traveling through my groin, pounding like the water, harder, harder inside but wanting to get out, almost unbearable, then out, no longer in, but out. I can almost feel the march, the waves, from my testes all the way through me out my penis and into my wife. It reminds me of that movie *Fantastic Voyage*, but I'm not detached. I'm more there than ever. We should tell Masters and Johnson and those pleasure people about making love to your wife when she's pregnant."

There was also an increasing incidence of awareness of what was called aftersensation. "For the first time I felt an ache afterwards. There was a kind of rhythmic contraction sort of just inside my ass. I felt as though something inside me was letting me know I have insides, too." Or, "There's something in me that has to do with this baby business. It's not just my prick and balls, but farther back. I mean really inside, not just out there." Or, in more prosaic terms, one physician told me, "Look, if you are 30 and if you are screwing a lot more than usual, your prostate is going to let you know it's around. God, mine's constantly reminding me that it is there."

MIDPREGNANCY

Several fathers reported more concern with gastrointestinal symptoms, in particular a feeling of fullness in the upper and lower GI tracts. I wondered if this trend, which seemed to be most evident around midpregnancy, had to do with the reworking of a successive stage in the caretaking line—a stage in which identification with the mother blends with the boy's "inner-genital" or maternal phase

(Kestenberg, 1975), when he becomes aware of early prostatic and seminal vesicle contractions. These are used to fuel his still powerful fantasies of being able to bear children (cf. Little Hans [Freud, 1909]). Residue of this phase of development often includes concerns about the order and connectedness of such things as body parts. One father reported, "I kept having these dreams of all these diagrams, a giant maze. Only I was both inside and outside." Another said, "How are all the parts of me connected? I've got to figure that one out. What I'm feeling, the baby, Ruth, my insides, and outsides."

This inner-genital stage appears to be followed by a hermaphroditic stage (Ross, 1977). In childhood, the boy is likely to see himself as able both to fertilize and to bear a child, as able to carry a baby, like mother, while sustaining his identification with the male role. Fathers in the most attuned group reported the wish that they could have it both ways. Several described new sexual techniques that allowed them to feel penetrated at the same time that they were penetrating—to give and get at the same time. One of the fathers related a dream in which an elephant reached around to his anus with his trunk and blew air into himself. He swelled up and ached. The father indicated that this was how he felt after he ejaculated now—both full and very empty. Men who reported that they felt empty when they were in touch with prostatic contractions also spoke of fears that they would not have enough to give their wives or that they would not be good-enough fathers. Many reported that they had begun to eat more, and several fathers gained significant amounts of weight during midpregnancy. In the less and least attuned groups, I did not find evidence of this reawakened inner-genital or hermaphroditic stage. There were some accounts of GI symptoms, and several of the men indicated recurrent bouts of nausea. These were variously attributed to "the bug," its being contagious ("I caught it from my wife"), and a somatic metaphor ("I'm sick of the whole thing").

THE TURN TOWARD FATHER AND FATHERING

At this stage of the pregnancy, roughly between 15 and 25 weeks, many of the men in the most attuned group reported an increased pressure to sort things out with their families of origin. A common preoccupation was that their own fatherhood would be blighted by difficulties in their relationships with their fathers. Over and over again, this motif was evident, often in terms of reestablishing connections: "How I hook up with my old man determines how the kid will hook up with me." There were analogies to plumbing, circuitry, and other kinds of connecting; thus this sorting-out phase, too, seemed to bear an earlier inner-genital imprint. There was another quality too. In order to envision themselves as good fathers, many men strove to revive and reestablish contact with the good father of old. Often, this was the preoedipal father, but also present was the mentor or masculine guide of the oedipal and latency years. Once more, I found that a male's caretaking line of development is fatefully affected by the presence of a good-enough male mentor/father who helps the boy grieve the loss of his earlier identification and helps him to see what a man is and what a man does.

I have come to think of this turning to one's own father in a "straightening-out" or even "refueling" manner during midpregnancy as a fateful landmark in anticipatory fatherhood. It is almost as if such an event signals a more masculine or less maternal quality associated with the second half of pregnancy. It is interesting to think in terms of Abelin's (1977) postulate that a boy is biologically programmed to turn away from his mother and toward the father at around 18 months of age to help dissolve his primary femininity and to embark on his anatomically determined masculine course. Something analogous may, I speculate, occur in midpregnancy, when the turn to his own father helps to launch the father-to-be on a more paternal course.

Men who did not go through this sorting-out phase (primarily men in the less attuned and least attuned groups) seemed to become progressively less able to participate in their expectant fatherhood or what Max Deutscher (1971) called the alliance of pregnancy. Often these were men who had no father toward whom to turn. Much of their lives could be understood in terms of his absence. Those men who were father hungry, who had experienced a felt absence of their fathers or of those qualities associated with maleness in their growing-up years, seemed now to make a career of the pursuit of males and maleness. Paradoxically, such men were both most intolerant of their own feminine identifications and longings and most vulnerable to these in the second half of the pregnancy. Rather than being able to turn at this critical point, with the help of an internalized male mentor, to a paternal role that was nurturant, involved, and masculine, they tended to fall into bisexual adventures, competitive strivings with their wives, or flagrant promiscuity. So striking was this finding—that the ability of a man to participate in expectant fatherhood is inversely related to his state of father hunger—that it emerged as the third general conclusion of this study.

FANTASIES ABOUT THE COMING CHILD

Sometime after quickening, a change in the fantasies and preoccupations of the father-to-be occurred. First, men began to think of the fetus as a child, separate from both themselves and their wives. For example, the sex of the child was now routinely conceptualized: in the most attuned group, approximately two-thirds of the men "expected boys"; in the other two groups, this figure approached 100 percent.

Blatantly aggressive fantasies also now made an appearance. One man reported a dream at 24 weeks' gestation. He was in Israel and saw a sign, "Ben Ramtitski." Where was this place? As he mused on his dream, his associations started with "Ram." He thought of Ramses, the prophylactic, and wondered why he had not used one. Then his thoughts turned to "ram tit," which called up sadistic feelings toward his wife. The "ski" meant "son of ram tit," as did the "Ben" before. Assuredly this place was where he was going, but that it was in the promised land did not seem at all clear. He was aware of a wish to hurt the baby as well as to welcome it. After all, he had placed it safely in Israel, rather than in Eastern Europe, the land of origin implied by the "ski" form of the name. The baby was now distinct and protected from his wrath by his wife's body. He had thought of wanting to hurt her body and then of wanting to venerate it. He remembered that he had felt a little afraid of making love to his wife then, lest he hurt her or the baby.

Many men reported variations of this theme from around 22 weeks onward. Their remembrances were especially vivid because of their closeness to the unexpectedly early arrival of the babies and because, in a not insignificant number of cases, labor ensued in rather close proximity to these kinds of thoughts, feelings, fantasies, and dreams, as if they were responsible for the premature parturition.

As one possibility, this material might be seen to recapitulate the next developmental stage, when the oedipal little boy is forced to acknowledge the presence of three people and to bring together wishes to love and to hurt, to be nurtured and to be punished. In this vein, several men in the well-attuned group began to be bothered by stories and news having to do with child abuse. One pediatrician found it increasingly difficult to start intravenous infusions on his little patients. A number of men recalled having dreams in which they were administering well-deserved spankings to older children. One man reported that such a dream had been quite sexually exciting, although to the best of his knowledge he had never previously been aroused by such material. Variations on these beating fantasies involved the notion that the kid would beat out the father himself. "The little pisser," said one dad, "just wait till he's old enough to make me squirm."

Urethral and urinary imagery was quite pronounced in several fathers. One father reported the recurrent thought that he might now urinate into the vagina during intercourse, either drowning his baby or otherwise washing up the pregnancy. This father recalled having been a bed wetter until the age of 10 years. This material, which occurred after 26 weeks, is especially interesting to compare with Kestenberg's (1976) description of urethral reworkings in the third trimester in women. Once more, it was harder to form impressions of the period after quickening in the men in the less and least well-attuned groups. It was my sense that there were hostile currents in these men, but that these were principally directed toward their wives. Two of the fathers mentioned their plans to get their digs in when the kids arrived, but this did not appear to be a phase-specific wish as it was in the most attuned group.

THE END OF PREGNANCY

Some of the pregnancies ended with the arrival of very small, often sick, but usually viable babies weighing 750 to 1,000 grams at around 26 to 28 weeks of gestation. In those pregnancies which lasted longer, the third trimester seemed to bring with it a new kind of experience: the sensation on the part of many of the men that something "powerful and magical and big" was going on, something beyond their ability to control. The intrusive fantasies seemed to decline, as did the frequency of lovemaking. There was a perceptible shift toward readying things in the real world for the child's arrival. Observations of children, concerns with patterns of childrearing, and preparations and activities related to the actual arrival of the child seemed to replace the preoccupation with inner processes of the previous months. "It's out of my hands," one father reported, "I've done what I could; now nature will take its course."

The theme of magic or mystery was echoed again and again. It varied in individuals from an emphasis on the sinister to an emphasis on the sublime. Also at this time, there reemerged a more defined notion than before of the differences in reproductive roles in men and women. Earlier sexual theories and reproductive fantasies seemed to be replaced by a general feeling of awe. Truth was more astonishing than individual fiction; the actual miracle of birth surpassed the childish fantasy. "Out of something that feels so good," one father said, "something that really has to be worked on. I have my part; she has hers. Together we make something new. The last eight months have been hard work, but nothing, I'd wager, compared with the next 400."

In this later stage of pregnancy, men in the most attuned group seemed to be working on the differences between inner and outer, slowly coming to understand what could be ordered and interpreted, while continuing to marvel at what lay just beyond their grasp ("the eternal feminine draws us on"). I wondered if I were seeing a replaying of that stage in a boy's caretaking line of development when he sadly but surely gives up his maternal inner riches and invests his penis and the outside world with ever-greater importance (Ross, 1977). Thus, the expectant father gets back "in touch with his insides" and to some extent with those of his wife; yet he maintains his valuation of his penis, his exterior, and the outside world. Thus he grooms himself for his future role with his children as the representative of the outside world (i.e., the world beyond the mother–child symbiosis), but as provider who is also respectful of this symbiosis. As such he also serves as an external beacon to his wife, who may feel that she is being submerged in her own inner processes and concerns at the time of parturition.

THE PREMATURE DELIVERY

For all the 35 men in the most attuned group, expectant fatherhood ended sooner than expected as a consequence of the premature births. All experienced varying degrees of anger, distress, fear, and grief. In this group, however, these affects were compatible with the ability to empathize with comparable feelings in their spouse. These men instinctively felt that their wives needed more rather than less after the production of a premature infant. It was as if the process of expectant fatherhood, linked as it was to the shared intimacy with the wife, enabled the man to parent his wife at the very time when she most needed care. In this group, there seemed to be none of the gross disorders of attachment and parenting that have been noted elsewhere in the literature (Klaus and Kennell, 1976). The reciprocal fantasies and concerns of the new mothers have already been reported (Herzog, 1977).

Premature delivery triggered somewhat different behaviors in the men of the less well-attuned and least well-attuned groups. A variety of affects were reported, but two feelings predominated: intense anger, usually directed at the wife, but sometimes at the obstetrician and other health professionals; and the reaction that I, borrowing from Greenberg and Morris (1974) who defined engrossment as the father's rapt response to his full-term infant, have called "superengrossment" with the newborn. This reaction occurred in fathers who had often been conspicuously uninterested in the pregnancy until this time. The baby looked "angelic," "full term," or "just beautiful" to these new fathers. In contrast, the fathers in the well-attuned group were often horrified at the fragility of their newborns and were greatly concerned (and justifiably so) about their lack of maturity and resilience. Among these so-called superengrossed fathers, what emerged was a competitive struggle with the wife for the baby's affection. Bitter denunciation of wives as "unfit mothers with bad insides" occurred with considerable frequency. The results of this state of affairs for the future of the family and for the initial mother–infant bonding were often disastrous (Herzog, 1977).

Was the orderliness of the fathers' reworking of old issues in caretaking disturbed by the lack of the prerequisite feature of a well-developed intimacy and empathy with their wives during the entire pregnancy experience? It was as if issues relevant to becoming a father surfaced in a less distinct and thus less workable fashion. In these cases, the strong affects aroused by the unexpected early arrival of the baby were turned against the spouse rather than being used as signals to strengthen the family unit. Missing in these men was the decisive turning from feminine to masculine conceptions of parenthood at the end of the second trimester and, with this lack, the experience of a mysterious external force: that nature, or a miracle, or the sum is greater than the individual parts (the one becomes the two, the two becomes the three, the three becomes the one) that most of the well-attuned husbands had experienced around the seventh month. Interestingly, Jessner and others (1942) reported a comparable feeling in pregnant women at this time of gestation. Instead of feeling awe, the women experienced themselves as responsible and culpable and, in a very real sense, punished by having been deprived of their babies. Less well-attuned men seemed compelled to act out what they were not able to remember or experience during pregnancy. In almost none of the cases did these fathers remember fantasies or feelings about feeding and refertilizing their wives or fetuses. Nor did they grapple with the wish to bear a child themselves, to hurt a child, or to hurt the woman who had had such great power during the previous pregnancy. Instead, they manifested unintegrated aspects of all these urges in their superengrossment and competition with the "culpable-bad insides" mother.

CONCLUSIONS

As I review my impressions of the 103 men whose wives delivered prematurely, it appears to me that certain characteristic stages of expectant fatherhood can be identified in at least one subgroup of these fathers-to-be. These stages involve a getting-ready period, which is followed by a time of fullness and ecstasy after an infant has been conceived. I then discerned a characteristic set of fantasies and feelings that clustered about the theme of nurturing woman and fetus, along with an attendant worry about the adequacy of one's own supplies.

This stage gives way to one in which old issues from the inner-genital period of development and hermaphroditic fantasies come to the fore. And this phrase, in turn, is followed by a time when the dialectic between the notions of a nurturing and of a punishing penis ensues. It is here that the father-to-be is most aware of his own ambivalence toward the child and toward its mother. Concomitantly, a strengthening of the relationship with the man's own father serves to give prefatherhood a more masculine cast near the end of the second trimester. The mentor of old is revived. This stage is followed by an uncanny kind of feeling. That which was willingly initiated has become larger than the sum of its parts, larger than the residue of past conflicts and resolutions (including perhaps the oedipal conflict), and large enough literally to become a life of its own. This feeling, which is often not exclusive to expectant fathers but, rather, is often shared with expectant mothers, strengthens the alliance of pregnancy and brings with it an appreciation of the division of labor in reproductive functioning and in subsequent parenting. It is almost as if this appreciation of the reality principle is ushered in by a recapitulation of earlier attempts at solving the "Mystery of the Sphinx," the quandary of sexual differences and functionings (Freud, 1905).

A striking feature of this study is that this sequence seemed to unfold with greatest clarity in those situations where the expectant father participated in an expanding mutual intimacy with his wife. Biological changes occurring in the wife were lent, as it were, to an expectant father. His attunement with her in turn allowed the father to use these compelling occurrences to regress, reassess, and reintegrate erstwhile elements of his own caretaking line of development.

The second general impression gleaned from the work is that individual life experiences, both inner and outer, exerted a powerful influence on each man's experience of prospective fatherhood.

A third general impression, a corollary of the first two, has to do with an apparently inverse relationship between the intensity of a man's father hunger and his ability to attune to his wife and to participate both intrapsychically and interpersonally in the progression toward parenthood. If you are always searching for a father, it may interfere with your ability to become one, although some men may make their own reparations and compensations for their defective childhoods by endeavoring to become superior parents themselves. In fact, a significant percentage of men in the less well-attuned group, and an even higher percentage of men in the least well-attuned group, came from families where the father was absent during part or all of the first five years of the son's life. Without a father in one's personal past, it is difficult to reconstruct a father in one's own prefatherhood, and this situation seems to have fateful implications for both intimacy and caretaking during adulthood.

16 | TOMMY AND THE BLACK LION

THIS CHAPTER ADDRESSES THE ISSUE OF NEUROSIS in childhood as it is differentiatable from other developmental disturbance. Anna Freud (1945) spoke clearly and cogently about the importance of diagnosis in childhood treatment while advocating for therapeutic interventions that take cognizance of the nature of the problem with which the specific child struggles. I discuss the issue of neurotic process as it emerges in child analysis.

Analysis of children as well as adults is a process in which consent is given by the analysand that an intimate encounter may occur in which the person's developmental line of personal meaning is examined with and in the facilitating presence of the analyst. It is a situation in which the nature of the analysand's representational world can be assayed, sometimes even recreated, as it informs the various contours of the transference, as an intermediate space is jointly constructed by both players to provide needed safety and a setting in which that which is most painful can be played out. The analysand discovers his psychic reality and recognizes himself as he is recognized by his analyst. Analysis heals by reconstructing a coherent narrative. It illuminates what is to be seen and what can only be inferred by offering the possibility for modifications in intrapsychic structures and by facilitating mimetic mobility and fostering the possibility that new representations, specifically those of self-with-analyst, may find a constructive place on the representational stage.

In all these therapeutic aspects, self-recognition, as it occurs in the presence of the analyst, is a crucial component of the healing process. Both adult and child analyses are informed not only by the former but also by the ongoing actual and the transformed activities of primary objects. We are accustomed to thinking about the parents' role in child analysis. Their pathology and their health are critical factors in the efficacy of our work and in the formulation of a treatment plan that features analysis.

Interaction with each parent, accompanied by affective coloration, is stored in a cumulative and yet paradigmatic fashion. The harmonic or cacophonous nature of the various pentimenti of representations of self-with-mother, self-with-father, and self-with-mother-and-father populate the internal stage on which intrapsychic dialogue and conversation ensue (Herzog, 1995). These conversations form the substrate for what I call internal enactments, that is, affective-relational conversations between and among the three primary categories of self-with-other representations. (One could consider also, self-with-siblings.) Similarly, they can serve as the scaffolding for external enactments or even interactive enactment in situations of play deformation or psychological exigency. Here I present material from the beginning and the ending of a four-year analysis of a boy who was involved in an enactment when he came to see me and who because of his functional structure and/or because of the analytic process (or perhaps both), moved on in the analytic *Spielraum* to evolve a neurotic process in which an internal enactment replaced an external one; thereafter, play in displacement predominated over interactive enactment.

Tommy was almost five when his parents first consulted me. He was a bright and accomplished boy who had weathered the birth of his sister, Abby, a year earlier with only the "mildest of regressions." For about a month after Abby's birth, he had stained all his underpants after defecating and stated that he could only drink Ma-milk, the name he gave to the nourishment that little Abby imbibed. He stated that he needed white Ma-milk rather than the chocolate milk that had been prepared for him as a special treat during his mother's brief stay in the hospital and immediately after her return. He suggested that his underpants were made brown by the chocolate milk. Prior to Abby's birth, he had loved chocolate milk and chocolate in general. Now he would not eat it at all and moreover had developed a number of other eating peculiarities. He insisted that each food that was placed on his plate be clearly separated from all the others, and he would only eat one food at a time. Thus he would eat all his carrots, then his potatoes, and then his meat.

The real reason for the consultation, however, was not this eating style but, rather, that Tommy insisted on wearing a Superman costume each day when he went to kindergarten. He also spoke frequently, his teachers thought excessively, of the danger of kryptonite. In fact, his school day was largely taken up with ferreting out this danger or avoiding it. In addition, he would periodically bark out a sound that had a guttural, "Germanic" quality and that had led his parents to consult a pediatric neurologist before seeing me to explore the possibility of Gilles de la Tourette syndrome.

Tommy had always enjoyed dressing up, his mother reported. For a while, right after Abby's birth, he had particularly enjoyed wearing his mother's clothes and shoes, but this behavior had abated, much to the relief of both parents. The interest in Superman had seemingly followed on a friend's wearing this outfit for Halloween. Tommy had worn his Superman outfit at home occasionally when playing. When kindergarten began, he started to insist that this was to be his daily garb and, as mother stated, "This sounds strange, but it is almost impossible to dissuade him. He gets so upset that it seems like it might also be unwise." Father concurred, although he told me with a slight smile that he could, of course, make Tommy wear another outfit, if that's what the situation required.

Tommy's parents were both academics. His mother's family were Holocaust survivors and his father's parents were from the American mid-West. The parents had been married for six years prior to Tommy's birth. He was a planned child, named for great-grandfathers on each side of the family, one of whom had been murdered after his deportation from Holland, the other having survived intact into his 90s. Each of the parents had had some exposure to psychoanalysis: the mother, through her work and immersion in a child-of-survivors group that had an analytic focus: and the father, through his friendship with a colleague who had completed analytic training. In addition, the mother had heard of my work through an associate who had participated with me in a seminar on psychoanalysis and literary theory. The parents asked me to evaluate Tommy and to advise them about what role they should play in this process and subsequent treatment. Neither parent had been in individual psychotherapy, and both reported some history of depressive illness in the family.

Tommy arrived at the first hour in full Superman regalia. He was an attractive, slim boy with blond hair, strikingly long, dark eyelashes, and large and beautiful eyes. He was accompanied by both parents and little Abby. He carried a magnifying glass and a curious-looking device that he identified as a cider counter. He moved decisively from the waiting room into my office without a backward glance at his family, loudly saying, "Kryptonite, I'll find you." I wondered where to position myself and, not yet having introduced myself, said, "Hi Tommy, I'm Dr. Herzog."

I was instantly shushed by Tommy, who said, "Quiet, I can't hear the cider counter." He then proceeded to canvas the entire office. His affect was interesting to me. Tommy was totally attentive, intently and intensely concentrating. He hardly seemed to notice that I was in the room. I continued to wonder if I should make myself useful and how. He responded to a couple of questions from me in the same way as he had my initial introduction. These silencings did not feel hostile or even dismissive to me but, rather, as though I were interrupting or distracting Tommy. About 20 minutes into the hour, when Tommy began systematically to remove the books from the shelf that was at his arm level, he turned to me and addressed me spontaneously for the first time: "Would you get a ladder?" he asked, "I can't reach higher."

I felt relieved at being included and offered a foot stool. "Is there any other way that I can help?" I wondered.

"Do you have your own cider counter?" he asked. I paused, thinking, and then Tommy said, "Next time, I'll bring you one. I have six million."

I was struck both by Tommy's offer and by the rapidity with which he had answered his question to me before I could decide how I might answer it and by the number six million. My thoughts turned to his mother's family's Holocaust history, and I thought that this could well be my association rather than his. I said, "Please do bring the cider counter. It sounds as though you have a lot of them." And then, "What is a cider counter?"

Tommy stopped taking out the books and looked me straight in the eye. "What did you say your name is?" I repeated my name. "You don't know what a cider counter is."

"No," I answered.

"It finds the kryptonite. How can you help me if you don't know?"

Tommy's face started to turn red. His breathing became deeper and somewhat uneven. He dropped the book that he was examining and then began to cry. During the preceding several seconds, I had been quite uncertain as to what was transpiring. I considered that I might be witnessing a neurological event, although the possibility of such had not been mentioned by the parents when I inquired. As he began to weep, I actually felt quite relieved. This was frustration, I thought, or some indication of how much he needed me or someone to help him with something. I said with a certain amount of conviction in my voice, "Tommy, please tell me what a cider counter does. I want to know. I think that you thought that I already knew and that it worries you a lot that I don't."

Through his tears, Tommy nodded. I was struck with the tableau of his huge, now weeping eyes, the long, dark lashes, and the intensity of his distress. "It hears the noise," he whispered, "It hears the noise even in the dark. If you hear it first, then you know it's there."

"It can hear even when it's dark?" I asked.

"Yeah, in the night," was his reply.

I was very interested in what Tommy was saying and had the thought that kryptonite might mean something in the night, perhaps a tomb, perhaps a secret. Again I noted that these were my associations and that a not-yet-five-year-old boy would probably not know either the word crypt or the word cryptic. Again, my thoughts turned to the family history and the six million cider counters. Now I pondered the "cid" in "cider" and wondered if this could possibly refer to killing, as in "cidal." I said to Tommy that I was glad that he could tell me about the cider counter and that I hoped that he would tell me other things that I needed to know to be helpful to him. This, I said, was always a good way for me to find out how to be helpful. Tommy looked at me in a very serious fashion and then said, "Are you sometimes afraid?" As I again began to contemplate my answer, thinking that I would probably say yes, he said, "I am. Every night and—and turn on the lights, it's getting dark in here." Together, we turned on several lamps, and Tommy continued his examination of the books.

I thought that Tommy was making the frightening and noisy night visit present in our playroom and introducing a way to illuminate it. I noted to myself that I already had many of my own associations to what might be the nocturnal danger and that the idea of the primal scene or of sexual noises or fears had not even crossed my mind. I could help in the illumination by following his instructions, and it seemed that he would be willing to tell me more of what I needed to know so that my helpfulness could continue. I conjectured that his style of asking me a question and then answering it immediately himself must have defensive as well as adaptive significance. I wondered if my asking him the question about the cider counter so early in our interaction had evoked this style, heightening an extant pattern, or, to the contrary, if it had little or no effect on what I was observing.

When I told Tommy that our time today was almost up, he stopped his study of each book. He asked me if I could remember where he had left off. Again, before I could answer, he said, "It's this green book, next to the brown one, I'll remember." Having been just thinking about this pattern of question-asking, I said, "You asked me if I could remember and then before I answered you said that you would remember. Do you also still want to know if I can remember?" Tommy looked at me as though he did not understand what I had asked. I wondered if my question had been premature or too complicated or for some reason off base.

"Can you remember?" Tommy then asked.

"I will try," I said, "It's this green book next to the brown one."

He looked at me quizzically. I had the fantasy that he might again ask his question about whether or not I was ever afraid, but he did not. I told Tommy that we could meet again the next week. He said good-bye. I thought that our parting was much more formal than the beginning of the hour into which he had launched himself with such alacrity.

I accompanied Tommy as he left my office and returned to his family in the waiting room. He did not greet his parents but instead said, "I am searching for kryptonite. I have to come back and search more. He remembers."

A week later Tommy returned, again in his Superman attire. He brought with him a stuffed animal that he called Alfred. Alfred was a sheep, with a baby inside, a lamb. I wondered about this couple.

Tommy did not respond to my initial questions as he returned to the green book next to the brown one and the search for the kryptonite. When I was told that Alfred's baby was crying, I asked what I could do to help. "He likes milk," was the response. I asked for directions in procuring the milk, and Tommy asked if there was any one here with Ma-milk. I recognized these as allusions to what the parents had told me and also again felt the curious tension that I had encountered with the questions the week before. Who would articulate the evolving scenario now, and would I need to be instructed, through my questions, as to every step while another drama, the kryptonite search, played itself out? I began to consider the meaning of parallel dramas, two stages on which two performances were being conducted. A little later, Tommy asked if the baby had gotten *her* milk. I confessed that I was still searching for Ma-milk, and he said sadly that this was a problem because Alfred, of course, had none. "You don't have any either?" he asked. I thought sadly. "No, I guess you are a man, aren't you?" he answered the question in the familiar fashion.

Although, in retrospect, it seems not surprising, I was completely unprepared for his next suggestion, which was that the baby should be offered cider if there were no Ma-milk. He gestured to a pencil holder on my desk. The cider counter went crazy in his hand, and he said, "It's there. Give her a drink. I'm busy." His tone was suggestive to me of that of a distracted or even annoyed parent. At the end of the second hour, we turned on more lights again as the baby, called Ruh, was afraid in the dark. I remembered out loud that we had together addressed this night fear in the previous hour. To myself I noted that cider, a substitute for Ma-milk, was detected by the cider counter. This made sense. How was this related to the seemingly driven search for kryptonite, which was also conducted with a cider counter? Was Tommy saying that Superman was endangered by a substitute for Ma-milk?

In the third hour, Tommy returned with all his accoutrements. In addition, he brought some Ma-milk, although, from its packaging, it looked like a nutritional-health food kind of snack. It was, in fact, a kind of trail mix consisting of nuts, raisins, and grains. He wondered if I could provide this kind of Ma-milk, and I said that I would try to get some, although his parents, and he, and I needed to think together about what he wanted to do. As I spoke, addressing my comments to the question of our ongoing relationship, he continued expressing his thoughts, which seemed concurrent: "I brought the Ma-milk even though it's not the real thing, so that we would have something to give to Ruh. You're not a mother, but you've got to have something to give him when he's hungry. Just because you're not a mother doesn't mean that you've got nothing to give to Ruh." I vaguely understood that he was talking about my not being female, not a mother, and that he was addressing the issue of what I had to offer. Was he saying that he needed to provide me with what I gave the baby? What might this mean? I wondered if it could be a commentary on his perception of the role of the father and some conclusion about the dearth of a father's endowment.

A little later in this hour, he had Alfred—was Alfred the mother of Ruh?—suddenly create a big row and roll over on Ruh. Ruh was very seriously affected by this encounter. In fact, he seemed to have been rendered unconscious. I produced my dream machine, a pen that we held up to the unresponsive Ruh's head and that enabled us to see what was going on inside. Tommy told me that Alfred was furious that Ruh had been given first cider and now something called Ma-milk, which was clearly no such thing. That's what caused the big row and rollover. I asked how Ruh knew this. Tommy looked surprised and told me that he was looking into Ruh's head, that's how he knew it. Then he said that Alfred was a strange critter. When I asked what he meant, Tommy said, "Have you ever met a mother called Alfred?"

I said, "Now that you mention it, no."

Tommy said, "Alfred's not a mother, stupid."

"What is Alfred?" I asked.

"Alfred is a daddy, stupid," was the response.

I noted to myself that Ruh had been called both a him and a her and that the parent, Alfred, was also somewhat confusing. There did not seem to be a third character, as in a family of mother, father, and child, and simultaneously there were possibilities that either of the two characters could change gender. I remembered my earlier thought of dual stages.

I thought that Tommy was presenting an elaborate schema of self-with-other that included the enabling or disturbing possibility of gender change—that he was suggesting that there were major dangers that might besiege him either from within the mother or by virtue of some substitution of what came from her for him. I thought that the preoccupation with kryptonite was related to this constellation and that the emitted noises might also feature some reference to the night or the dilemma of the maternal nutriments and their ersatz equivalents. I puzzled about the role of the father and felt both drawn into and invited into Tommy's efforts to make sense of things and his evident need to fight off some difficulties that had now taken center stage, at least in school and in my office. I proposed to the parents that Tommy and I continue to learn together about kryptonite, and we began our further explorations.

At this time, an unexpected event occurred. Tommy's mother called to tell me that she had developed a deep attachment to me with erotic tinges. She voiced concern that this might in some way interfere with Tommy's treatment or even be designed with that purpose in mind. After a consultation, I referred the mother to a colleague. Three weeks later, she called to tell me that she had straightened something out and was at work on much more. She apologized for the "intrusion" and stated that it was probably better that it had arisen when it did rather than later. I did not inquire further but recommenced my work with Tommy.

Initially my schedule permitted only two meetings a week. Tommy kept asking if we could meet more frequently. What he actually said at the end of each hour was, "Tomorrow please." As soon as I had a free hour, we added it, and five months after our initial meeting we achieved a schedule of four meetings each week.

The following material is from the eighth month of treatment, the third month of four-times-per-week meetings. Tommy now calls me Stupid all the time. Whereas this appellation was originally clearly derogatory, it now seems less so. It has become my name. I cannot say that I am completely neutral about this turn of events, but I have accepted it after inquiring a number of times about its choice. I imagine this to be an attribute describing not only me but also, perhaps, the transference persona whom I represent. Ruh continues to be one of our interests. He is growing and is very active. Sometimes he needs cider and sometimes Ma-milk, the ersatz kind. We follow these dietary alterations with the help of the cider counter, which has become, with regard to Ruh, an instrument for predicting hunger, not a global hunger but a specific need for cider. It also retains its function as a kryptonite detector.

Simultaneously, by using the dream machine, we continue to study Alfred's psychology, which can be accessed by looking into Ruh's head. I have come to say that it seems as though what goes on in Alfred has an effect on what we see in Ruh's head. I express puzzlement over this phenomenon. Tommy says that I have gotten it right. Alfred's issues affect Ruh's psychology. We continue to tolerate the ambiguity of both Alfred's and Ruh's gender. I feel that Ruh is not quite all right, although I don't know why. Perhaps, it is because the inside of his head is so filled with Alfred; perhaps it is the matter of gender variability. When I voice my concerns about Ruh to Tommy, he looks serious and says, yes, there is a problem.

In the previous hour, a new character appeared called Cecil. Once he or she was also called Cecille. I remark that Cecil seems to have certain things in common with Alfred and Ruh. Tommy says, "Like all in the family." Not infrequently now, Tommy blows me a kiss. His gesture at such times is particularly striking, as it is feminine and quite delicate, creating a kind of amalgam between Madama Butterfly and Superman. I am reminded of another patient, Davey, whom the reader will meet in a later chapter and who frankly announces that he is Madama Butterfly.

The hour begins with Tommy telling me that Cecille could not come today. I ask why and am told that he had to go to work. I note, to myself, that Cecille is a he. Tommy continues that Cecil works in a garage. He has just shifted the names. Tommy is playing on the floor and reaches for a car. He turns it over and takes my dream machine and applies it to the car's underside. "What is happening?" I ask. "Fixing the car," is the response. I try to orient myself. Is this Cecil, or is this just a coincidence? I wait to see what will emerge. "This car has been given bad gas," Tommy then says, "How can you expect it to drive if you give it the wrong stuff?"

"What should it have gotten?" I inquire.

"It needs good stuff." He hands me the dream machine and directs me to look into the underbelly of the car.

"I can't see very well. Will you help me?" I ask.

"See that pipe?"

"Yeah," I say.

"It hasn't grown because it doesn't get what it needs. It's getting rusty."

"Is that why the car is in the shop?" I ask.

"Yeah, stupid," says Tommy. "How do we fix it?" I then ask.

Tommy smiles at me. "Get that bottle over there." He points toward my analytic chair.

I move toward the chair and then say, "Which bottle? I haven't my glasses on so I can't read the labels."

"The green one next to the brown one, don't you remember?"

I feel a rumbling of memory, and then it comes. This is what he said in the first hour while conducting the search for kryptonite among my books. "Here is the green one," I say. "What is it called?"

"It's Pa-gas," Tommy says. "If we pour it in, a lot of it, then maybe the car will be all right."

I hand Tommy the imaginary green bottle, and he begins pouring. I am feeling confused, but excited. Pa gas, something growing with it, stunted and rusty without it, yet amenable to repair, all sound very promising. I wonder why this enthuses me so. My thoughts are interrupted as Tommy says, "Oh no, it's Cecil."

"He's come?" I say.

"What are you doing here?" Tommy says to Cecil. He takes out of his pocket a figure that looks something like Kermit the Frog. The puppet represented Cecil in the preceding hour, too.

"I told you to go to work," Tommy continues.

He now has Cecil say, "You don't know how to fix that car. Don't give it Pa-gas. It needs Ma-milk or cider." Tommy turns to me and says, "You saw that pipe, didn't you."

"Yes," I say.

"It needs Pa-gas," he then says.

"Well, we have given it Pa-gas," I say.

Tommy then throws the Cecil figure across the room, and the cider counter begins to click ominously. I ask what the clicking means. Tommy emits a series of noises, guttural and sounding something like Ach ach ach. This is the Gilles de la Tourette-like sound, I think. It has never before entered our play space. I consider how to respond to this sound. Tommy does not look distressed. I say, "What does it mean?" thinking that this question can be applied to either the clicking of the cider counter or to the Ach ach ach.

"Cecille wants to wreck the car," Tommy says.

"Why?" I respond, noting the change from Cecil to Cecille, but thinking that I would stay with the syntactical elaboration. "If you give it the wrong gas, it won't work," is Tommy's next statement, "It doesn't know how to drive. It doesn't know what it is." There is intense feeling in Tommy's voice.

I respond to this feeling, perhaps prematurely, by saying, "Giving the car Pa-gas now will help."

Tommy looks at me and says, "Stupid, there's still Cecil. Don't you hear the cider counter? There must be kryptonite in here."

"I'll turn on the lights," I say as we have agreed that doing this is necessary when kryptonite is present.

Tommy searches for the offending kryptonite. He brings his counter over to where Cecil is lying. "It's here," he says. "Get the box." I get the shoe box that he and I have devised as a kryptonite container. Once we put the kryptonite into this container, it is effectively neutralized. Tommy takes Cecil and gingerly puts him into the box. As all previous kryptonite deposits have been imaginary, this seems quite momentous to me.

"Look, look," Tommy then almost screams, "He's gotten out and he's giving the car Ma-milk. I told you there's still Cecil. Get him, get him, Ach ach ach."

Together we capture Cecil and return him to the box. Tommy asks me if we can take a couple of books and put them on top of the box. "I mean really," he says, "He'll get out and give Ruh cider or Ma-milk."

"Ruh?" I say.

"You saw him. He gave Ruh Ma-milk. Ach ach ach."

I say to Tommy that we will find a way to keep Cecil in the kryptonite dump so that Ruh won't be given the wrong food and so that the car won't get the wrong gas. Tommy says, "Good, cause kryptonite isn't good for Superman either."

I note the interchangeability of Ruh and the car as there has been interchangeability of gender. As Tommy has not responded to my "Ruh?" I say nothing. I also note that the play involves both displacement and enactment. Tommy, too, or at least Superman, Tommy in costume, is vulnerable to what Cecil is, also a form of the dangerous kryptonite.

The next hour Tommy comes without his Superman costume. His mother is beaming in the waiting room.

"Is he still in there?" Tommy begins.

"I think so," I respond, "The books are still on top of the box."

"Get the Pa-gas, a lot of it," Tommy says, "I'm glad that you have a full tank."

"It's what is needed," I venture.

"You remember," Tommy says.

I follow him as he gets the car. Today he has the car speak. It says, "I am so thirsty. I need that gas so much. I want to be a really fast car, win races, beat the other cars."

Tommy says to me, "He wants to be a real car, not half car, half, Ach ach, I don't know. Just a real car."

"Pa-gas will help," I say, "It sounded like you were starting to say Ach ach like you did yesterday."

"He'll need a lot. He'll need it every day," Tommy goes on, "At least you've got a lot of Pa-gas here."

"Yeah," I reply.

For a few minutes, we continue administering the right gas. The car expresses relief, and then Tommy asks, "Is it growing?" Tommy asks me to look. I ask if we know how long the pipe was yesterday. Tommy answers that it was a mile long. He then takes the dream machine, looks in, and says, "Oh-oh, it's still a mile. We need an operation."

"How come?" I wonder.

"It's not longer," says Tommy.

"Shall I get ready?" I ask.

"No," says Tommy. "Get Cecil."

"What!" I say, "Isn't that dangerous?"

"He does the operations. Get Cecil," Tommy says.

I move to the box and remove the books. The cider counter begins to click ominously, and Tommy starts to Ach ach.

"We've got a problem on our hands," I say, "Is he the only person for the job?"

"Yes," says Tommy with very great seriousness, "Get him out, now. Ach ach ach."

"Let's just think about this a minute," I say. "The cider counter is going crazy. You are saying Ach ach ach and you know you're not even wearing your Superman outfit."

Tommy's eyes widen. He looks down at himself and begins to shake. "I'm not," he says, "I'm not."

I feel very surprised with my intervention. Instead of simply following orders, I resisted. Why? An antipathy to surgical solutions come to mind, followed by concern about the appearance of the Ach ach ach. Moreover, I had decided earlier in the hour not to mention the change of garb. Now I brought it up in a show-stopping manner. Listening as Tommy now says, "Maybe we should measure the pipe again," I feel that I can reverse my determination to keep Cecil, the mother-milk and cider-giving kryptonite poisoner, imprisoned in the dump and allow the surgery to occur. "It's longer. The Pa-gas is working," Tommy shrieks loudly, "He'll be able to beat the other cars and win the race."

"Does he want to beat the others?" I ask.

"Every car wants to win," Tommy says, "unless it gets the wrong gas." I nod. "Sometimes, a car gets the wrong idea, some other car's idea, like a truck, not a car," he continues.

"How does that happen?" I wonder.

"Don't know. Well, maybe like Alfred and Ruh, remember?"

"I remember, one's thoughts inside the other's head."

"Maybe it's because of an operation," he says.

"What do you mean?"

"Like the car gets a bus insides, I mean a truck. You take out the car insides and put in the truck's. Then the car wouldn't want to win. It wouldn't want to beat the others, right?"

"I can see how that might be," I say.

As I think about this rapid series of events, Tommy suddenly begins running toward me, crashing with his head into my crotch. I think of Alfred having a row and rolling over onto Ruh. "Ach ach ach, I hate you," Tommy shouts. Then he begins to cry. "Don't give the car cider. Don't give it Ma-milk," he wails.

"I gave it Pa-gas, didn't I?" I say.

"Cecil wants to give the car cider, Ma-milk."

"Yes, that's what we learned yesterday," I say.

"I hate him. I hate him. You have lots of Pa-gas."

"How much do we need?" I ask.

"A lot and we have to keep Cecil in the tank. He can't get out."

"Not even for an operation," I say.

"No, not even for an operation." Tommy looks very worried.

"Why would the car need an operation anyway," I ask.

"If he has turned into a . . . girl," Tommy whispers.

There are then a couple of seconds of silence during which I again try to sort out what is happening. Once again Tommy starts to butt with his head in my direction. "I hate you, I hate you, you pussy," he screams. I stop him this time before he makes contact with my midsection and say, "What's happened to this car makes you very upset and I guess you feel that I had something to do with it."

"You have the Pa-gas," Tommy replies, "You have the Pa-gas."

I feel that Tommy is saying that whoever had the Pa-gas either gave it to the little boy car or withheld it and substituted something else. I try to think of the many meanings of Pa-gas—something needed, paternal farting, whatever it was that had asphyxiated the paternal great-grandfather. These thoughts bring to mind again my thinking of cider as being related to "cidal" and the six-million comment of the first hour. I ponder the eruption of physical aggression toward me, a first, and the appellation Pussy. It seems to me that I have been regarded as both a withholding or possibly repairing father and as a degraded female, perhaps something like what Ruh or the car or even the uncostumed Tommy, a perhaps very emasculated Clark Kent, might feel.

All these thoughts prompt something like a summary statement, probably to frame my agitation, and I say, "A lot has happened yesterday and today. I think it is good that we can help the car to recover and that we need to find out more about how it got into the jam with the wrong gas."

"It was the operation, I already told you," Tommy says. He then blows me a kiss while backing somewhat coquettishly away from me and starts to hurl himself in my direction.

I again stop the charge and say, "This is confusing. You seem to be both coming and going at the same time."

"The car doesn't know whether to be in drive or back up, and Ruh can't tell if she is a boy or a girl," Tommy responds, "Alfred doesn't know either."

"What about Cecil-Cecille?" I ask. Tommy shrugs and the hour comes to an end.

Let us examine the events of these two hours. An enactment has occurred that is vitally important to the ongoing work. I interrupt the play, changing the story, so to speak, as I become anxious about Cecil the surgeon. I experience myself as perhaps constituting a paternal presence, certainly as being designated as the provider of Pa-gas. But simultaneously I repeat something already encountered in our syntactical play and putatively significant in the pathogenesis of Tommy's disorder. Like Alfred's thoughts populating Ruh's head, my anxiety, ideas, and wishes have now altered the scenario. Importantly, Tommy does not, or is not able to, resist such an intrusion. Equally importantly, I recognize that I have repeated something and that this reiteration needs to be explored and acknowledged. Here is the enactment: in my becoming anxious and prohibiting the surgery, I am like Alfred to Ruh, like ersatz Ma-milk instead of Pa-gas. I am also being protective as in encountering the father; Tommy complies, in that the pipe grows, but it also actually grows in its multiplicity of meanings, as the content enters the transference and he actually barrels into me.

Over the next several months, we continued to work on the car. It shifted from being interchangeable with Ruh to a different sort of relationship with him. They could be regarded as one, but they were in fact not the same. Ruh was the baby; the car was the car. I had to tolerate a certain amount of ambiguity about this sameness and difference; it did not seem to bother Tommy. I would ask for clarification, and we would get only so far as to learn that they were both the same and different. I developed the hypothesis that my coming to understand the developmental line from Ruh to car might constitute a goal of the treatment. I pondered the connection between this thought, that is, that my increasing understanding might correspond to Tommy's treatment goals, and pondered, too, the complicated relationship between the content of Ruh's thoughts and Alfred's issues. I felt comfortable, more or less, with this way of thinking, which was something like making a virtue out of necessity. I vaguely grasped the importance of the same and different motif but did not yet know where it would lead. Tommy eventually gave the car the name Night Rider. This appellation seemed to evolve through a series of successive approximations, which I heard as nigh, nighrye, and nigh ride her.

I think that this evolution of the name reflected was not only my placing the material in a sexual context, but some process in Tommy by which he shared with me the pentimenti of this uncovering, and simultaneously forming, representation of an interactive and intrapsychic object relation depiction. There had not been a repetition of his butting me in the crotch, although now I wondered if this might be some form of "nigh ride her." Were this the case, I would then be the ridden her. I also thought about his turning into what I experienced as Madama Butterfly immediately after the attack. Did this change represent a female attack on a hapless male, or was it the punishment for, and an act of undoing, the forbidden, or at least unintegrated, assertive and penetrating thrust?

The alliance between us during this unfolding seemed secure. Tommy would play, would talk to me about life at school, and had begun to tell me about his worries about his mother. She sometimes would cry, saying that it was about work and telling Tommy that she had her own doctor with whom she discussed her problems. Tommy thought that his mother should come and play with me. Clarification of this though led to the realization that his actual idea was that she should play with us. He also told me that his mother cried mostly at night, as she came out of the bedroom where she and his father had been talking. When Tommy talked about his mother, he, too, seemed sad. I felt concern about her well-being, and I had to remind myself that I had referred her to a very competent colleague. I wondered what it would be like if Tommy did bring his mother into our sessions. This possibility seemed to resonate with her earlier statement about her feelings toward me.

Regarding the car, I thought of a crypto-night rider. Night Rider was irascible and sometimes downright mean. Whereas our sympathies initially were clearly for and with him and his deprived and vulnerable state—no Ma-milk and an absence of Pa-gas—they now became more ambiguous as he ran over Ruh, played tricks on Alfred, and was particularly sadistic to Cecille. In these moments, I wondered about representations of the primal scene or at least of interaction between a man and a woman. I, of course, considered that this play could also represent fantasized interaction between a boy and his mother. I found myself remembering my initial response to the father's statement that he could make Tommy wear other clothes, were that necessary; I recalled particularly that I had felt something vaguely sadistic in the laugh that accompanied his statement. I conceptualized Night Rider as being a representation both of the sadistic father and of Tommy's own aggression. I opted for the paternal rather than the maternal representation because we continued to regard, measure, and then shine Night Rider's nether pipe—a masculine image, I thought. Somehow, its continuing growth and general good health, in response to daily portions of Pa-gas, seemed reassuring. I was also influenced by the concomitant reports of Tommy's mother's distress and need for assistance. Night Rider did not seem to me to care about his sad mother who also needed to play. Tommy's attitude toward Night Rider was mixed. Sometimes he seemed admiring of Night Rider's arrogance, sometimes abashed by his "unbridled audacity."

During this period of the analysis, I commented about the salutory effect of the Pa-gas on Night Rider's pipe and expressed continuing interest in his motivation to be difficult. I noted that the Pa-gas did not seem to change Night Rider's behavior and proposed that we learn more about what was going on inside of him. I wondered if Night Rider might need something more than he was getting, like Pa-gas with some special additives. I expressed continuing resonance with Tommy's worry about his mother and found myself echoing her statement that she had a helper whom she consulted.

I wondered about this response of mine, remembering her erotic attachment and her statement about derailing the analysis. Was this earlier event being repeated? Or was I unable to listen sufficiently to what Tommy was bringing me in the "service of protecting the analysis?" I knew that I was managing a more positive set of feelings about her and her needs. I wondered about the complexity of all of this and about the power of her presence in our *Spielraum*. Tommy seemed genuinely concerned about his mother and repeated a number of times that she should come with him to his hours. He would often follow such a suggestion by moving the play into displacement. Here we would admire Night Rider's pipe or follow his latest outrageous misadventure. What did Tommy need from me in order to be able to help his mother? What were the many reasons that he had taken, or had to take, this task on himself?

Eventually I took up the subject of his mother with Tommy

directly. I asked why his mother should join us rather than seeing her own therapist. I was quite startled by his reponse. He told me that his mother should be married to me rather than to his father. I was nicer, and I had Pa-gas. He said that his father was mean to his mother. He then took that back, saying that his father was not mean but, rather, big and strong and just too busy. Tommy was very anxious. There followed some thoughts about wanting me to be his father and then finally a statement that he could take care of his mother alone, especially if they got rid of Abby, his sister. After this conversation, which was not displaced, Tommy began Ach ach aching and started to butt my crotch again. He also blew me kisses and did his Madama Butterfly imitation. I spoke with Tommy about how anxious he became when he talked about his feelings about his mother and his feelings about me, especially those in which he pictured our being together. He asked me if I remembered the last time that he had said Ach ach. I recalled the sessions with the car and its non-growing pipe, the question of surgery and my reluctance, and the problem of Cecil. He said, yes, that was right. He looked very sad and said, "I need some Pa-gas." He seemed to become younger and kind of snuggled up in my direction. I told him that it seemed to me that by moving closer to me he was saying that it was good that I was around to help sort out these feelings and to be with him when they felt overwhelming. I did not mention that there might be another side to his feelings, involving either the defection from his own father or the fuller range of what closeness with me might entail. Tommy smiled at me and nodded, yes.

Over these sessions, I felt that we were making progress in seeing a connection between Tommy's inscape, the ways in which remembering and documenting aspects of kryptonite were related to earlier and current wishes and experiences in the dialogue between mother and father. He not only played these themes out in displacement but also spoke about them directly. Our talking about his wish to "have" his mother here in our playroom seemed enormously helpful. During this time, his mother never contacted me, nor did her analyst. I thought of our situation as reflecting the dilemma that Tommy needed to manage involving his own father hunger, my role as competitor or provider, his mother's need for Pa-gas, and the question of whether, he, the father, or I should provide that. There was also, perhaps, the questions of whether "we" should do the providing and how these issues affected gender identity, the organization and modulation of aggressive drive and fantasy, and the vicissitudes of his oedipal configuration.

I wondered about the intensity of forces that might eventuate in Tommy's being willing to give his mother to me or even to us for her sake and for his. I tried to sort out the transferences as preoedipal father, a comrade in arms, and oedipal rival. I kept in mind that the central issue seemed always to be what was needed and how this might or might not be sufficient, even before the question of conflict was elaborated.

The following sessions are from the end of the second year of the analysis. Tommy is seven. He comes in and starts to tell me about his soccer practice. He has gone out for the team at his private school. This initiative delighted his father and has seemingly sparked a hope in Tommy for something more from his father, whom he mentions every time he mentions soccer. We have talked together about Tommy's wishes to see more of his father and the complexity of feelings connected to his father's unavailability. By contrast, the soccer worries his mother, who says that boys are rough enough without contact sports. Tommy has reassured his mother that he is strong and not very vulnerable. During the hours, he has attributed this strength, in displacement, to Pa-gas and by so doing has in a certain sense identified himself with Night Rider. I have inquired about this, and he has told me, as he often does, that I jump to conclusions and I shouldn't. "That's why I called you stupid," he says. Tommy has told me that it feels good to tell his mother that he is strong and not afraid. He has even suggested that it helps her. When I asked about how this might be, he told me that his mother cries less now that he is stronger and on several occasions, he has gone still further and stated that his coming to see me has helped his mother. I have asked him how this feels and how this might work. Sometimes, in such discussions, we return to the Alfred–Ruh experience. Sometimes Tommy speaks of wanting to bring his mother here so that she can be with both of us. This always evokes anxiety, and both he and I have come to be able to anticipate this reaction.

"Joey is a whiz on the field," he tells me, "He always gets the ball away from whoever has it. He doesn't care whom he kicks."

"He is very strong," I venture.

"Yes, and not afraid. It's like he's full of the right kind of stuff. He's got strong man in him."

"Could one say that he's got Pa-gas, a good-enough supply?" I ask, "Is that what it is?"

Tommy says wistfully, "Yes, I don't see why not, except he doesn't know about Pa-gas; only we do."

I appreciate this reminder of the boundary of our work and also have the feeling that Tommy is saying that Pa-gas is not to be shared with Joey. I also hear the wistfulness and think that the Pa-gas is not the whole story. I say, "Whatever it is that allows Joey to play the way he plays is different from what we play here. It is not the whole story."

"Yes, I think so. Joey is actually mean sometimes. At this afternoon's practice, he kicked Barry really hard. Barry's leg was bleeding and Mr. L____ was really mad. He shouted at Joey to control himself. Joey got real red in the face, and then he ran up and down the field by himself."

I am thinking that Night Rider was sometimes really mean but decide not to say this. I am aware of needing to listen more to what Tommy is trying to say about Joey and not be so eager to fit it in with what we have already talked about.

"Joey's father came to the practice. We heard Mr. L____ yell at Joey. When the practice was over, he put his arm around Joey in a funny way. Not friendly. I thought something was going to happen."

"Like what?"

Tommy looks down. "Oh, I don't know. You know."

"I don't," I say, "I wasn't there."

"I thought that Joey was going to get it from his father, a spanking."

"Did he?" I ask.

"I think so. I don't know. His dad sort of hurried him to the car."

"And what did you think about all of that?" I ask.

"I don't like Joey very much. He once tried to take my homework paper and say that it was his. I hope that his dad spanked him. Mom says that grownups should never hit a kid."

"What do you think?" I ask.

"I hope that Mr. C____ hit Joey." His mood during this exchange has become animated and did not reveal, I think, either anxiety or fear after he raised the topic of spanking.

Tommy then says something about calling Joey up when he gets home. I respond that maybe he wants to find out what happened. Tommy says no and that he wonders what time practice will be tomorrow. I know that practice is at the same time every day; we adjusted our schedule to accommodate it. I consider pointing this out to Tommy and then decide not to. I have some feeling that the unfolding of the Joey–Dad drama, or at least Tommy's interest in it, will be less hindered by my silence than by my inquiring about the defense.

Tommy then moves on to the cars. I wonders if this is a hoped-for deepening or has the defensive move interrupted the material successfully? Tommy brings out Night Rider and with him a second car, which he has named Bad Sort or Bad Sport. Night Rider now seems to be a more civilized auto, and, generally speaking, he monitors Bad Sport's behavior. On one occasion, he even told him that all these bad things that Bad Sport insisted on doing were signs that something was hurting him inside. We established an automobile diagnostic center, called ADC, and it was to this facility that we now repaired. I consider the possibility that Night Rider might be coming to represent me or even Tommy together with me. This last thought is especially intriguing: the consolidation of a masculine identity through the process of man and boy working together. Why am I being the father in this important developmental process? What does it mean that I conceptualize things in this manner? Am I being competitive with Tommy's real father or reciprocating his mother's interest—or both? I recall that Tommy mostly spoke longingly about his father and has never before discussed spanking, and that I know of no relevant history.

"Well what is our work today?" I inquire. A line I have learned through much practice.

"Bad Sport has got a sore rear bumper," Tommy answers.

"How did he get it?"

"A big truck ran into him, on purpose. He had been bumping into a lot of other cars."

"Sounds like he was kind of asking for it," I say.

"Yeah, but he got it worse than he can take. His bumper is really bashed in. Won't be able to play for a long time."

I seem to recall that Tommy felt Joey's spanking had been very severe, perhaps too severe. Knowing that Tommy also felt, at least in part, that Joey should be spanked by his father, I venture, "Is the problem that the truck overdid it, that Bad Sport could have used a whack, but not getting his bumper banged in?"

"Something like that," replies Tommy, "But it's worse. Another car should have bumped him, not a truck. Night Rider would have been perfect for the job."

"It's important that the bump be given by the same kind of vehicle," I say, searching for a word that embodied the whole class.

"That's what I said. Night Rider is older and stronger than Bad Sport, and he knows more. He would have been the right car to bump him. I think that we should arrest that truck right away."

"Even before we fix Bad Sport?" I ask.

"Now," Tommy says, "What are you waiting for? Get him now."

He converts a nearby book into the truck and places it under arrest.

"What now?" I ask.

"He has to be punished."

"Should we find out his side of the story?" I ask.

At first Tommy says no and then he reverses himself, saying, "Yes, let's have a trial."

I ponder this problem of lack of modulation in Bad Sport's spanking and the question of its being administered by the wrong kind of vehicle. Tommy seems to be saying that modulation arises from alikeness rather than from difference.

We return to Bad Sport, who is lying in a heap on the floor of the diagnostic facility, ADC. He is wailing, "I know that I am naughty, but my bumper, my bumper."

Night Rider moves rapidly into action and begins the examination. He looks very worried, Tommy tells me. "Why?" I ask.

"The pipe, you know, it runs right under that bumper."

"So?" I wonder, again aware that this is probably something that I shouldn't have to inquire about.

"If the pipe has been wrecked by the truck's bump, then Bad Sport will never be the same," Tommy says, "I know that you know that. I wish you wouldn't be so stupid. This is very serious. Get Cecil, we need a surgeon."

I have a distinct feeling of déjà vu. I wonder if the cider counter from which we have not heard in almost 18 months, will now be reactivated and if more Ach ach achs are just around the corner. I am not inclined to resist this call to surgery as I was the previous one; and, as I head toward the case in which Cecil resides, the doorbell rings announcing the next patient. Tommy says, "We have to wait until tomorrow."

I feel both relieved and disappointed and a kind of hurry-tomorrow feeling, which reminds me of his "tomorrow, please" good-bye in our early meetings.

Tommy then turns to me and says, "Is it that black man who is in the waiting room? I'm afraid of him." The next patient is a blonde woman with a very fair complexion. She always follows Tommy in the schedule.

"What do you mean?" I ask.

"I am really afraid of the black lion," Tommy responds, "and of black lions."

"I didn't know that," I say, "Has it been true for a long time?"

"For six million years," is Tommy's response.

This is entirely new material, not placeable by me in any hitherto constructed category. I have no referent for either black man or lion, although my thoughts turn to the soiling and chocolate avoidance around his sister's birth. Once again I find the number six million to be evocative. I say, "That is a very long time. I think that you also told me that you had six million cider counters."

"You remember," says Tommy, "Black lions are really mean. They kill because they like to, not just for food."

Our time is up, and I say something to that effect. Tommy asks me if I can accompany him into the waiting room as he is afraid. Feeling that there is no time to explore what this might be about and also inclined to say yes, I walk with him into the waiting room. He seems apprehensive and quickly grabs his coat and departs. The woman in the waiting room, whose ringing of the bell had interrupted us, says, "He looks so scared today. Is everything all right?"

The next hour with Tommy was filled with references to the black lion. Everyone was terrified of him. I felt uncertain who or what a black lion might be, although I understood, at least putatively, that it had to do with killing, that is, aggression, and that its appearance as either a phobic object or new character in the play had followed on material that seemed to be about punitive responses to aggressivity or sexuality. Was this a regression or a further elaboration or, more likely, both? I wondered about Tommy's guilt over giving me his mother and being willing to be my son. Would this evoke retaliation from his own father or augment Tommy's own rage even more. Was homosexual anxiety mobilized by Tommy's interest in spanking and its effect on the pipe? I rechecked both my memory and my notes as I recalled some mention of a black man—he had imagined one in the waiting room yesterday, now there was only the lion. I asked Tommy whom he had been afraid of yesterday.

"The black lion," he responded.

"Only of the black lion?" I asked.

"There's nothing in the world that's scarier," said Tommy.

I realized that I had been shaken by Tommy's anxiety at the end of the last hour. I had never seen him so frightened and had had some other kind of response to his comment about a black man. Some feeling of guilt, I think, was stirred in me about the predominantly Caucasian nature of my practice. Also, this unanticipated change in his mental status, if that is what it was, reminded me of an earlier episode in which I had considered the possibility of petit mal.

The ADC was the scene of general pandemonium as automobile patients and doctors alike were frantic with terror about the beast. Bad Sport's case had to be put on hold; the same was true for the trial of the truck abuser. Tommy asked me if I would board up the center's windows.

I said sure and then added, "This black lion sounds really dangerous. Where does he come from?"

"No one knows. Africa, I suppose, but no one knows," was Tommy's answer.

"Does he have a family? They might know his origins."

"He has no family. He is the only black lion. There are no others, just him."

"One of a kind," I ventured.

"Yes, that's what makes him so deadly and dangerous. He has nothing to lose," Tommy said.

"It must be hard to have no family," I said.

"Even harder to be one of a kind," Tommy replied, "No one else is just like him."

"That's what is hardest for him? Why is that?" I asked. "It helps to have someone who is like you. Everyone knows that, stupid."

I was thinking about the black lion's appearance and its effect on our work. I wondered if we would now get to know more about him or if he would remain an externalized representation of terror. What was the mechanism of his first being a man, then becoming a lion—disguise or transformation? I was aware of a wish to bring the black lion right into our play so that we could learn more about him. I did not act on this wish but thought that it might reflect either my attitude toward bringing mother in, which seemed on the positive side, or my feeling about the return and inclusion of the real father. Did I want him there more, now that I considered that Tommy was internalizing us together as the father–son representation? I also heard the reference to one of a kind and associated to yesterday's material about spanking. It was better to be spanked by someone who was like you. Who could or would spank Black Lion? Was this his problem?

My thoughts were interrupted by an overwhelming barrage of clicking and Ach aching.

"What is it? What is it?" I asked.

"Let's see," replied Tommy. I thought that he seemed strangely calm, given the indicators of alarm and my own startle response. Tommy proceeded to survey Night Rider, Bad Sort, and the too-hard bumping truck. They were all shaking with fear, he said. Again I noted that Tommy was not shaking with fear. Could he be showing me that *with me* he could manage, but that when he left the play room, as in going into the waiting room, things went less well and new symptoms arose?

I said, "They seem really upset, but the situation is O.K. right?"

Tommy smiled at me and said, "We'll manage, boss."

"Boss?" I said.

"Yeah," grinned Tommy. "It's the black lion. You told me yesterday that you know a lot about those critters, so you are in charge today, boss." I thought about this attribution and how unusual it was for Tommy to use this mechanism. There seemed no point in contradicting what he said, and I remembered his earlier pain around my not knowing what a cider counter was. I said nothing and waited to see what would ensue.

Tommy got up, lurched around the room, and then collapsed in a heap at my feet. "I'm so tired I can hardly roar," he whispered.

"Who are you," I asked, even though the roar was a dead giveaway.

"My name is Wrecks," he replied. "Black Wrecks. You know a lot about me."

"Yes" I said. "We have learned a lot together." I was aware of answering ambiguously, neither accepting nor denying my expertise regarding black lions, but also hiding behind the ambiguity of Tommy's now becoming Black Wrecks rather than depicting him in displacement. It always seemed to me to signal a crucial moment in our work when the play shifted mode and Tommy became the character we were examining.

"So how can I help you, Mr. Wrecks?" I inquired.

"I hear that you know more about black lions than anyone in the world. It's true, isn't it?" said Tommy.

"I've heard that, too," I replied, "What is your problem?"

Black Wrecks started to growl and then he roared very loudly. "I'll eat you raw," he growled.

"Do you want help or don't you?" I replied. I was trying to think about what would be helpful in this situation and seemed to be guided by the notion that Tommy needed someone like him to help him learn to modulate his aggression. Always when one has such an idea, it is a cause for uncertainty, and this was no exception. I could also hear that what Tommy was saying might, in fact, be his problem.

"I'm going to eat you up," Wrecks continued, "I eat everything."

"Raw?" I asked. I am not sure why.

"I'll kill you and then eat you," roared Wrecks.

"Are you very hungry?" I then inquired.

"Not at all. I do nothing but eat, kill and eat, kill and eat."

"Is that as boring as it sounds?" I asked.

"Totally," he said, "What else is there? Besides which I like to kill."

"Do you need some help, Mr. Wrecks, so that you only kill to eat and so that you don't overeat?" I asked.

"Is this a joke?" Wrecks replied, "How can you help me? Only another black lion could help me, and I am the only black lion in the world."

I said, "I can see how you might think that, and surely another black lion would know from the inside what it felt like to be a black lion and to have to deal with a black lion's problems. *But*, as you've heard, I know a lot about black lions, so I may be able to help."

"Yeah," said Wrecks, "Let's see what you can do. But I think that I am going to eat you."

Tommy then got up from the floor and walked over to the ADC. He reported that everyone there was terrified. No one could sleep while the black lion was in the neighborhood. Night Rider had taken out a cider counter to serve as an alarm. I wondered if we could say anything to the cars that would help to set their minds at ease.

"Yes," said Tommy, "Tell them that Wrecks is making his sleeping noise."

"Oh," I said.

"Ach, ach, ach, don't you hear it?"

"Yes, I do now. He's asleep," I said.

"He's really got a problem," Tommy said, "I hope that the doctor can help him. It's his only chance, and there are very few *black* lion doctors. Actually he may be the only one."

As Tommy said this I heard black, as in African American lion doctors as opposed to doctors for black lions. I was reminded of my earlier response to his saying that he was afraid of the black man in my waiting room. I now felt quite certain that this black man or boy was intimately connected to him and that our job was to learn more about his problem and what might be done to aid in its resolution. I understood that it was connected to the love of killing and to overeating; also that it had to do with being one of a kind and therefore being unable to modulate one's aggression. I felt cheered by hearing black lion doctors. There were possibly two blacks, which might, in and of itself, be salutary in assisting Mr. Wrecks and thus helping Tommy to manage better.

The arrival of Mr. Wrecks was both sudden and overdue; his presence had been long standing. It had apparently been present in the Ach ach ach of his initial symptomatology, in the putative Gilles de la Tourette, and, I gathered, in the very imagery of crypto-night and Night Rider. I recalled the tune: "In the jungle, the quiet jungle, the lion sleeps tonight." The initial appearance of Mr. Wrecks in the analysis, coming as it did around the question of the car's pipe's growing or not and the corrective or punitive need for surgery, which I had interrupted, seemed to depict the complex melding of sexual and aggressive drives and their derivative fantasies and the feared consequences and the resulting attempted defenses. The cider counter had been and clearly still was some kind of recognition of the sleeping lion's presence or nocturnal behavior.

Tommy had now arrived at the point where he could claim the black lion as a part of himself, or at least he was almost there. This step seemed to become possible around his interest in Joey's spanking and his expression of uncensored aggressive interest. It was also in the context of his struggling with the implications of giving his mother to me as a way of either helping her to "feel better" or as a way station to taking possession of her himself.

There was another very important aspect to this new development. For the first time in the analysis, I was given a particular and highly delimited role. I was to be black, the black, black lion doctor, expert enough and similar enough to the black lion to understand him and to help him, even though he was *one of a kind*. This seemed to me to be a very important transformation and, in a sense, a brilliant move. I was needed for this job of helping the lion tame his instincts and moderate his appetites, but that was not the same thing as marrying Tommy's mother and being his father.

The work now became a two-person dialogue involving Tommy and me. The black lion was, as it were, in analysis with the black-lion doctor. Eventually, Tommy even lay down on the couch. We began by exploring the black lion's dreams.

"I am very tired, I have to sleep," Tommy said as he came into the office. I understood that this was the black lion talking and sat down behind the couch. Tommy gave a feeble roar and then lay down on the couch.

"A terrible day, just a terrible one," he continued. "I ate 20 children and 50 grownups. I have a terrible stomach ache."

"That's less than yesterday," I said.

"It's not easy to diet," the black lion replied.

I waited to see what would come next and, when there was silence, I said, "Have you gone to sleep already?"

"No, I'm just lying here. I know what you are going to ask. Go ahead," the black lion said.

"You ate less. How many did you kill?" I asked.

"Not good, not good at all. I killed 100," the lion whispered.

"That's more than yesterday, yesterday. If I recall, you only killed 87," I said.

"You remember," said Tommy.

"What made you want to kill more today?" I asked. "Don't know. Just felt like it. Now I feel terrible. I think maybe it was because Dad's away again and Mommy was sad this morning."

"That'll do it," I said.

Another remarkable aspect of this phase of the work is that Tommy has begun to move easily from displacement to direct communication. He often identifies aspects of his daily life and interactions that motivate the black lion to strike. I always accept these statements of cause and effect and never question the relationship between Tommy and the black lion. I think that my doing so provides him with maximal freedom to explore and to employ fantasy in this manner. He chooses the play mode or the communicative fashion, and I follow suit. In this way, I understand myself to be more homeostatically attuned, that is, in the maternal mode, while I am simultaneously in the more disruptively attuned, that is the paternal mode, by being the black-lion doctor. The transitions from one to the other and how these are signaled by him or initiated by me remain extraordinarily interesting.

Additionally important in this period's work is that we have begun to think about the relationship between loving and hurting. This movement has occurred around the motif of too much and too little, taking off from Joey's spanking and Bad Sport's bumping. Tommy has articulated the feeling that, if a dad loves you, he won't spank too hard; if a truck bumps a car, there may be no love involved and thus no modulation. Tommy has even said that he doubts that Mr. C. really beat Joey. "He's his father, after all," was his comment. This formulation has been associated with Tommy's feeling better about his father, who often has not been at home and therefore has been unavailable. Although always intrigued by the possibility of engaging his father on the sadomasochistic level, he has come to be more and more interested in his father's interest when the father is present and more and more interested in what the relative earlier deprivation produced.

"I'm really tired. I'm going to sleep now. Ach ach ach." With that signal the lion is sleeping.

I say, "Are you dreaming?"

"Yes. It's like yesterday. I am a little lion and Daddy and I are
hunting. Oh, there's a zebra. Daddy starts to chase it, and I run with
him. It feels great. I run faster and faster. Then I trip. Daddy stops,
and the zebra runs away. I'm scared that Daddy will be angry because
of my falling down. I'm going to get hit. He comes over. He's pant-
ing from the run. 'Are you O.K., little guy?' he says. I'm so glad that
he's not mad. Daddy helps me up and says, 'Come on, I'll show you
how to run and then we'll get another one. I wanted antelope for
dinner anyway.' "

I say, "That's how a little lion learns to hunt. You know he needs
a teacher."

"Yeah," says Tommy. "Someone who is like him and knows how
it feels to run fast and then to jump and strike."

"How does it feel?" I ask.

"Wonderful. You know that. It's the best thing in the world. I
know that you feel that too when you hunt," Tommy says.

This is a familiar kind of lion dream. A good one, so to speak.
In this genre, there is a helping father. He is not angry but functions
as accompanier and teacher. This is very different from Joey and his
father, but, then, the little lion is different, too. He is not hypera-
gressive but, rather, not yet expert enough to do the job. He is in an
apprentice mode. I say, "The little lion is happy when he has a teacher.
It's good to learn running, jumping, and striking with someone who
also does it and knows that it feels wonderful."

"Yeah," says Tommy.

"Now it's getting worse," Tommy continues, "I'm not in Africa
anymore but here, all alone. I am killing and eating all the time." He
starts to burp and belch and makes farting sounds. We have come
to understand that these sounds signal indigestion and accompany
overeating and overkilling, a sort of generalized superdrive discharge.
These burps and belchs and farts all sound something like Ach ach
ach and click, click click. I think of Pa-gas, which must be discharged
rather than being nutritive. This kind of dream segment is very familiar to us, too. "Where are you now?" I ask.

"Here, I think. I want to do it. No, I don't know. I just keep
doing it, 10, 30, 70, I'm not even hungry."

"Isn't there anyone who can help?" I wonder.

"No one stops me, and I won't stop," the lion goes on rather mournfully, "Now I've gotten 97."

"Where are the police, the doctors, the fathers?" I ask.

"I don't know. There are none of those things in here," Tommy says.

"Why not?" I ask. "You were once in Africa, weren't you, and you had a father then?"

The black lion often speaks about where he is now as an internal state. This, too, represents an important accomplishment for Tommy. He recognizes that the black lion represents a self-state in which he feels out of touch with other aspects of his experience that might exist in counterpoint with his aggressive urges.

"I left because I was mad. Daddy stopped hunting with me. He went away. I thought if he can do it, so can I. I made Mommy sad. The jungle's a tough place."

"So you left because you didn't have a helper anymore," I say.

"Yeah, it just wasn't enough. I couldn't wait for him to get home and, when he did, he was too tired for me. Besides which, he didn't want to hunt at night, just to go to bed with Mom and sometimes he would even go to sleep on the couch"

"No wonder you felt frustrated, left out and like you weren't getting what you wanted," I say.

"One day I was really naughty. I broke four dishes on purpose. Mommy was really upset. They had come from Holland. I had heard her say that this was all she had from her family there. She said, 'When your father gets home, we'll have to all deal with this. He will. I'm too mad to know what to do.' She was crying. I broke them because I was really mad but also because she always cried when she took out those dishes. Now she was crying that the dishes were gone. I was afraid, but I wanted him to get home. When he finally got there, Mommy told him. I was shaking. Daddy said, 'I'm too tired to deal with him. Those damn plates, who cares. Let's just get this baby born and get on with things. Good night. Behave yourself, Tommy, or somebody will really give it to you.' Then I went away."

I say, "You really needed your father to help you even if it meant punishing you. That sort of reminds me of Joey and his father, and of Bad Sort and Night Rider. But he said that someone would give it to you. Is that more like the truck and Bad Sort? The naughtiness, breaking the dishes, Did you say you were trying in some way to help your mother in addition to being mad?"

"Both, both," Tommy was now crying, "I hate it when Mommy cries and I did it wrong. I needed help to know how to help. *Sometimes a boy has to do it, but doesn't know how to do it.*"

"I can certainly see that. When you were so mad, you struck out and did something because you were mad, which also had another meaning," I say.

"But it just made Mommy sadder. She kept saying there's nothing left, nothing. 'Oh, Tommy you've broken my heart. I didn't know that you had such blackness in you. They broke everything and now you've done the rest.'"

I then say that it seems clear to me that being accused of breaking a heart and not knowing how to do it right are heavy and horrible burdens for a boy. I can see that he has to go to great lengths to manage such feelings, but it would be impossible for a lion to control himself in such circumstances.

"Yeah, he just got worse and worse," Tommy replies.

This hour deepened our understanding of Tommy's pain. His anger at his mother and her immersion in her family's pain had conjoined with a concomitant rage and resulted in his "breaking her heart," destroying the Dutch plates. She, in her despair, had likened him to the family's former persecutors and had called him black hearted. His father could not, or would not, help him with this anger, this tangled effort to undo the past, and this loss of control. The father seemed to be ambivalent at best about this part of his wife's history. He had simultaneously abdicated his role as Tommy's teacher, helper, and organizer and modulator of aggressive drive and fantasy; more, he threatened his son with limit setting or punishment from another. The mother, who was usually very present except when preoccupied by her Holocaust memories, could not moderate her response in the light of Tommy's act and perhaps her own unsupported state as she neared the end of her second pregnancy. Tommy was left on his own. The delivery of Amy, which followed closely, only heightened his sense of isolation. He left Africa, where he felt there was adequate help with his development and attempts at mastery, donned his Superman garb, and, manfully/boyfully alone, struggled with the problem of the black lion.

Now, with the help of the black-lion doctor, an accompanier who was alike enough and available enough to stay with him as he told his story, further work on resolution and integration could occur. As the play continued, we learned that he seemed to borrow some from the memory of the lion father in Africa. Thus, lying on the couch and speaking as the black lion, Tommy would say, "You used to help me so much. That's before I became the black lion and when I was just a lion cub. I need help even more now."

I wondered whether the black lion needed help from his doctor or from his father.

Sometimes the black lion would say, "But you, doctor, are my father." Sometimes he would say, "Well, what we do is like what I used to do with my father." Sometimes, "You know about how wonderful hunting and striking feels, and that makes you close enough."

We were exploring the evolving relationship between the two of us and how both the transference and the alliance were forged from the interchangeability and individuality of the other for Tommy as he struggled to sort out his derailment and his restitutive isolation and symptomatology. Tommy said, "What has happened means that I need a doctor." I agreed with him that we had to find a way for the lion to deal with this blackness business. "It's more than my father can do. I need you." Tommy said. Then he added, "My dad does help me. He has become a soccer coach, and he and I watch sports together on television."

In fact, the relationship between Tommy and his father had improved dramatically. The father, too, had decided to embark on an analysis. He had told me in asking for a referral that Tommy's treatment had been so successful that it had persuaded him that he should try one, too. In talking to me about a referral, father had shared with me that, having had a great deal of trouble with his own father, who was physically abusive, he wanted to see a woman, and he was struggling himself with sadomasochistic fantasies that involved other men. I did not ask for further information, but wondered about the pathways by which this data had entered Tommy's fantasy life, as had his mother's family's painful and traumatic history. At about this time, the mother also shared during a joint meeting that her analytic work was most helpful and that she felt much better about herself and about the marriage. Both parents discussed their contributions to Tommy's difficulties and cited, in particular, that they had had monumental troubles in the year before Tommy became symptomatic. The mother had immersed herself in Holocaust studies and become more painfully in touch with her family's history and pain, and Tommy's father had become involved with a male colleague and felt less interested in being with his wife. I furthermore learned that mother had confided frequently in Tommy during her pregnancy that she was sad and alone, needed support, and received none. She had said to him, "Here I have a baby growing inside of me and no man to help me with it." I now began to understand more of the Alfred–Ruh dilemma and the Pa-gas, Ma-milk, cider infusion/confusion concatenation.

Tommy felt both called upon to be his mother's man and inadequately equipped to perform this role. We were to understand that Night Rider's growing pipe represented both Tommy's arousal and excitement over this invitation and his formulation that, to help his mother, he needed a longer pipe, more man in him to be more of a man. We further came to feel that his attempts to be Superman, which he felt he needed to be in order to help his mother, were constantly undermined by his noticing that his mother wanted his father with her and not him, especially at night.

In an important episode, Tommy, or, rather, Tommy as the black lion, became furious with the black lion doctor for not understanding a comment of his about killing. I said that I did not follow what was being said, and the black lion began to roar and thrash around on the couch. He accused me of paying attention to something else when I should be helping him. When I asked attention to what, he thought that I was more interested in grownups than in little lions. Again, I was puzzled, and he mentioned the blonde woman who came to see me everyday after he left. I suddenly remembered that the fear of the black man and then the black lion had first appeared when that very woman had rung the bell too soon for us and taken me away from Tommy before he could spare me; he had been left with unmanageable feelings and, transiently, the seeming phobia and then, more importantly, the black lion himself. I was about to say something about all this to Tommy when he said, "I'm going to eat you raw, so that it will hurt the most. I'll knock your bumper off and your pipe with it. I want to kill. Don't you get it, stupid?" he screamed, "I want to kill you."

Tommy got up off the couch and then stood as if paralyzed. Now I was reminded of his much earlier butting into me and then ogling away as Madama Butterfly. I had not been able to acknowledge the antecedent of this intense feeling then but did recognize its importance. I said, "Yes, you do want to kill me, black lion. But you have other feelings about me too, I think. You are stopped in your tracks because you feel both."

The black lion was silent for several seconds, and then Tommy said, "I need you, I can't do it alone. I get so mad that I can't stand it."

"I know," I said, "That is the dilemma."

I thought that this interaction, played out in both displacement and in the transference, mirrored Tommy's exacerbated oedipal dilemma at home at the time he became overtly symptomatic and "left Africa."

He went on: "I used to feel strong when I went to Kindergarten in my suit, but then as soon as I got there, I had this feeling that there was kryptonite, that I could lose it."

"So you would search for the stuff," I said.

"Yeah, but the feeling came from inside, you know, that I couldn't do it, no matter what I wore. We've learned that, right?"

"Yes, but you were searching for something," I said.

"Yes, but it wasn't there," Tommy continued.

"I wonder if you were actually saying that I am so mad at Daddy for not helping Mommy or me, and just when I try to be Superman, he comes home and is with Mommy anyway that I could kill him."

"How do you know?" Tommy asked with genuine surprise.

"Well, you got that mad at me, or at least the black lion did before, and you said that you could kill me, and you said that it was because I didn't pay attention and preferred the blonde lady."

"Yes," said Tommy, "It's the same. I said that I needed you and—I needed Daddy, too." He began to cry. "I still do. I need help."

I thought that Tommy was saying that he had to undo whatever power Superman might have by preoccupying himself with the search for kryptonite to retain the father; at the same time, he needed to strive to become Superman in order to have a long-enough pipe to try and please his mother. It was an impossible set of conditions and contraindications to accomplish simultaneously. The Ach ach ach and the very name kryptonite, later Night Rider, seemed to allude to sexual sounds and a theory of what father and mother did together at night or of what was needed from him to help his mother. Simultaneously, he felt that the way to acquire this knowledge was from his father, that is, with Pa-gas, and he struggled with the idea that there might be a need for either punitive surgery—power-diminishing and thus father-preserving cutting—or, at the very least, some sort of moral surgical scraping or debridement.

I said to Tommy, "No wonder the black lion calls himself black and feels that he is out of control. His mother calls him black when he is really trying to help her even though he's very angry and he wants to kill his father. And he feels that there is no father there to help him with that feeling, to show him how to manage it so that he can still have a father and not break everything that is valuable. He must have felt that it was pretty hopeless."

"You said it," Tommy replied.

"And if that weren't difficult enough, there was also the problem that your Mommy really did want your father when he came home," I continued.

"I did, too," Tommy continued, crying. "I wanted to take care of Mommy, snuggle with her, and make her feel better and I wanted a Daddy, too."

"I know," I said, "Those are all reasonable wants, but every boy needs help in sorting them out and figuring out what he can do and what he can't and how to do what he can do and how not to do what he can't do."

"How do you know all of those things, about lions, about boys?" Tommy asked.

"I learned it from you," I said.

"I know," Tommy said, "But you also know about boys and lions yourself, from the inside. The black lion and the black lion doctor did it together."

"They are a good team," I said.

"Yes," said Tommy "because they are alike, right, both are black."

"Well," I said, "you and I both know about having to deal with what you call black, with the running, striking, killing, and wanting to have, to help, and to hurt feelings. All boys and men know about those—as you say, from the inside."

"Yes, that's why there are fathers, right?" Tommy then said.

"I think that you are right," I answered.

"And doctors," he added.

"Things are a lot better now. I want to go to soccer camp this summer, and Mom and Dad want all four of us to go somewhere far away for our vacation. Do you think that we could be going to Africa? No, probably Amy is still too little, but I sure would like to go back."

"I think that we have," I said.

"I do, too, but I mean really. Don't be stupid," Tommy replied.

In this work Tommy found both his father and his mother in the analytic setting. How did he do this and why did it occur? Is this a standard feature of the analytic process or at least of the analytic process with children, or is it but one of many possible analytic templates that may evolve in a productive and healing—or disruptive and demoralizing—fashion?

Tommy's search for and refinding his father is apparent in the content of the work as it evolved in each of the play modes he employed. He checked me out for my attributes and capacities from the beginning of the first hour. He was aghast that I did not know what a cider counter is and was immensely gratified that I "remembered." He stated that I am male and therefore not possessed of "Mamilk." Later, around the spanking sequence and the appearance of Joey and then Bad Sort, he advanced the notion of likeness and the problems of being one of a kind and articulated a boy's need for another who is like him to show him how to manage his drive and how to modulate it. This need extended to the concept of punishment, here spanking or bumping, and a recognition that learning about aggression may involve the use and experience of aggression in the father–son dialogue. When black lion was on the scene, Tommy became even more explicit: a boy needs his father to show him how to do it and how not to do it even if the impulse is very strong. "Sometimes a boy has to do it but doesn't know how to do it," he had black lion say.

Tommy conceived of the black-lion doctor as just such a father figure, like the black lion, in that he too knows the joy of running, jumping, and striking. Yet he did not insist that the black lion doctor or I in any other of my guises do it in the fatherly manner; that is, I mean that I was not called upon to participate in rough and tumble play, to be attuned disruptively, or to administer a spanking in the service of using my aggression to help the child with his own. Some children whose father hunger is very great do *ask for it*, do push the analyst to be paternal in these action modes. Tommy did not. Rather, he asked me to be maternally attuned, to follow what he described and prescribed rather than to use my own aggression to change the dominant but derailing scenario. In this fashion, Tommy found the mother in the analytic setting, too. This was the mother of attunement and accompaniment. The mode of engagement was thus maternal, although the content of the material was primarily paternal.

Is this conjunction of paternal and maternal functions typical of analytic work and, if it is, of what kinds? I think that the answer is that it is typical of analytic work in what might be termed the primarily neurotic realm. By this I mean in analytic work in which the primary play mode employed is displacement and the press for enactment and for interactive enactment is not predominant. I have previously argued (Herzog, 1993) that the ratio of these three play modes—displacement, enactment, and interactive enactment—is highly correlated with the intensity and pervasiveness of traumatic experience, which deforms the play function and initiates a shift to the left in the ego function of play. This shift to the left is conceptualized as the reciprocal of the developmental process normally occurring in the maturation of the ego function and thus constitutes a reversible regression.

Goethe (1954) wrote, *"In der Beschränkung zeigt sich der Meister,"* in limitation, the master reveals himself. Analysts encounter different kinds of limitation and subsequent variations in restitutive or self-maintaining strategies. Deficiencies or traumatic deformations with their resultant manifestations in narcissistic development or in play-mode predilection may push the analyst into a primarily homeostatic attunement or into a stylized interactive enactment, where he must behave in a prescribed fashion in order for the child's play to continue.

Tommy is a neurotic boy and his analysis is the analysis of a primarily neurotic child. Such an analysis, I propose, means encountering both the mother and the father in the *Spielraum*, both homeostatic attunement and disruptive attunement, as necessary analytic technical stances. Mother and father are both in the playroom because both have figured prominently in the child's development and their intrapsychic representations are available both for analytic investigation and for transference elaboration and exploration.

In fact, it may be possible to define neurosis as the intrapsychic situation when self-with-mother, self-with-father, and self-with-mother-and-father representations are all available to and usable by the child or adult in the analytic situation. The kinds of internal enactments available to the analysand feature flexibility and variability among these representational schemas. The analyst is then able to play both the maternal and the paternal roles, employ both maternal and paternal modes of empathy, and simultaneously interpret and enact, not being confined to either mode. This definition of neurosis is an analytic or interactive one, in that it is made by the analytic process rather than as a statement about the composition of the mind by itself.

> *"Yea and Nay, each has his say, but God, he keeps the middle way!"*
> —Herman Melville, *Billy Budd*

17 | HOW DO MEN GET INTO ONE ANOTHER?

THE FATHER–SON RELATIONSHIP SERVES AS one paradigm for male–male interaction. Fraternal interactions might be regarded as another. As we study various aspects of each of these man-with-man associations, developmentally and dynamically, we are able to understand something of the problematics, potentials, and entelechy of the associative relations between men. Ways of being together involve doing, watching, accompanying, teaching, validating. How are these similar to and different from female–female relationships or male–female relationships?

The body in male–male interaction is both the theater of operations and curiously taboo. Fathers touch sons and vice versa. Brothers interact physically. By its nonpenetrative way of being, this physical contact is distinguished from the modal male physicality that is penetrative. Men do not get into each other physically although they are very physical with one another. How *do* men get into each other, given the modal thrust and the prevalent taboo? How are drives and their penetrative implementation converted into compromises and compounds that permit closeness, cooperation, and play rather than only fucking and killing? Where do beating, beating on, and beating up fit into this schema as male aggression, in all its direct and sublimated aspects, is explored?

Eddy, a seven-year-old boy in his third year of analysis with me interrupts the syntactically elaborated play to inquire, "What did you have for dinner last night?" I answer roast beef. The boy goes on to say that he had roast beef last night, apparently not noticing that both he and I had enjoyed a similar menu. I probe a bit, and it seems clear that the boy has not registered this coincidence. The boy then returns to the play that the question seemingly interrupted.

The play is about a fight between two crocodiles in the Everglades. They are brothers and bitter enemies. The analysis has focused on how this inimical state arose and how it is managed by the two now. There is a great deal of biting and beating of each other with powerful tails. Eddy has proposed that the two crocodiles never really learned how to fight at home. In fact, he states, this tail beating is kind of ridiculous—their father didn't show them how. He was too busy being one of the boys. Eddy wants me to help the brothers. He will set up a fighting school, but I need to be the principal. "After all, someone has to run the show," Eddy states. The school is established, and it turns out that it is an institution with very intricate rules. The principal's job is to see that all hitting and hurting is done according to precise regulations. "He can enforce them because he's the boss," Eddy says, "The boss is bigger and stronger, and so he doesn't have to be afraid of the brothers. That's how come there can be a school for fighting."

Another patient, Ralph, comes to consult with me about a "developmental problem." He is 28 and has moved in with Dan, a 38-year-old military man. "Dan teaches me discipline," Ralph tells me, "How to cut the grass, rake leaves, take initiative, and be a man, I guess." Ralph feels love for Dan and would like to express it physically. Dan rejects his advances and tells him that sex would be a diversion and that he is helping him become a man "because someone needs to." Sometimes Ralph goes to gay bars anticipating that he will try to have sex with another guy. He always decides at the last minute that he really doesn't want to go home with someone but, rather, needs to go home to Dan. Sometimes he dates girls. This endeavor, too, has remained unconsummated. Ralph and I decide to try and understand more about his situation. As he states it, "I'm amazingly lucky to have found Dan. It's the best thing that has ever happened to me and naturally it happened at the gym. But I want a sex life, too. Can't I have both?"

Art, a 29-year-old lawyer, talks with me about the novel *August* and a patient who came and slept at his analyst's office. "It is heresy to think of coming and sleeping with you," he says blushing. With deep embarrassment, he proceeds to stammer about the sexual meaning of his comment and then tells me that what he meant to say is that he comes here to work and to work hard with me, with my help. It would be a waste and perhaps even insulting to both of us, if he were to take a nap, "lay down on the job," he continues. He is then surprised by a memory from 20 some years earlier when he shared a room with his brother, three years younger. He had been lying in bed thinking about Jesus and how nice it would have been if he had risen triumphantly from the cross in front of all the onlookers. His reverie was interrupted by Joey, whom he thought to be asleep. Joey asked him if it felt good when he, Art, played with his penis as he was now doing. Art was very embarrassed and said something like "Shut up and go back to sleep." Joey, who adored his older brother, muttered that he was sorry. "I didn't like being taken unawares," Art now says, "It's the same here with you and the comment about sleeping with you. Later Joey and I talked about masturbation. We even jerked off together, for Christ's sake. But for him to see me doing it when I didn't even know that I was. . . ."

We might say that in a sense Joey got inside of Art without Art's issuing an invitation, something very different from the way two men, even brothers, might be together with their penises. In our work, too, the question of how we might both try to understand what went on inside of Art needed to be defined and carefully constructed. A slip could threaten mortification, an interpretation feel assaultive.

Yet another young man, Nathan, first came to see me following his graduation from medical school. He was tall, handsome, and well built. He, too, wanted to talk with me about "developmental issues." He was about to go to the West Coast to begin an internship and "worried" about gay culture in the city where he would be working. He told me that he had had a girl friend during medical school with whom he was still involved and yet another during his undergraduate years. "I was never a lady's man," he said, "but girls like the way I look, actually the way I am, and I like them, too. My problem isn't girls. It's guys," he went on. When I inquired as to his meaning, he looked very sad and told me that he had "kind of been involved" with one of his attendings in his last subinternship. The attending, Joe, was very good looking and highly charismatic and seemed to take an interest in Nathan as soon as he came onto his service. Joe and Nathan had spent a lot of time together. At first it was talking about medicine and Nathan's career. But then it got more personal and eventually, he told me, almost in a whisper, they had had sex. "I really liked it, but I can't handle it," was Nathan's next comment and then, "Besides which I don't think that I can sleep with Joe and with Amanda at the same time."

"I need to figure out what this is about," Nathan continued. I don't think that I am gay, but, then again, I liked it, and I like Joe. He knows how uneasy I am, and he tries to be supportive. I've told him that I have got to straighten this out and that I was coming to see you. He knows about you somehow and thought that it would be a good thing. Joe is not a predator. He is a real man." Nathan and I agreed to talk together to see what we might learn.

Over the next several weeks. I learned more in our weekly sessions about Nathan's background and the events leading up to his being with Joe. He was the third son of physician parents, both of whom had emigrated from Germany just before the onset of World War II. His father had succumbed to a myocardial infarction when Nathan was 19. "Always the impeccable and unflappable officer and gentleman," Nathan told me, "He simply said one day, 'I shall recline,' and proceeded to lie down and die." Nathan's two older brothers were already in medical school and he followed suit. His mother continued to practice psychiatry and to travel and lecture widely. Nathan wanted to know if I had ever been her student and seemed relieved when the answer was no. He described his father as aloof and very Prussian, whereas his mother was warm and romantic and "revealed Slavic as well as German blood." Her exposure in Zürich to Jung had been decisive in her development, and she "really is a kind of mystic," her son said. "They were a very odd couple; he being so cold, she being so hot. I don't think that much happened between them, and mother as much as told me that theirs was a platonic relationship except for the obligation to procreate."

In response to my wondering about his relationship with each parent, Nathan told me that he had none, "emphatically none," with his father and that he and his mother had been "unbearably close." He recounted, "Father looked like something out of a history book. He even wore a monocle on Sundays. It was impossible to have a relationship with him. When he spoke to us it was to quote Goethe; otherwise he went to the hospital or worked in his study." I wondered if there were exceptions to this reserve and distance. Once again Nathan looked very sad as he told me that there were none that he knew about. His mother, on the other hand, was totally different. She laughed, always had time for him, especially for him, but also for his brothers Felix and Heinrich. Her favorite expression, he told me, was that for flowers to bloom, there must be plenty of manure. This he said was an indication of how earthy she was as well as fun loving, this axiom always being delivered as though it were simultaneously utterly profound and totally ridiculous.

In medical school, Nathan did well as a psychiatrist-to-be, but then, in the clinical years, he had found himself increasingly attracted to surgery, his father's specialty. Joe was a neurosurgeon, like his father, and seemed irresistible in his warmth and earthiness. I remarked upon hearing this that, from the words that Nathan used to describe him, Joe sounded like some optimal combination of both parents. "I melted," was Nathan's response.

I also learned about Nathan's relationship with Amanda, a medical student colleague who was planning to become a psychiatrist. They enjoyed each other's company, had an active and pleasurable sexual life, and came from comparable academic backgrounds. Sometimes, when they made love, Nathan told me, he would fantasize about being with a man; but, before Joe, the closest he had come was some mutual masturbation with a buddy when he was in the ninth grade. "I really never thought of myself as gay. I'm not homophobic, but this is just not how I picture myself," he said. He told me that these fantasies about men were mostly about erect penises and then gushing orgasms. He was embarrassed about these images but seemed to recover himself as he said that, when he ejaculated, the scenes looked very similar to what he fantasized, during lovemaking sometimes. Amanda knew about his closeness with Joe and encouraged him to sort it out with professional help. She, too, by prearrangement, was continuing her postmedical school education in California. She had told Nathan that he needed to decide whether he was ready for them to live together in San Francisco or whether he needed to keep his options open.

I concurred with Nathan's and Amanda's thoughts that it would by useful to explore all this further and referred Nathan to a colleague in San Francisco whom he saw on an irregular basis during

his internship and residency. He returned to Boston to pursue neurosurgical training and again came to see me. In the interim, he had
married Amanda, and they had a one-year-old daughter, Tatiana.
Nathan told me that he still had the same concerns that he had struggled with when last we talked. He had maintained contact with Joe
during his time on the West Coast (they had spoken to each other
regularly) and now was working with him again. There had not been
sexual contact between them in over three years, although they were
physically affectionate with one another. "The reason for the absti-
nence, I think, is his doing. He is involved with Jeff now and is basically monogamous. I am grateful, because it takes me off the hook.
But I feel that all he would have to say is, let's do it, and I would hop
into bed with him before you could say Jack Robinson. This is in
spite of the fact that Amanda and I are very happy and that the arrival
of Tatiana is totally wonderful." After talking together for about
three months and exploring the lack of success of the California referral, Nathan and I decided to embark on an analysis.

The material that follows is from the third year of our analytic
work. Nathan is nearing the end of his fellowship, Amanda has established a successful psychiatric practice, and Tatiana has a new brother,
Helmut. Nathan has developed an intense transference in the analysis which seems now to be paternal. This evolution has followed a
long period in which I seemed to resemble his mother. He felt that
he was my favorite, "preferred above all the other blokes who frequent this couch," and he found my comments either profound or
comical. We had come to recognize this as the *blooming flowers and
manure notion.*

There was an aspect to this phase of the work that had a romantic quality, but as he told me, "It is without passion, more like you
are an earth mother and I burrow into you than anything to do with
real fucking or passion. I guess you could call it love amongst the
archetypes."

We had both come to feel that this state of affairs was really quite
sad, and Nathan felt very upset, but pleased, that his feelings for
Amanda were quite a bit more physical. He also pointed out to me
that he could do a certain kind of thinking with me, given that I
liked him the best, that it was almost as if he were in psychiatric
training and I was his teacher. Together we explored the multiple

determinants of this somewhat blunted relationship. It was "cozy," as things had been with his mother, and "collegial," as things had not been with his father. "I like it this way," Nathan told me, "Safe enough for our work and nothing weird rocking the boat like my becoming attracted to you."

In pursuing this "neutral" aspect of our being together, Nathan once told me that I seemed genderless, that, like my gray hair, I lacked sexual color and thus did not evoke a sexual response in him. "No juice in you and so no juice in either of us," was his way of putting it. I responded by agreeing that he seemed to feel that his sense of masculine aliveness was very much connected in our hours to his sense of where I was in this regard. We had discussed together that his seeing me as so gray was both a defense and replayed a painful deficit in his masculine development.

A major shift was signaled by Helmut's birth and a very strong feeling that overcame Nathan about his son's name. He felt that it should be German, like his father's and brothers' and like mine. His surname was, in fact, very German, too, although the name Nathan was ambiguously German and also Jewish. It had been given to him after Lessing's *Nathan der Weise*, in contradistinction to the names of his brothers, Felix and Heinrich, or even to Tatiana's. He had the thought that Helmut Herzog would sound very nice, as though the two names went together. This made him very uneasy, as he wondered why his son would bear my name. Then he seemed to move away from this topic by thinking that Herzog might be a euphonious, albeit otherwise peculiar, middle name for his son.

I returned his attention to my inclusion in the family tree with a question wondering about where I belonged in all this. I even quoted Goethe—a potentially dangerous activity (*Grau, teuer Freund ist alle Theorie, Und Grün des Lebens goldenr Baum*—Gray, dear friend is all theory, but green life's golden tree)—as we discussed a seeming change in my grayness, a perhaps greening or otherwise coming alive. He thought about it a little, feeling, he said, confused. And then he became persistently and doggedly focused on the names of my children. He began by asking me if I had children and what they were called. His tone had become solemn and somewhat distant. I responded by wondering what his thoughts were. I noted the change in his tone while assuming that this was an extension of his thoughts about his connection to me and our *naming* of fathers and sons and the relationship between them. To the surprise of both of us, he felt intensely wounded by my response and then enraged. "Who do you think you are to say what do you think, some Freudian asshole?" he shouted. This kind of reaction was new (though it was perhaps also old), and we both recognized the sudden shift. Recognition and even interest in the meaning of the strong affect did not dissipate it, however.

Following this session, which concluded without my supplying the names, Nathan dreamt that he was trying to build something with his erector set. The dream was confusing, because this seemed to be happening in the operating room and an aneurysm in the circle of Willis was being repaired at the same time. He was being told to keep his eyes on the surgical field, which he didn't want to do, and anyway how could he watch and also hold the retractors and build the tower, which it now seemed to be. Immediately after telling me about the dream, Nathan said to me, "Your pants are really tight this morning. I could see your bulge."

I sort of checked myself by looking down and then said, "What could you see?" "Your dick," he responded, "It's long and thick."

I remained silent. Nathan did, too. Then he said, "It looked as though you had a hard on and you might be looking for some help to take care of it."

Nathan and I had talked a lot about penises, his, his brothers', his adolescent buddy David's, little Helmut's, and a lot about Joe's penis and the fact that Joe got hard when he talked with Nathan, something that pleased, excited, and bothered Nathan. He always felt irritated with himself that he noticed Joe's erections, that he might, in fact, be looking for them, even awaiting them. I wondered if something about Joe had been stirred or if this were related to the dream and to our interaction about my children's names.

"I see that you are silent again, just like yesterday. What does it take to make a guy like you open up? You're so tight, so cold and distant," he said.

I recognized the probable reference to his father but chose to comment on his perception of my aroused state.

"But I seem to be hot, too. At least that might be why my dick is hard," I said probably prematurely.

"Oh, don't say dick," Nathan said with intense feeling, "It's a penis. You know the word, don't you?"

I had used the word dick because he had; now I recognized that whatever was happening in this enactment, the differences, at least in vocabulary, between us were as important as the similarities. I remembered, somewhat uneasily, that I had recently quoted Goethe to him, in German no less.

"It was the wrong word to use," I said.

Nathan spoke rapidly, "You wouldn't call a guy's brain 'squash' while lifting up the lobes to get to the base and the circle of Willis. You would refer to the lobe by name or at least say gray matter." We seemed to be back in the neurosurgical operating theater. I knew that the cast of characters there could include Joe, my patient, and, when he was a little boy, Herr Professor, his father (or another Goethe quoter).

"I should not have used that word," I said.

"I never knew the right words," Nathan began, "It's a problem when your parents don't speak the language. You know anyway that he used to call me *dick*; it's the German word for fat. I hate the word and if you cared about me at all you wouldn't have said it."

I felt very much like apologizing. I had known that his father called him *dick*. Years of working out had been designed in part to make sure that he was not *dick*, but, rather, trim and in excellent shape. Now we seemed to be approaching something having to do with the difference between dick (penis) and *dick* (fat) and how the two might be transmuted in a dialogue between son and father. I was clearly participating in a process with him in which what I was saying was a part of what was being repeated.

Nathan then thought about a recent experience in the operating room when a cerebral artery that was being coated prophylactically to prevent subsequent aneurysmal rupture began to ooze. He told me that he had stared at the whitening field until Joe had said twice, "Clamp it now." The word prophylactic reminded him of my penis and its perceived tumescence and he said, "There's no way of preventing it. Once it's in that state, you've got to come."

I had noted that Nathan described the oozing artery as whitening the field and that his thoughts then turned to my irrepressible ejaculation. I did not know how to put the components of this apparent condensation between semen and blood in a usable place and so I waited.

"The fucker was absolutely bloodless. You couldn't get anything out of him, like—what's the expression?—getting blood from a stone. He would correct my vocabulary and tell me not to be vulgar or call me dick. That was the extent of it." Nathan was crying. "And she was always telling me that I was wonderful, her little *Furstchen*. That means little prince, but not in the Saint Exupéry sense. If I was so wonderful, then why didn't he love me? Help me. Show me what to do. Now I can't even clamp off an artery without Joe's having to practically shout at me and, and I hate my name."

The not entirely German name Nathan seemed to be connected to his having chosen Helmut for his son and to the current pain around my children's names and my having returned his question rather than answering it. Could my not answering have somehow been similar to his own father's not giving him an entirely German name? And what of my speaking in German to him earlier? We were both working on issues of an interaction between two living men involving the penis-penis dialogue, the difference between deadness and love and aliveness, and the question of what to call a thing, and, at least in the operating room and when building with an erector set, how to do something.

A long period of work was thus ushered in in which a father's not loving, a bloodless relationship, lily-white flowers, blooming in surrounding manure, and an absolute fascination for an engorged penis (a truly bloody field coaxed by a son or lover into a different kind of whitening) could be untangled. Nathan's defenses against the analysis' becoming as hot as the hospital could become with Joe were eased by our antecedent "neutral relationship" but jarred by the arrival of a son whom he wished to name in a patrilineal (*nom de père*) fashion. My choosing to note that I was becoming less gray by quoting Goethe, a response with multiple levels of conscious and unconscious determinants, seemed very important, too. The sexual, aggressive, and narcissistic components of father search, father hunger, and father availability could no longer be contained. They emerged in enactment, in intense affect, in dream, and in interaction for our mutual understanding in the analytic *Spielraum*. The way that Nathan was with me allowed him to begin to address and redress the way his father had been with him; analysand and analyst together were thus both revisiting and doing a new man-with-man dialogue.

DAVEY

Another analysand, Davey, is brought for consultation at age four by his parents after the preschool he attends raised a question about his unhappiness and about his sexual orientation. The parents report that he and his brother, three years older, both love pretend play and that Davey, in particular, likes to dress up as a girl and play female roles. In giving the history, mother tearfully discusses the death of her mother when Davey was two and the family's coping with a melanoma that was removed from her husband's back—he is in remission at the moment—when the boy was almost three. Both parents confide that they would not be seeking consultation were the school not concerned; they find Davey's pretend "girlness" pleasant and assume that he will grow out of it.

The mother mentions her aversion to certain boyish behaviors and to the fact that boys get "so sweaty and smelly." She states that she has to keep after her husband to shower frequently. In the first hour and in subsequent play, Davey says that he is Madama Butterfly and, in fact, wears something like a kimono. Puccini's heroine has appeared more than once in my office courtesy of more than one little boy. He tells me that he smells just like cherry blossoms and invites me to sniff. This invitation is accompanied by his bending over, his bottom being the intended sniffing site. He also tries to sniff me. Shortly thereafter he tells me that girls smell of a delicious blend of natural perfumes, whereas boys smell gross, that there is just their sweaty butt smell. We learn more of the multiple meanings of the name butt-erfly. It seems to combine his need to fly away from his butt smell, an identification with his mother's sentiments, and, if you will, scentiments, if not her person proper, and a terrible fear that his father's melanoma, which was on the lower back, was connected to his aroma and to what his mother deplores.

One day in the seventh month, we are playing out a familiar scenario. There is to be a wedding; Davey is the groom. (After the third or fourth meeting, he stopped maintaining that he was a girl but stated that I should call him Butterfly anyway.) In the play, he takes seven showers, scrubbing himself repeatedly. The bride, we learn, has a bad cold and can smell nothing, so this intensive bathing is for him, not her. He then tells me a story about the nose people. They are quite a bit like dogs, in that they gather all important information olfactorily, but, they also "sex" with their noses. In fact, it turns out that they are only noses, and, when one nose gets into another nose, they wrestle and then it makes a new little nose. He then tells about sleeping in his mother's bed, but only after a shower, and her telling him how sweet he smells. "You smell just like a cherry blossom," she coos to him, "not gross like your Dad."

"I shower and smell the way my Mom wants me to because I can sleep in her bed if I do," Davey says, "Sometimes, when she is not looking, I put her perfume down there." Later we learn that among the nose people really nosey noses are sometimes punished by having their tips snipped. Also this is the way that you can tell boy noses from girl ones. The boys are longer; the girls, shorter as if snipped.

So we infer that Davey is a really nosey nose. This image represents his own drive derivatives and his parents' collusion: mother's seductiveness, denigration of father, and active efforts to mold her son's character figure in this; so, too, does father's depression, abrogation, and adaptation to his wife's agenda. The so-called gender identity problem, and the nasal-anal fixation, are, likewise, seen to be endogenously and exogenously shaped. We might say that there was a superego lacuna that permitted Davey to display all this material in school and in his first meeting with me. He tried to sniff everyone and offered up his own bottom promiscuously. We might wonder about his ego's capacity to assess reality, and we could speculate on the intensity of id cauldron pressure, at least as it was seemingly manifested in his behavior as an apparent drive derivative.

In fact, the intensity of drive derivatives seemed more related to hyperstimulation in the absence of paternal buffering than to hyperendowment; and the ego and superego aspects seemed to reflect external guidance that was inadequate to prepare Davey for social contact outside of the family, not to mention in school, or even to consolidate his own core gender identity. In the presence of an analyst who did not impose an agenda, his compromise formations became clear and his own capacity to be the groom developed.

Later in the analysis, Davey elaborated the story of three brothers: the always hungry and angry Buck, the more savvy Brad, who kept an eye on the neighborhood, and the careful and stringent Bart. Buck is involved with wanting to do it and doing it; Bart with not doing it, with the don't; and Brad with balancing these forces, getting the lay of the land, and figuring out what can and cannot be done, what will fly. The three B. (B. for Butt) boys were to occupy a great deal of our analytic attention. Their resemblance to the tripartite model, and their emergence in the analytic play, of course interested me greatly. I also thought that Buck might represent self-with-mother; Bart self-with-father; and Brad, self-with-mother-and-father, although these putative formulations required continual juggling and revision. Brad came to be called the "lookout," although there was something wrong with his vision; and Bart, the "judge," although he had some serious problems with judgment.

Davey simultaneously became very aggressive in school. The school psychologist called him id driven (Buck in the ascendency) and thought that he must have an ego defect as he seemed not to be able to anticipate the consequences of his actions or learn from repeated punishment. Meanwhile, the analysis saw the playing out of more material about the B. boys and how they could not do anything together, although they tried to, especially when Brad, aided by wearing special glasses that seemed to neutralize olfactory and other overwhelming distractions, organized a game that was not too exciting or too scary. The one exception entailed their love for fighting.

In play conducted contemporaneously with Gulf War, they especially liked to gang up on unsuspecting Iraqis, in order to conduct what Davey called "the mother of all turkey shoots." For this activity, the three B. boys could cooperate even without Brad's donning his special spectacles. Sadman Hussein appeared in this play. He wept so much, we were told, that he could not organize himself enough to escape the turkey shoot or even to fight back. Were he not crying, he could be very powerful and then the three B. boys would be in "deep shit." Cleverly, they had sprayed onion juice on him, and so he wept continuously and could not fight. There was a vivid discussion about the aroma of onions in this play. They smelled rotten. The exploration of the origins of this rotten smell and how it enraged and rendered Sadman impotent were particularly interesting. We came to understand that this rotten smell could be inflicted, could be a self-state, could be used toward other ends, and could even come to be integrated into the self-schema were it to be valued and regarded as a part of one's equipment.

We learned that Davey was now a boy, no longer Madama Butterfly. At home he was not sleeping in his mother's bed, although he showered religiously and sometimes the mother would lie down in his bed at night. He liked this but always felt scared afterward and would sometimes have nightmares. His father was ill again—the melanoma had returned—and was almost totally unable to intervene at home between him and the mother or to help his son with his aggressive or fantasied sexual dyscontrol. I told Davey that I thought that he was so naughty at school because he felt that he needed a father to intervene.

"Yeah, kick me in the butt and make me fly," he said returning to the earlier Madama Butterfly motif. "Sadman Hussein could be really tough if he weren't crying all the time," he added. "Who sane who insane?" he then said. As he spoke, he bent over to reveal an apparently suitable posture for the kick. It was the same position as the one assumed for the original sniffing invitation.

In the play, the three B. boys could get along better when there was a coach to see that no one got out of hand. Sadman could be strengthened by the coach, too, in displacement. Here the coach first provided tissues and then helped him build an onion vapor-resistant shield. We worked on the amelioration of Brad's visual problem so that he could be a more effective lookout, and Bart was sent to Judging School so that he could learn how to be a fair judge. Sometimes Davey called me "the coach." There was, or could be, triadic interaction and defensive organization in the presence of a modulating and organizing father.

Here are, in Davey's experience and actual *Umwelt*, life's calamities, indeed. The actual players are very much affected in their parenting, and the resultant internalization and drive derivative interactions are played out in the analytic *Spielraum* and in real life. How are life's calamities represented? How do they heighten sexual and aggressive pressures and conflicts? How do they affect the resonance between inner and outer or what is otherwise called reality testing? How do moral prohibitions arise? How does the child master the don't-do-it along with the let-it-all-hang-out? Kagan tells us that the don't-do-it is a cognitive capacity appearing in the second year with an unclear relationship, if any, to parental disapproval. For Davey, maternal disapproval of masculinity, combined with hyper-stimulation, was most apparent and the father's standards could more easily be intuited from acquiescence than from prohibition. A theory of the Sadman's plight had been formulated, and the need for his recovery and active presence was enacted. Parts of the mind, of the self, of the person were depicted as the three Butt boys and as the drama of the deranged and then restituted Sadman Hussein.

Yet in fantasy, in the presence of the analyst, the modulating and organizing father is constructed and a drama with him or the real dying father is enacted in the school setting, just as the playroom was previously a stage for the snipped-nose girl–boy Madama Butterfly production. Once again, the butt is the scene of the action, although its penetration, its saliency, has been somewhat modified. Typically, anal-stage ambivalence and issues of gender differentiation and aggressive modulation are all being organized and reorganized in the second year. That the mother lost her mother during this period and that the father fell ill seem highly pertinent. Libidinal, aggressive, and narcissistic parental availability, normally nutritively available to the developing child, are all intruded upon when life's calamities befall caregivers, too.

DR. P

Dr. P is a 42-year-old pathologist who cannot keep a job because he is too slow. He studies each slide for hours. It is critical, absolutely critical, that he get it right, that he miss nothing. He specializes in the detection of malignant cells. "Only a few can pollute the entire body, wreck what otherwise is good and pure," he states. His diagnoses are, in fact, ultra-accurate; his productivity totally unacceptable. He may pore over a single slide for several hours. "Every single cell must be seen, must be rooted out for the body not to succumb to this tremendous evil," he asserts.

Dr. P is the only child of a physician father of Polish extraction and a German mother. The mother oversaw the family's chemical factory during World War II and had special responsibility for making sure that the Jewish slave laborers worked to full capacity. In the

American mid-West after the war, she continued this regimen with her son. He was to be productive, never make a mistake, and above all be ultraclean. Toward this end, she regularly scoured both his nose and his anus with a tooth brush.[1]

"We must remove every trace of dirt, every last trace," she would say solemnly during these ablutions. Dr. P continues these activities currently, along with a 40-minute shower each morning. He could not be cleaner but also has a chronically abraded and bleeding anus and nostrils. Dr. P's social relations have been dramatically affected by his fear and the efforts he mounts to counter it. No woman is perfect enough for him. When he married a Jewish girl, the daughter of a prominent jurist, he found her disturbingly unclean. He used to pour Paco Rabanne, an aftershave lotion, on her bottom to obscure the smell of perspiration, which offended him. He divorced her when she decided not to become a judge. He wished not to be married to a "lazy woman."

In his work with me, he is hypercritical of my lack of "sharpness" and finds it difficult to associate. He says that it is too scary to do so and that I might kill him if he were to say something untoward. In psychopharmacological consultation he has been helped by large doses of fluoxetene, 80 mg/day, but remains almost totally crippled by his relationship with his mother and his father's inability to intervene protectively. Sometimes he rails against the Jewish influence in his field or the fact that the news media are biased in their reporting of the atrocities committed by the Israelis. He alternates between believing that I am a German or supposing I am a Jew. Both these attributions are problematic for him. We have come to understand that he feels both frightened, as were the Jews whose work his mother supervised, and excited by the possibility of assuming her stance. The possibility of murder is always close at hand.

I find his particular dilemma not only compelling from the clinical perspective, but also enormously meaningful in terms of mechanisms. How often is it the case that those who kill other chil-

---

[1] Here we have the "excremental assault," from Terence des Pres (1976), *The Survivor*, prophylactically reversed. Des Pres postulated that the systematic efforts of the Nazis to deprive their Jewish prisoners of access to hygiene caused them to become dehumanized in their own eyes and certainly in the minds of their captors.

dren in the name of ideology are simply displacing a profound hatred of their own progeny? Dr. P's mother helps us to appreciate this dynamic as she shifts her operations from Jewish prisoners to her own son. He recalls her declaiming how filthy the Jewish prisoners were and that their uncleanness was the basis for what happened to them during the Third Reich. Is it far fetched to ponder the dynamic in the other direction—to consider the wish to murder one's child as the basis of the killing of Jewish children, Gypsy children, Bosnian children, Cambodian children? Do studies of the children of Nazi parents corroborate this hypothesis? Can Dr. P, with me, embark on a process in which he can be with a man to learn something of how to be a man?

Is there a chance that what wasn't there with his father while he was growing up can now be coconstructed with me in the analytic situation? Is it really conceivable that he can regain control over his own aggression in a modulated enough fashion that his murderousness would be neutralized—and the psychic murdering of a child brought to a stop?

Each of these boys and men shows us how men work on being together in order to manage themselves internally and interactively. Aspects of the father–son relationship, of peer interaction, and of the teacher–pupil or coach–player paradigm can be seen to involve that which penetrates without actual penetration, that which hurts, yet with adequate safeguards. Men need to be with men in order to learn how to become men. This need requires careful and ongoing care and monitoring, often, but not only, provided by a woman if the need is to be optimally met and result in improved integration and function.

> *Choreograph the passage from complex*
> *Clairvoyance to some ultimate blind x,*
>
> *Raw luster, rendering its human guise.*
> *The lover shuts, the actor lifts his eyes.*
> —James Merrill

18 | BOYS WHO MAKE BABIES

BY ACCIDENT OR BY DESIGN, ADOLESCENT MALES sometimes father children. By trial or error, with greater or lesser success, some adolescent males parent their offspring. Little is known of the psychological determinants, internal or external, that account for either of those phenomena. Until recently, the whole area of male caretaking and its relationship to male sexuality was a relatively neglected and understudied one. A change is now occurring as fathers have been discovered—by themselves, by academicians, and by women's liberationists. A fairly consistent picture of the way in which fantasies, experiences, identifications, and interactions are forged into a nascent view of the self as provider and progenitor is beginning to emerge.

The connection between sexual behavior and caretaking in adolescence is far from understood. The rising adolescent birth rate, particularly in the face of widespread contraceptive availability, is particularly noteworthy. In those cases in which the father of an infant born to an adolescent mother is himself adolescent, is the conception and subsequent birth accidental or intentional? If intentional, whose intention does it reflect? The boy's, the girl's, the couple's, or someone else's entirely?

My own work with adolescent fathers has been in the context of studying male caretaking from a developmental perspective. In early work (see chapter 15), I suggested that the caretaking line of development in boys and men differs from that occurring in women. For men, a condensation of aggressive and libidinal components can be clearly identified at each stage, and in suboptimal circumstances the emergence of these constituent components can be seen with frightening clarity. I have also suggested that an ongoing heterosexual intimacy that permits expression, titration, and containment of sexual and aggressive drives seems to favor the emergence of optimal male caretaking (Herzog, 1980). This last concept has been stated succinctly as: adult–adult interaction predicts adult–child interaction.

The clinical data I present in this chapter derive from my leading four groups of junior and senior high school boys in a middle-class suburban high school over a four-year period in a nonclinical setting. The groups were billed as seminars in sexuality and intimacy. Corresponding groups for girls led by female mental health professionals were available simultaneously. Each group had eight to ten participants and met weekly for approximately 30 weeks. The participants in the groups corresponded to no specific diagnostic category, nor was there a predominance of any particular character type. The dynamics of these groups were highly instructive. Transferential issues were very prominent, as were issues of status and competition among the group members. Information about the boys' sexual lives and practices emerged only slowly and in the context of growing familiarity, trust, and a group ethos. The manner in which these data surfaced raised many questions in my mind about personal sexual data obtained from adolescents by survey and questionnaire protocols.

From the data, I have culled material pertaining to adolescent male caretaking from six of the boys. Since 32 boys participated in the groups over the four-year period, this number represents almost 20% of the group who were actively involved as 16, 17, and 18 year olds with issues directly related to male caretaking. My sample included young men who would not ordinarily be considered to be adolescent fathers. The reader will need to judge the wisdom or error implicit in these groupings.

In the first-year group were eight boys, all white and middle class. Three pregnancies were reported during the year, and all were to be terminated by abortion. This led to some discussion of the abortion experience. Matt, who was very involved with his girlfriend, Sharon, and had been with her before and after the procedure, described a dream about Abraham sacrificing Isaac at the Lord's command. However, at the last moment, the knife was plunged into Sarah, Isaac's mother. Matt commented on the fact that Sarah was both the name of his girlfriend and the name of the biblical Isaac's mother. One of the other group members, himself not yet the source of an abortion or conception, told Matt not to take it so seriously—that it "was just a fluke" and wasn't it "nifty that a kid could be gotten rid of almost as quickly and easily as it could be made"? At this point, Matt became very angry and then, quite suddenly, sad. He told us that he had almost intentionally not used a rubber, that perhaps he had wanted to make Sharon pregnant—but he certainly didn't want to become a father.

Later, when two other boys in the group impregnated more casual girlfriends and those pregnancies were to be aborted, the discussion came up again. "You win some, you lose some," was the prevalent group attitude. Matt challenged the two who were intensely involved in this issue—Jack and Joe—with, "How does it make you feel?" "Cocky," Jack answered with a grin. "Like handing out cigars," was Joe's reply. "You know, I sort of felt like a father or a father-to-be when Sharon was pregnant," Matt said, "But I couldn't imagine our having the kid, or taking care of him." The entire group of 16 and 17 year olds agreed that they did not want to become fathers, yet all agreed that it would mean something to make someone pregnant. This feeling coexisted with the feeling that the worst thing that could happen was to "knock someone up." There were jokes about shotgun weddings, irate fathers, and the law. The mood of the group was lighthearted and partylike until Matt recalled that Sharon cried sometimes when they talked about the abortion and that he sometimes felt that she didn't enjoy lovemaking now as much as before.

Then a rather startling occurrence was reported. Joe came to the group very shaken and reported that Liz, his casual paramour of some months earlier, had not had an abortion after all. He had happened to meet her, and she was very visibly pregnant. Joe told us that he was very angry with Liz. She had deceived him. Then he told us that he really hadn't had very much to do with her decision making and certainly not with its implementation. Joe was clearly troubled. He developed a sleep disturbance and started to drink excessively. He asked if he could see me alone and then told me that he didn't know what he was feeling or what he should do: "There was really a kid inside Liz. What should I feel about that?" He thought he hated Liz. But he couldn't just shrug it off. That kid was his, whatever that meant. He felt that he should do something, but he didn't know what. Then Joe, who was in some ways the most "macho" member of the group, began to cry. He expressed a strong wish that I contact his parents. He particularly wanted his father to know, but he felt afraid of his father's reaction. At the next group meeting, Joe told about his meeting with me. He said that he felt "all screwed up about this father thing" and had decided to go into psychotherapy. The reaction of the group was quite mixed: Matt was very supportive; Jack made a wisecrack to the effect that one paid his nickel and took his chance. Then the group moved on to other topics.

In another group, Brad told us that he was the father of two children, a boy of six months and a girl of nine months, and each one lived with its mother. Brad was friendly with each of the mothers but had now fallen in love with Belle, a third girlfriend. Belle did not want to get pregnant, and Brad was relieved that she was on the pill. He said he certainly wasn't "going to wear anything or pull out early with a girl. You might as well use your own hand then." Brad told the group that he didn't see much of the kids now, but maybe he would when they got older. His mom, the grandmother of his son and daughter, kept in touch with the mothers of his two old girlfriends. "It sort of keeps it in the family," he said. The other boys in the group did not know how to respond to Brad, but this was uniformly so, not only with regard to his attitudes toward fatherhood. Brad was from a different racial background than the other boys and was bused to the school from an adjacent part of the metropolitan area.

Two years later, Brad, now almost 20, brought his now two-and-half-year-old son to a successor group. He seemed proud of little Sam and was invested in him. When Sam knocked over another group member's books, Brad picked him up and gave him a spanking. This event resulted in a number of discussions among the group members on themes of anger, limit setting, corporal punishment, and fathers. There ensued one of the most detailed discussions that had ever occurred about the boys' relationships with their own fathers, particularly with regard to discipline. At first there was great embarrassment when the boys discussed lectures, spankings, and other punishments they had received. Later, embarrassment seemed to give way to camaraderie and backslapping. One of the boys wondered if I, the oldest male present and a father, was a spanker and, if so, what kind. This question was followed by almost raucous laughter and speculations that ranged from my being the gentlest and most nurturant of men to my being a direct descendant of the Marquis de Sade.

Arthur was the quietest boy in his group. He spoke not a word as we talked about masturbation, intercourse, contraception, or venereal disease. There was general snickering when the topic of the day was homosexuality, and Arthur developed a gastrointestinal disturbance and had to leave. When the topic was children, however, Arthur became more vocal. He shared with the group that he helped to care for Ricky, the two-year-old child of his unwed sister Jane, who lived in an adjacent neighborhood. Arthur saw Ricky and Jane daily. He babysat for his nephew and took him to the park. Ricky called him "Ar Ar" and told his Mommy that he "loved Ar Ar more than anyone else in the world." Arthur blushed as he told us that Ricky wanted to pee in the toilet just as he did and that his sister had told him that he, Arthur, was a wonderful father. When asked how he felt about Ricky, Arthur said, "I love him." "It's good practice for you Art," one of the group members said, "Most of us don't get to practice being dads ahead of time."

Another group member, Frank, told us that he and Milly had been going together for a year and wanted to go to the same college to continue their close relationship. They hoped to marry after college and then, after law school, to have two children, a boy and a girl. Frank said that he and Milly had recently become intimate. Together they had seen Milly's gynecologist. They had to be very certain to delay the arrival of Amanda and David, their future children. Both Frank's and Milly's families knew about the relationship, but neither family knew that a 10-year projection complete with grandchildren existed.

"I CAN DO IT"

Matt, Jack, Joe, Brad, Arthur, and Frank are six young men who might be called adolescent fathers. Each boy's "fatherhood" was different. Their experiences ranged from abortive to actual to substitutive to accidental to anticipatory. These cases tell us something, not only about the varieties of adolescent fatherhood, but also something about the constituents, components, and conflicts characteristic of the male caretaking line of development during adolescence.

In thinking about fathering, we tend to have in mind a series of functions: the way the father takes care of his child; the way he interacts with the child; the way he loves the child; the way he guides, teaches, and disciplines the child. Generally speaking, these activities are separated into discrete entities so that they will then be suitable for observation and study. In a naturalistic setting, it is highly probable that male caretaking is not performed in discrete quanta of definable functions, although its inherent rhythmicity may be less tonic and more staccato than that characterizing female caretaking. Rather, there is a relationship between the male adult in the family and the children in the family that features both direct and mediated effects, substantially influenced by the adult female caretaker who is also present. That mothers mother, fathers father, and children develop in a context that is triadic at a minimum is now a generally accepted point of view, even though it runs contrary to certain views of development that emphasize the essentially dyadic nature of early experience. We also know that parenting, both male and female, is an activity that grows better with practice. The very act of parenting seems to predispose to better parenting over time, provided, of course, that serious psychopathology is not present and exerting a deleterious effect on caretaking. Adolescent parents tend to have relationships of shorter duration than do older parents and, by definition, a shorter time-experience of parenting than do older parents with multiple children. There are no data, however, to suggest that adolescent male parenting is different from that of older fathers. Kinard and Klerman (1980) and Bolton, Lane, and Kane (1980) suggested that the incidence of abuse perpetrated by adolescent parents is no greater than that committed by older parents.

There are data on what fathering is, as distinct from mothering. Parke (1981) reviewed the studies of Lamb, Clark-Stewart, Pederson, Yogman, Kotelchuk, and others, which demonstrated infants' recognition of the father in the first months of life and an attachment relationship to him often as powerful as that with the mother. Since then, attachment researchers (Main, 2000; Hess and Main, 2000; Slade, 2000) have documented in great detail that the infant-toddler develops an attachment to the father independent of the mother. In the attachment tradition the focus is on the overall quality of the relationship, that is, whether the child is judged to be securely attached to the specific parent or caretaker independent of gender of either child or adult. My own focus has been on fathering as a distinctly male form of caretaking that can be thought about independently of quality of attachment, although obviously it also operates inside of a particular attachment bond, be it secure or insecure. In a study of eight middle-class families (see chapter 5) consisting of a father, mother, and first child in the second year of life (neither parent an adolescent), I detected some of the ways that fathers, by virtue of being secondary rather than primary caretakers, appear to evolve a quite identifiable style of interaction and functional uniqueness with their children.

These interactions are often energizing, activating large-motor activities that both disrupt and delight the child. They appear to disorganize him by disturbing the status quo and as such may mobilize intense affect, which facilitates radical reorganization and further developmental progression. I have suggested that the radical reorganization-change of perspective paradigm may be the precursor to the quality I call ego resiliency, which may be a hallmark of children who are fathered as well as mothered.

This same mode of interaction—changing gears, jazzing things up, gross-motor play—seems to be a modality by which fathers teach children not only how to mobilize drive and affect, but also how to modulate it. Within the play framework, and by departing from it, fathers model and express in more direct preverbal and verbal forms the range of expression of affect and action that they and their community will sanction.

It is very important to emphasize that these fathering functions can occur only in the presence of a mother. Such interactions with a child would be catastrophic if they were the only kind of interaction. The child would be driven to distraction in two hours if the only component of his developmental diet were stimulating, gear-shifting, disruptive, limit-setting play. The fathering I have been studying is entirely contingent on the presence of homeostatic-attuned caregiving by the mother. In fact, male caretaking in a variety of settings seems to bear an important relationship to adult–adult male–female interaction. It should be noted, however, that there are circumstances in which the male can become the primary caretaker. Then his style becomes more responsive and attuned. The father then comes to resemble more closely the homeostasis-maintaining maternal caretaker.

But what of the six boys whose experience with "fathering" I have reported on here? We know almost nothing of their actual inter- action with their children since the only "observation" was of Brad with Sam, the only report was of Arthur with Ricky, and the only affective male–female relationships of Matt and Sharon and Frank and Milly, did not involve an actual child. On the basis of my data I cannot discuss the actual fathering of these young men. I can, how- ever, advance some views on the meaning of the fathering concerns, plans, and fantasies of these six young men. My discussion draws on a nosology of the meaning of sexual behavior that I have developed.

I have classified sexual behavior according to its predominant meaning to the persons participating in it: declarative, recreative- interactive, procreative, parentogenic, and integrative. Of course, any sexual episode may contain elements of some or all these meanings as well as a large admixture of more idiosyncratic meaning.

Declarative intercourse is "I am a man. I can do it." The part- ners' value need not be stressed and the empathy-intimacy dimen- sion can vary from nonexistent to profound. Recreative-interactive intercourse stresses the hedonic and social aspects of the act. Obviously, depending on the particular dyad, one or the other pole of this form of intercourse may be stressed for the self or for the part- ner. Procreative intercourse features the wish, often unconscious, to make a baby. It often also contains the opposite wish, to get rid of the baby once made. Parentogenic intercourse differs from procre- ative in that the wish to make a baby is coupled with the commit- ment to care for it. In my experience, parentogenic intercourse almost always occurs within the context of a relationship that features sig- nificant future orientation. Integrative sexual intercourse involves a feeling of oneness and wholeness with one's partner, a permeability of ego boundaries, and a resolution that leaves each participant feel- ing renewed and complete.

From a developmental perspective, it is not clear whether or not there is an intrinsic order to the aforementioned distinctions. In some ways it seems that a parentogenic and integrative sexuality corre- sponds to the later Eriksonian (1950) stages of generativity and integrity and might thus be considered a postyouth-early adulthood phenomenon. Declarative and recreative-interactive intercourse, on the other hand, appear to be the most common forms of masculine adolescent sexuality. Surprisingly, perhaps, I differentiate procreative (or conceptive) sexuality from parentogenic sexuality. The former appears to exert considerable influence on adolescent masculine sexuality. Complicated forces from earlier developmental epochs appear to motivate the sexually active male to try to make a baby—to show that he can, that his stuff is adequate. For some boys, particularly those without other accomplishments, this seems necessary to maintain self-esteem. The procreative form of sexual activity sometimes also contains, in quite clear view, its opposite, the wish to get rid of or throw away the baby. This feature of male caretaking sometimes seems to contribute to instances of abuse or neglect. I have applied a similar scheme of categorization to adolescent females' sexual behavior.

In the examples I have presented can be observed a wide range of reaction to the occurrence of an "unwanted" pregnancy. The nature of the relationship with the girl appears to impart the most important immediate component of the response, as with Matt. But even the macho Joe reacted to "his baby" when an abortion did not occur. Joe's reaction is particularly significant because it did not seem to be relationship dependent. Brad's experience tells us something about the different definitions of fatherhood that some cultural settings allow an adolescent male. Procreating and parenting are not necessarily closely linked temporally, but the right of fatherhood, once established, persists. Also, the father's role as modulator of aggressive drive and fantasy, often through the actual use of aggression, was clearly called forth by Brad's spanking of Sam and resonated with active currents of interest and concern in many of the boys. A theme of adolescent caretaking seems to be: can I do unto another what is still being done unto me? This permutation on the Golden Rule appears to apply both to libidinal and to aggressive caretaking issues.

Arthur's experience seems to be an example of either preparing for parenthood or a situation in which massive psychological inhibitions favor the emergence of a substitutive behavior at the expense of more age-appropriate exploration and play. The number of adolescent males caring for children but who are not their own is unknown. Clearly, this is a very interesting group of young men for further study. A subgrouping of this category may be adolescent boys in fatherless families with younger siblings.

Frank's anticipatory fatherhood is equally intriguing. One cannot help but wonder if Amanda and David will ever arrive, how the discrepancy between what has so long been imagined and what actually occurs will be handled, and what the purpose of the decade-long gestational period really is. This is not to suggest that Frank's anticipatory fatherhood is abnormal. It is another variant of adolescent caretaking encountered in this setting.

None of the adolescent "fathers" described resembles the stereotype of the father in his late 20s, 30s, or 40s. Some may say that these boys were not actually fathers at all. By examining the experience of each of these boys, however, we may achieve greater clarity as to what fathering actually is and of what it is composed. The admixture of sexual development and meaning, of the capacity for intimacy and relationship, and of caretaking appears to be illuminated. As these men are in the earliest stages of their caretaking careers, we can perhaps more clearly appreciate the components, constituents, and conflicts that constitute the paternal posture.

19 | JONAH: Someone Is Being Beaten

JONAH, A VERY TALENTED PHYSICIAN, FIRST CAME to see me in his early 30s after a particularly distressing quarrel with his wife. We embarked on a four-year analysis during which we learned much about his family of origin, his pain in growing up, and his modes of engaging with both men and women. We were able to sort out, using the transference and his associations, why he needed to be constantly reassured by many woman that he was attractive and sexually interesting and why he fought continuously with men, especially those in authority. These issues are not unique, and, although they bore Jonah's distinct signature and the contours of the way he and I could play together, there was a quality of the average and the expectable about the first piece of analytic work, which suggested that much still remained to be learned. We ended our first go-around together when Jonah received a significant promotion and elected to move to a distant city. As he and his wife had divorced during this time, and his mother had succumbed to a virulent illness, he felt an itchiness to explore new places and new opportunities. I was left with a feeling of both wishing him well and anticipating his return. He had raised many unanswered questions, and it felt to both of us as though we had completed round one of what might be a multiple-round encounter.

Jonah and I had played in the transference with questions of who makes whom do what and how this power or authority is enforced. Some of this play seemed to be about questions of family structure and generational boundaries of the sort that every boy must sort out and struggle with if he is to understand reality and consequence and to master his own impulses and grow to manhood. Some of Jonah's play with me also had homosexual overtones. There was a feeling that these same concerns might have something to do with how two men get into each other. This concern was playfully negotiated—"Herzog has his hands in my pants"—but seemed to be highly cathected. In addition, Jonah was very concerned about bettering me and by so doing triumphing in the game of life and, as the victor, being entitled to all the spoils, including my wife. These fantasies contained competitive ambition, immense excitement, and considerable fear of retaliation. Toward the end of the first piece of analysis, Jonah decided that he wanted to keep me as a loved object, so he would try to find a new wife of his own and she would likely be even more lovely than the woman I must be married to.

Still, there were intriguing loose threads. Together we wondered about his not wearing underpants when he came to his hours, a happening that had begun early in our work and continued until the end of the first phase. I also wondered if the interest in how fathers made sons behave and, more directly, Jonah's recurrent idea that I was making him come to analysis and that he would never submit, were only the tip of an iceberg whose lower stratum was a conscious or unconscious beating fantasy that had not yet emerged for analytic exploration and understanding.

The following is from seven hours from Jonah's second period of analytic work. Like Michael, he has found it especially useful to have this return engagement. Together, he and I are able to learn more about what did and did not happen for him in the first piece of our work and what was shared and what was not. These process notes contain not only the verbatim exchange between us, but also my unuttered thoughts during the analytic hours. This manner of presenting Jonah's analytic work allows us to see how what happens evolves, as the process between him and me is very much the scene of the action.

FIRST HOUR

"The weekend was really difficult. I had to come in to assist in an emergency myelogram and the patient was an old friend of my father's, Dr. K, who wrote the treatise on abortion. When I checked the catheter, I thought about his leg. There wasn't very much hair on it. It was kind of hairless. And now my aunt's rubbing herself in the bathtub as she washed her hair and making me watch come up."

This screen memory, which he had called sexual abuse in the first round of analysis, had not made an appearance earlier since his return. I wondered about the reference to abortion. I remembered that he had told me that Nelly, a girlfriend at one time, had had an abortion and that one of the reasons that his first marriage had ended had to do with making or not making babies. I waited for more of the dream.

"He called me Jony, and I blushed. I just had the feeling that I would blush if you called me Jony. It might be nice. Jony, Jony. Then the idea that you might blush if I were to call you Jimmy. You don't seem like a Jimmy to me. More like a Jim."

"Oh," I say, noting to myself that it has switched to us. What about the screen memory, abortion, babies?

"Well, Jimmy is like a term of endearment. I'm beginning to get a little flustered. You are dear to me, but it makes me feel that you will turn on me. I just had the idea that one could spell Jim as G-Y-M, you know, gay young man."

This is something new, but related to "Herzog has his hands in my pants," which was more like as a meddlesome father. But I had expected something about heterosexual excitement; he had been talking in the previous hours about needing more penis excitement than he was feeling with Marge, his new wife. I am aware of shifting gears. "Is that how I seem?" I ask.

"No, actually more like a GOM, G-O-M, gay old man. Now I thought of my old man. Actually, I always wished that he would call me Jony. But something funny is going on, I really think that this is about you, not him. I was just thinking about not wearing underpants, back then, you know when I saw you the first time. I think, no I can't say it, I would like us to be naked together, like you not to wear underpants either. I just had the idea that you would send me away."

"Oh?"

"But when I said that it sounded to me as though the send me was sexual. Like you send me. Did I ever tell you about Dan Collucci? Do you remember?"

"No."

"Well, he lived next door in Palo Alto. I just thought about being a boy, Sir Real, you once said, instead of surreal. I am a real sir, not a girl but a boy. I had a gender identity disorder, not really but in my psychology until the analysis. Well, anyway, Danny's father was a cop, big and brawny, what a physique. I don't think he worked out; he was just built that way. And he used to spank Danny with his belt. Danny's mother would say, "Wait till your father comes home." There was something about her saying that, wait till your father comes home. I would get excited. I thought it would be interesting to be a Collucci boy."

"Why? What happened when he got home?" I was thinking about the change in his own mother when the father returned, that it constituted a loss for him, Jony, when his father returned to the house; in the Collucci house it was apparently different, involving spanking. "Do you mean to get the belt?" I ask.

"Yeah, sort of, from him. I mean it was exciting then."

"When you were a child in Palo Alto?"

"Yeah."

"And now?"

Maybe I was still orienting myself to the switch in material from the heterosexual to the homosexual, if that is what this was, from penis to backside. I realized that I was quite unsure what this was. Just listen, I told myself.

"I'm not talking about now," he said.

"No?"

"Well, it certainly wouldn't be exciting to get the belt from you, pervert. I'd haul you up in front of the board even faster than you could get my underpants down."

I considered not saying anything but then did say, "You were mentioning not wearing them."

"Don't get your hopes up or anything else Jimmy. I am wearing them. I called you Jimmy."

"Yes," I said.

"I've never done that before. Even in my thoughts you have been Dr. Herzog, no, sometimes Jim. You know we have been here before, but it feels different. I just thought, thank heavens for Marge. She's a protection for both of us. I hope that you are still married to that beautiful woman. I could never talk this way."

"With anyone?"

"No, it feels as though not even with you before. Now I'm going to say something strange. It feels as though you are different. I don't know what this means, but more like a Jimmy. You know, my father speaks academese, almost like being a lawyer and speaking legalese. It's like he is always preparing a brief. Underpants are called briefs."

"Is that the kind that he prepared?" I asked.

"No but it feels to me that it is the kind that you do. No, I take it back, maybe that we do."

I wondered if I were being flirtatious, with the underpants retort, having some difficulty keeping up with him, and perhaps being awkward in making the transition. This felt sort of like fun. Maybe two guys horsing around together—latency, no earlier, sexual, not really, some kind of play that we had not experienced before? I wanted neither to fuel it nor to thwart it.

"Actually, I think that I am different. I could never have talked before about wanting to be over your knee. Don't write this down. This must come from a long time ago. I used to think about Mr. Collucci sometimes when I would masturbate. Then I would get scared that I was gay and get my Mom's *Vogue* and look at the pictures of women. You know how I've said that I can only masturbate by looking at pictures. Now I am wondering if that means I need to look at pictures in order not to think of Mr. Collucci."

I wondered about Mr. Collucci, about what Jonah thought when he masturbated. This did not feel sexual to me. What did that mean? Am I defending against this, denying the sexuality, that is, the homosexuality? He is talking about being over my knee, overlap. Why is this hard for me? Is it? I have a slight feeling of being one of those slow-to-warm-up kids, slow. Then I feel a sort of staying with the warming, bottom warming. He is talking about its being exciting to be told by one's mom that one is going to get it from one's Dad.

Jonah said, "I just had a very disturbing thought, something like that Marge is like him. This seems crazy. But in a certain way, Nelly and Linda were men. They both ended up beating on me and then I had to leave."

"And you worry now that you will feel that you have to leave when Marge gets angry."

"Yeah, so, do you think that this is connected?"

"What is your thought?" I ask.

"Strange, I would think that I would feel that you were about to throw me out," he says.

"Do you?"

"No, but I feel as though I have to get out of here. Actually, this is very embarrassing. I have to get up and take a shit."

He gets up, sort of grins at me with embarrassment, and goes out to the bathroom. I had the image that his gut was convulsed by what he was thinking and feeling, I wondered how I was feeling and wondered if my self-preoccupation was a defense against the excitement or the regressive pull. He had noticed groddeck's *Book of the It* on the bookshelf in the first round of analysis. I thought further that, unlike his fear in the first round of analysis, now he wasn't waiting for me to throw him out, which I wasn't feeling like doing in any case, but rather that his gut wrenched and he took himself out or at least interrupted his thoughts and the play. My thoughts turned to our termination 10 years earlier and the fact that this material had not come up, I wondered about readiness. Had I thrown him out? Did he get up and shit to interrupt the regression? Was there a collusion? Was I being too much in there with my question about his underpants? What was the "it" I shouldn't see?

A couple of minutes later he returned. "I had to shit so badly I didn't think that I would make it. I might have plugged up your toilet, so much came out. At least you can't smell it in here, can you?" I thought about answering yes or no, but I did not know which, if either, and remained silent. There was no actual smell, but could I get the scent, sent, you send me, scent me? I felt that I was doing a little better, had the image of Telly, my dog, sniffing, which I always like. Then I recalled my patient saying something before about his dog, the Asian maid, and the dog's shit, perhaps smelling it.

Back on the couch, he said, "I just thought about my uncle's irritable bowel and how he used to announce that there were going to be dire results when he was having diarrhea." I remembered his description of this with an emphasis on the smells and sounds of his uncle's defecation; it had been described as disgusting, in no way as exciting or interesting. "Are you worrying about dire results?" I asked.

"This feels very dangerous to me. I actually said that I would like to be over your knee and I had the feeling, no I can't say it."

"Yes," I said.

"Well that we could actually do it. It scares the shit out of me."
"Literally."

"Do you think it's defensive that I think of the women, you know, Marge and Nelly and Linda, like to manage the spanking, the gay stuff?" Marge is his second wife; Nelly and Linda were important women from the period before his second marriage.

"Is that how it feels?" I ask.

"Yes and no. Maybe it's both yes and no."

I thought about my just thinking yes and no and my thoughts about our previous termination–interruption. "You seem to be saying something about excitement but also something about how relationships come apart. Maybe both have to do with here and what we have talked about and what we didn't"

"What does that mean?" Jonah asked.

"Well, maybe having to leave when you get thoughts about being spanked, an overwhelming urge to move your bowels, or Mr. Collucci, or overlap. Beating on," I said, "is something that we need to learn more about."

I realized that I had extended or amended his thought by going from over the knee to overlap, but it felt right.

"This is too weird for words, but it feels right. I never could have talked about this with you in the 80s. We did a lot though. Christ, I've got to be able to both love and work, à la Freud. I never would have been able to do that without this. I didn't think about it with you then. It wasn't here, I mean in the room. What we're doing now, I feel closer to you and closer to me now or something. Like we are in the same place and I don't have to run off. Oh, I may be late tomorrow, I'm giving rounds. No, I think I'll make it."

"This is scary for you," I say. "You may both feel that you can stay and notice that you feel the need to be elsewhere."

"These are not good times to be gay, you know, and spanking is out of favor, too."

SECOND HOUR

"I felt very uneasy after I left yesterday. Like I was propositioning you to give me a spanking. I actually felt like a naughty boy who needs one. I hope that you don't think that I am totally insane. Oddly enough, this feels interesting, even important. It got worse. In the afternoon I was supposed to prepare my talk for this morning. You see I did get here on time, but I looked out the window and I saw this guy working on the roof across the quad. He was bending over and wearing tight jeans. I could clearly see the crack between his well-developed cheeks. I thought, he is in a great position to get the belt, I would enjoy spanking him. I got a hard on. I was disgusted with myself, but then it seemed sort of amusing. I know it's related to here."

"How?" I asked.

"Well it's what we're working on, isn't it? Say yes, or I'll think that I'm becoming a fucking S and M fag."

"You said that this feels interesting and important."

"It does, but how come you didn't just say yes? Are you checking out on me?"

I also noticed that I didn't just say yes, although I thought yes. Then I thought that this reversal from wanting to be spanked to spanking and having an erection might mean more than we had learned yesterday. I felt as if I didn't know what was going on and that I should just be quiet, but also that I should say something. I wondered about his mentioning the crack. Yesterday's thoughts about scent. What were we on the trail of? "What do you mean?" I asked.

"Well, I feel that I can only talk about this if you play with me too. Now I think of your not wearing underpants also, now of what it would be like to spank you. I need you to be here."

"Does it feel as though I am?"

"Just say yes," he said.

"What's the question?"

Now I felt as though I were being either withholding—the opposite of violent cramps—or provocative. Was it in reaction to his saying that he wanted to spank me, or was I trying to provoke it? This was getting extremely interesting. It had begun earlier with his first request for me to say yes, and I felt surprised at my sense of being drawn in.

"Looking at that guy and thinking abut belting his ass is connected to here. It must be. I felt like I could almost see the sweat between his cheeks, that I could see the dampness coming through his jeans, almost like I could smell it."

More overlap. I had wondered about our being on the scent of something, remembered his first wife's negative comment about his backside sweat-smell.

"Now I feel that I can't make you say yes, but you get the point, don't you? This isn't really about making. It's about our doing this together. Like a circle jerk. No, it's not about fronts, I think, but about backsides. I just thought about standing behind my mother and smelling her. Do you remember that?"

Again I was aware that I was not answering, not so much that I needed to, but that I wasn't.

"It had something to do with my sister Ruthie too. I don't smell like that from behind. I bet you don't either."

I mentally noted with interest that I had taken a shower and neither defecated nor exercised since then. I wondered why I was reassuring myself—why would I not want Jonah to smell me? Or what did I not want him to smell? It seemed to be either feces or sweat. Was I clean or dirty? Had I just been to the gym, gay young man Jim?

"This is going from bad to worse. Now I'm thinking about how you might smell back there."

I did not ask how I might smell, but noted to myself that we were thinking about the same thing.

"Sometimes, especially when I eat Mexican food, I develop such a strong smell between my cheeks that I think everyone must smell it. I actually like it if it's not too strong. Last night Marge was sucking me and she said, I like your strong smell. I didn't know whether she meant in front or in back. You're in back of me."

"Yes," I said.

"Good, now you said it. I was wondering if my smell is all right with you. You know if you spanked me, if I were over your knee, I could be sniffed. I think that I would want to be. Thank you for saying yes. I actually knew you would."

I too felt relieved that I had said yes, a sort of yes at last, still very curious as to what the dynamic is that is evoked in me—withholding, defending, thinking this is intrinsically interesting isn't it?

"Last night was interesting," Johan said. "Almost the usual disaster, with Marge."

I was relieved that the topic was now Marge, but also disappointed.

"Marge erupted. Something about a woman at work, and then

she snarled at me, said that I couldn't understand anything. I got this familiar feeling, I am out of here. Then I thought of us as comrades in arms."

"You and her?" I asked.

"No, of the spanking brotherhood, the gay old man and the gay young man, the two Js. I thought Herzog said something about things ending and feeling spanked. Then I just sort of smiled at her and said that it sounded like she had had a tough day. She started to cry and thanked me for not checking out on her."

"You worried that I might check out too," I said.

"Yes, this is a strange paradox. I know I said it, but I'm feeling just the opposite, as though we will see this through together. After all, I am back at Harvard now with tenure. I am not going anywhere. You have tenure too, don't you? Anyway analysts can't just pick up and leave. That would be malpractice, even the Freud professor only went away for a year. I worry that you'll do that too. It's OK. Maybe in five years, but you are forbidden to go now. Do you understand? I feel tearful. I wonder if I would cry when I was over your knee and you were spanking me with the belt. This is going to sound even stranger, but those would be different tears, tears of being with you rather than tears of going away."

Two gay men together, old and young, spanking and sniffing, help him to stay with his wife, not feel dismissed, beaten, or as though he has to check out.

"You know, having to go to the bathroom yesterday reminded me of something. That happened both with Nelly and with Linda."

"What?"

"Having to go to the bathroom like that, suddenly and no holding back. At the end, I had these episodes of like a convulsive emptying of my bowels. It was on Linda's father's boat, and I actually did wreck the toilet in Nelly's apartment. The boat thing was hilarious although it made me very edgy. Her father was talking about toilets while we were sailing the boat over to the vineyard, and suddenly I had this overwhelming urge. Uncharacteristically, I said something like I'm out of here and rushed to the head. I was in there for about five minutes and everyone looked at me kind of funny when I came back. This I'm out of here feeling was very strong. I could hardly wait for the boat to dock. I kept worrying that someone else would use the head and I would be found out."

"What would be found out?" I wondered what was in there to be found out.

"That I'm full of shit. That Mr. B _____ would kick my ass. Actually, even stronger than that, that something terrible would be found out that I am grossly abnormal or worse."

I didn't know what this meant and was about to ask when he continued.

"I was feeling that his daughter was real good at that, beating on me and, I knew where she got it from. You said something about things breaking up and also about things breaking up here. Did you mean when we stopped last time when I went to Stanford? No one could have kept me here. If you had tried, I would have simply checked out. That's a ridiculous thing to say, but we both thought that a good piece of work had been done. I moved from changing fields three times and girls even more frequently to becoming a full professor, having 150 publications, and being able to marry a woman I really love. That's a good analysis. I didn't get that all wrong, did I? Well, did I?"

"No."

I in no way wished to undervalue our past work or take anything away from him or us, but to leave room for the new play which was emerging.

Jonah went on. "We talked about us then, too, about your having your hands in my pants, but that was about my penis. Now it's about my rump. You know my dad occasionally spanked me, and his dad strapped him. There was nothing remotely fun or exciting about that. I said remote—that is how it was. I just thought of Billy Budd and that line, 'and Billy ascended and took the dawn.'"

I started to think about the Benjamin Britten opera and about Britten's relationship with Peter Peers. That was really making music together. My own feelings about men singing together were stirred. Now it seemed to me that I could listen a little better.

"I wrote about that in college. In some ways talking about this makes me feel that Jony is taking the dawn," he said. (He had described a particularly torrid fucking sequence with a girl named Billie, who had sat on him and provided him with incredible ecstasy. There had been some conversation between them like, "You've had this experience before." "No, never. It just dawned me." Something is dawning here that has never been here before.

He went on: "It dawns on me that this is very, very interesting. Now I remember coming here once at the beginning of my analysis and hearing opera and then a little girl came out of the office. I figured that you and she were listening to opera together. Like singing duets. I don't mean this disrespectfully, but this is similar. It's more like a child analysis than last time. I'm more like a child. I think that's good."

"And I?"

"You're a playmate, old man. All around the mulberry bush the monkey chased the weasel. The monkey thought it was all in fun, pop goes the weasel. You're not remote, pop. We can monkey around. Why don't you just sing with me, say yes." This was like a child singing.

"I wouldn't have wanted to marry Nelly or Linda, Marge is right for me, I think. Also I had this happen a lot before my analysis. But what a thought, that it might have been different if I had stayed. No, I don't think so. I couldn't have talked about this with you then. I was too young to do a child analysis. I had to be 40. How droll. Thank you for not checking out. It's funny, I hear you saying yes. You'd better cover your butt. Or uncover it, or maybe this is advice for me. I admired my English professor very much. He is the smartest man I ever met. I invited him to our wedding. Now I wish that I had invited you too. I never could have talked with him about this stuff. This is rather like cerebral angiography, but even more delicate. What would happen if you were turned off? Would you just ream out my gut?"

"You once spoke of a six-foot bayonet," I said.

"Now I feel like this is about a boyonet, whatever that might be."

"Something that helps hold up a boy?"

"Like, this feels—he can't stay up without it. I am he, Jony. But so are you, I can't do this without you. It warms me that we are talking about this."

I had been feeling somewhat withdrawn at the beginning of the hour and more at the end, wondering about the fantasy of mutual bottom warming, the two kinds of tears, the relationship between spank play, beating on, shitting, and checking out, including my comings and goings. That night I had a dream about Fred D, a man who beat his daughter when I was young. I recalled his saying to her at the Memorial Day parade, "You're going to get it." My feeling both worried for his daughter and very interested. Fred D seemed like a Neanderthal man to me; it has taken me a long time to be interested in Neanderthal men.

I sensed Jonah's different reactions to Joey Collucci, Dan's son. I marveled that Joey had never come up the first time around, thought about wrestling with Jonah versus wrestling with his problems, wrestling versus spanking, the soothing effect of putting it as music, why the need for this defense, a change from yesterday. It seemed as if that was setting the stage with the no underpants retort. Now, if I listened, he would define what this new alliance was of backsides, sniffing, spanking, and excitement—what its uses were to be, what its dangers might be. What is this gross and abnormal thing within? Should I have inquired about "head"?

THIRD HOUR

"Hi, are you still here?" "Yes," I answered. (I felt comfortable after the dream and my thoughts yesterday. Saying yes felt as if I could play safely, too.)

"Thanks for saying yes. This is like some form of code. I felt phenomenally embarrassed, I hear 'bareassed' yesterday, when I sang all around the mulberry bush. I think that I was trying to say that I am a little boy. Is it all right? And it is being bare assed, visible to you to sniff or spank. It is like a duet, or that opera with the little girl, but this feels like guy stuff. Marge and I made love last night. It was very exciting. It seems strange, but being over your knee in this play makes me more comfortable with her. [Both to love and to stay— why?] I was voted the best teacher in the second year. It pleases me a lot. They said I was knowledgeable, open, boyish but well informed. I just had the unpleasant thought that you know too much about me. You may have to be eliminated. Flushed. Maybe that's what all around the mulberry bush was about."

"What do you mean?"

"I don't know, a very unpleasant feeling. It has to do with checking out, like I can't bear or you can't bear for us to be this close. One of us is going to get eaten."

"Or flushed?" I said.

"Yeah, oral or anal. Why don't we add fucked and then we will have all three phases. This is really all too primitive, but very compelling. [So is the border of this excitement elimination, oral destruction, or being fucked?] Marge asked me if I had been taking technique lessons. I laughed and said from the Fuckmeister, from Herzog. [I noted that he was using German.] She was intrigued and said, 'That makes analysis sound better than I thought it was. Maybe I should meet him, too.' I just have the very strong feeling that I don't want her to meet you."

"Why?"

"Well, what occurs to me is that you would like her better than you like me. She smells better and all of that. But then on the other side, backside. I mean, you couldn't do this guy stuff with her. Did you do this with Jack too? [Jack was a former patient of mine who was a friend of Jonah's.] Somehow I don't think so; he is so uptight, and he was letting Regina beat the crap out of him when he was seeing you. How come you do it with me and not with him?"

I had a very sad feeling, of having failed Jonah's friend Jack. I wondered where this came from, but also a feeling that it was not only one sided. I marveled at the persistence of that feeling, which I had worked hard on and thought, not for the first time, about the effect of Jack's analysis on Jonah. The central issue for me in Jack's analysis had been what happened between him and me as it related to his first analyst, a colleague who had committed suicide.

"It must be coming from me, right? But what about when we worked together last time? It must not have been coming from me. I am different."

"It feels different now?" I asked.

"Yes, safer. Even more than that, like I can play—with you—or at least in your presence. Also like you play, too. I want to say that I have never had this before, that I've always wanted it."

"What?"

"To be able to play like this, to really let it all hang out without being shot dead for what is showing, this feeling that I am abnormal, gross. Now talking about playing with you makes it better, like I have a playmate, not an executioner. [I thought of his grandfather, who was an executioner of cows and pigs, also a strapper.] My uncle called. He and his girlfriend are going to Greece, to the Parthenon. I wonder what my mother would think. Or how about gym and gom seen warming ass at your office, a brush with the law."

"Dan Collucci's father was an officer of the law," I said. (I wondered why I was invoking the law—as a refuge I presumed. Why did I need it? I guess I thought the material was more about the law than about spanking or triadic excitement.)

Jonah said, "And he didn't use the hair brush, he used the strap. This press is unbelievable, but the thoughts still keep coming. Do you need to fasten your seat belt?"

"What's your thought?" I asked.

"Well, first, that all this might be too much for you. Then that maybe I was saying that you should unfasten your belt or your seat. I remember that we talked about toilet training, and the Shirelles. But this is too much, except that I keep feeling we're into something quite important."

I felt anxious about the press reporting on the action at my office. I was in touch with my both liking the play and being afraid of it, something about the effect on my patient of the overlap. I wondered if absent fathers and off-again/on-again mothers might produce something too similar in him and me. I reviewed the Collucci comment: it seemed to me that maybe I had focused on the law (on defense) rather than the brush (the impulse). Hair brush had not even occurred to me, but I thought of it now as I remembered that hair had come up, his aunt's, in the previous hour. I thought about Fred D. and his brother, Paul, also a belt user. Both were patients of my father, and Fred used to drive my parents to the train when they traveled to New York. To my great surprise I could picture their father and imagine him with both of his sons. Then, with a rush of sadness, I realized that I could not picture my father's father and my father with him, not to mention me with him. Next, Holocaust feelings; then an image of my other grandfather accompanying his son from Theresienstadt to Auschwitz. Fathers and sons in extreme situations. And then I thought that these paternal musings could bear the scrutiny of the press. It was quite all right, guilt and shame, even personal history. Developmental shortcomings were not determining my listening or my being with my patient.

"I had a dream this morning. It's hard to recall, but I think it had to do with Germany. Something about *Kristallnacht* or the wall coming down. It's that time of year. I think that Herr Willy Brandt was saying something, making a stink, shouting *schnell, schnell* or *langsam*, maybe *langsam*, something about Margarite and Schulamith, like in the Celan poem, the hair, Frau Brandt was with him. Was he even married?"

I felt startled, worried, and then warmed by the concordance of our fantasies—my Holocaust associations, his dream, the *"Todesfuge"* ("Death Fugue") reference to Celan, but alert to the fact that I needed to listen to what he had to say in the context of now thinking about overlap, and even over each other's lap. I tried to picture him over my lap, or me over his, but I couldn't. I noted the Herr, hair and the connection to a smell, here a stink, perhaps diarrhea rather than backside-sweat smell. My *klang* association: was this the origin of *schnell*, the fast and slow of the dream?

"I have always wondered if you are German. You look like you could be. My mother's family were North Germans and my father's family from Romania. The light and the dark. I was so afraid of being dark and hairy the way he is. Marge is blonde like you. It's all in the color of the hair. I just thought that we could sing Deutschland, Deutschland über alles together. [He sings a few bars.] I keep wanting us to sing a duet. I once read something where a spanking was described as the dad's making his boy's butt sing. [I felt unable to put together *Kristallnacht* and the guy stuff, some kind of being together stuff. I had the feeling that it was moving from spanking as warming to beating on, beating, hurting, like leaving the realm of excitement and entering the realm of horror, except for my private musings about hair, the screen memory and not hearing the hairbrush significance. Need to sort out if this is about gym or gom or has moved into something more deadly or just shitty.]

"Wait a minute, there was something horrible in the dream" [Again this seems strange; I say to myself, listen carefully.] I forgot it. About a Chinaman who was stabbing women. On the other side of the wall. Now I don't know if it was the Berlin Wall or the Great Wall of China. That part was decidedly unpleasant. He was sort of like Charley Chan, sinister. It reminds me of how I used to think of myself as an archeopteryx. Swooping down and gathering up girls, like King Kong. This is making me nervous."

"What?"

"Well, that my orientation switched, from being with you in Germany to abducting or ravaging women or worse."

"What is on the other side of the wall?"

"Yeah, tentatively. Remember that dream about the hole in the head. It's like that, and then I become afraid that you will really hurt me?"

"That goes beyond spanking?"

"Yes, beating, killing. [This is what I had been wondering about.] Where does this come from," he said with unusual emphasis. "I feel like I want to leave. Let's terminate. I probably just said that because we were talking about stopping last time."

"This seems very frightening to you," I said.

"Now the scene from Mr. Sammler in Poland comes up, where everyone had to dig his own grave."

"The Germans could be pretty deadly, too."

"I wish you wouldn't say that," he said, "because this is about your not being deadly but our playing together."

"The dream is about that?"

"No, but what we have been talking about. My God, it must have been absolutely horrible there on *Mistralnacht*."

"On what night?"

"What do you mean, what night? What did I say?"

"You said *Mistralnacht*." "What . . . I didn't."

Mistral was his first wife's name. He sobbed, cleared his throat. "I knifed her pretty brutally. She was German, like you. This is making me very nervous. This seems strange, but it is both more exciting and more soothing to be butt busters together."

"It seems that it is preferable to knifing and murder," I said.

"Well, you certainly aren't disputing that, are you? You know this archeopteryx thing was very vivid when I was young. A dinosaur bird. I went to see a skeleton of it at the Museum of Natural History with my mother. I think she said that there was one in Berlin. No, Gottfried, her father, told me; it wasn't my mother. He always sat in the last row when he went to lectures so that no one would breathe germs on him. Germs, many of them. Germany. Now I am getting oriented, or rather disoriented. I just had the thought that backside-sweat smell, yours and mine, pal, is caused by the many germs there."

"So another meaning of Germany and our singing together."

"Maybe, and with girls it's different, a blend of sweet fragrances. No, I think it's the same. But how do we put the archeopteryx and Mistral in the same place? They are both here. I wish I didn't have to be in London now. But I will be back on Monday. There is a lot of spanking in England. Just kidding. I've got my hands full with these fantasies here. I just had the distinct impression that you were saying, 'Whoa, slow down. Don't go after that guy on the roof and don't do anything in England.'"

"Didn't your father used to say cool it until the feeling passes?"

"Yeah, but that was about sticking it to women. Stinking it. The Chinaman and knifing. It makes me shudder. I think that everything will be fine on the trip. I wish that Marge could accompany me, but she is going to Buenos Aires. This sounds silly, but could I call you if I have any particularly distressing thoughts."

"Yes."

"Thanks, pal. I wish that I weren't going to be away now. It's not really that I am scared, but rather that this is so compelling here with you, I didn't have to walk out on Marge when she beat on me, the way I had to leave Mistral, actually throw her out." He sobbed. "Something about the difference between rolling with the punches and getting killed."

I say, "Something that we can learn about together."

"But I think actually do together. I mean, that's what we are doing I think," he responded.

"So we are learning something about being over the knee and something about what is on the other side of the wall, having to do with danger and hurting."

I felt that he was right. I was quite prepared to say yes and was not at all surprised about the inquiry about the call; and, interestingly, I was not worried about Jonah's well-being in England. I had a fleeting thought about caning in English public schools, which was associated with the image of a boy I had known in Edinburgh who had been caned and then an image of my friend Colin, also English, whose father regularly beat his sister, for which reason I was not invited to their London home. Then a story emerged about a murder in that family; I think it involved the mother. I felt that Jonah was talking to me about the relationship of libidinized interaction, erotic and aggressive, between father and son versus something far more destructive—murder, in Germany, in prehistoric times, perhaps involving the mother. I remembered that he had associated to his relations with women. I wondered if I was being experienced as the father or the mother.

I had associated mostly to men beating women—was this a reversal?—also to the murder of my grandfather. I felt that my unconscious was very actively present in this play. It could be an ally or might it represent the Axis; I hoped for the former and felt that this was quite likely. Also I could not fit in my lack of association to hairbrush, another form of spanking. As I reviewed this lack, I could not think of his describing it or what it might mean. I could hear, however, that he was saying that he was experiencing the fantasy of our playing together in this particular way enabling him to love Marge and not be beaten on by her so that he would have to leave. He seemed to need to confirm his continuing connection to me even in his absence, perhaps to counter the eliminating-eating-fucking thoughts.

My own thoughts turned to grimmer scenarios, and so apparently did his, albeit with their own particular markings. I felt the need to make a summary statement, a need I often feel, because of the upcoming break and also because so much comes up in each hour that it's as though a defensive multimedia show were being staged to obscure, or somehow make more tolerable, something that we were not looking at, or at least were not seeing.

FOURTH HOUR

"London was great. The meeting was about dye-assisted MRI investigations, and people were interested in my results. I got into a disagreement with Ronald. You know about him; he is in Edinburgh and thinks that the technique he developed is superior to the one that I developed—talk about phallic symbols. I think that all this is sibling rivalry—we all trained with Professor A____. He was a good father, but all the guys want to be his number-one boy, especially now that he is dead. You know, he was just a nice guy. This is strange. He was German really, like you I guess, another nice guy. I have an image of him with his blond hair and blue eyes, grinning. He didn't really look like you, but sort of. Everyone liked the way he looked, Mr. Good Citizen, especially with the ladies. He had a great build, too, kept himself in shape. He did Nautilus. He was a little thick in the middle, just like you, I wonder if that is a particularly Germanic habitus, the mesomorphs of *mitteleuropa*. Sorry. Once he was on the floor in the operating room, on all fours bending forward, I could see his butt outlined in blue and the sweat demarcated his crack."

"Like that guy on the roof in the quad last week?"

"Yeah, it was like you could almost see in, something about how taut his cheeks were."

"What could you see?"

"I don't know, I feel very uneasy. Professor A____'s ass is off limits. This is going too far. He was like a real father to me in my work, and in some way I went to him because of the work that we had done together."

"What do you mean?"

"Well before the analysis, I fought with guys, my bosses, all the time. I just couldn't help it. Then when I went to work with him, after we had finished, I felt like I understood something about that belonging to the past, to Palo Alto boy, not to Palo Alto man. I just had a most discomfiting thought something about that article in the New England journal about the guy who ate the bad sushi and had that huge worm in his lung. [I wondered to myself if this were an associative answer to my question about what he could see, a murderous worm in the crack? A penis? Also a reference to the ovarian cancer, the disease that killed his mother?] God damn it, look, I am interested in cracks. Sometimes I study my own."

"Oh . . . ," I say.

"Yeah I lie down on the floor in front of a mirror and I study it. [He brings his legs up as if in the lithotomy position.] Actually practically every day. [This revelation is completely new, and I was not expecting it, I feel a kind of flush of surprise and wonder if surprise is a pleasant feeling.]

"What do you see?" I ask.

"Not so much, dark hair, some pinkness, and what looks like stained or I guess pigmented mucous membrane."

"What are you looking for?"

"I don't know exactly," he answers.

"Just to see how it looks, to check it out. Is it the same as yesterday? When I had that convulsive diarrhea last week here, it reminds me of something. Like a colonoscopy, the feeling that if one is really all cleaned out, then you could really take a look."

"We seem to be really taking a look at something—there or in there," I say. (The colonoscope is clearly to see something inside, far inside. Why am I still staying on the surface?)

"This is going to sound very strange, but it feels to me that we are taking a look at something not in there but here." He gestures back to the space between the head of the couch and where I am sitting. I feel a certain increase in pressure, not entirely unwelcome, as if the scene of the action is again going to be the transference. But then I wonder if I am directing things to the surface, to the cheeks or crack rather than to the dark and hidden inside.

"In England, I kept having the over-your-knee feeling," he says. "It was very comforting; it was over your knee. A____ was not in a colonoscopy position, but more of a sigmoidoscopy one; you know, you lie on your side for a colonoscopy. [I note that he is now in the colonoscopy position as he is describing it.] You are not up on all fours or sticking your ass up into the air."

"And the over the knee position?" I ask.

"I feel embarrassed. There's that word again. It's cozy, warming, controlled, trusting, no bayoneting."

"What then?"

"Safe, like we can look at what is there. I have always been interested in men's cracks. I always look when a guy bends over. I have always thought that if they did one of those tachistoscopic studies of eye focus and movement I would be found out."

"What would be found out?" I ask.

"That I am a crack man."

"What is a crack man?"

"I don't know, not a fucking fag. I hope not a fucking fag," he answers.

"So we are learning something about what it means to be a crack man," I say.

"Yeah, if I can trust you and me enough to do it."

"Can you?" I ask.

"Well, over your knee, that's the paradox or maybe just the fact that if I feel that you are looking, sniffing, and spanking, then I feel safe. I can't explain it beyond that." [The conversation seemed considerably more focused on me. I wondered about the contributions of each of us to this situation.]

"So over my knee, it feels safer to talk about certain things."

"Yeah, and to say even more, well, here goes—I really hope that this is OK to say."

"Why wouldn't it be?" I ask.

"I don't just look into my ass. I rub the crack, mine, with a hairbrush and see if it gets dirty or if it just smells like ass-flavored sweat. I have the brush in my nighttable next to my bed, and I like to sniff it; sometimes I have to wash it off if it really gets disgusting. Marge doesn't know about it. I hide it."

"Is it a way of telling what is there?"

"Well sort of. I sniff after I rub my butthole, and I can tell what I smell like, whether it's too strong or just right. If it's really too much, then I whack my ass really hard with the brush. It seems only fair."

"What does?"

"To punish a butt that stinks."

"What makes it stink?"

"Shit, man, but it's not only that, it's when, I don't know, but sometimes it smells really good and sometimes it stinks. I've had the brush since before Dr. F____, since before I tried boarding school, I just couldn't tell you before. I thought that you would be disgusted or say that I wasn't analyzable or check out on me."

"You have been using that phrase, check out, over the last several days."

"Yeah, yeah, so?"

"Well, I wondered if it has something to do with checking on something as well as leaving?" I say.

"Maybe, maybe. Sometimes I think that a guy should be really spanked if his smell is too strong, and sometimes I think that spanking is an opportunity for checking the smell."

All this sounded clearer. Over my knee was a metaphor for his fantasy of my sniffing the brush or at least for my being told about it. I marveled at the absence of this communication during the first phase of our work or of my resistance to hearing it. Was the spanking simply a cover for curiosity about what was there? Was it a symptom in the sense of containing both impulse and defense, a way to the butt and punishment for the exploration? How was this behavior related to mother and father and to my earlier intuition, or at least my associations, which seemed to travel in a catastrophic direction? I noted that I had been surprised when he told me that he inspected his hole daily or nightly. Now there was this extension, the rubbing and sniffing and spanking. The material just seemed to flow: interesting, perhaps even amazing, no, for some reason not amazing. Am I more attuned, listening better?

"I'm interested in spanking," he says.

"Yes?"

"This is both the same and different." [I don't understand this remark.] "Where do you spank when the smell is too strong?" I ask.

"The hole, of course. That's what smells, not the cheeks."

I thought that he would say this. It seemed to me that he was describing something terrible, scary, unmanageable—un-man, too much man—on the inside and something different on the outside, perhaps excitement. I also thought about the triad, Mr. and Mrs. Collucci and Danny Collucci. Might this be cheek spanking? Is this what Danny got from his dad? And something about my seeing what would come out, and monitoring the border or the outside.

"Spanking the cheeks is what most spanking is about, you know, butt warming. Spanking the butthole is different. It's about the smell."

"What's coming out of the crack?" I ask.

"Yes. Is it O.K. or too much? You know when I was on the fuck it was really too much, sometimes I really felt like I was hurting all those cunts, stinking them. Now it's only a threat if I drink too much; then I begin to flirt and I get into trouble. My mother said that I had a weakness for drink, just like my uncle. He has it too, really can't drink. Nor can I."

"So this too muchness that is in there is like his?"

"I don't know," he says. "I see why you said that, but this sounds too intellectual. Are you blown away by what I've said? I never told Dr. F____. Actually nobody knows this. It has always bothered me that I couldn't tell you, but I really just couldn't."

"And now?"

"Well, it seems safer, like you can see, like you are strong enough to give me a spanking. No, like I feel that it is O.K. to tell you this.

I spoke about child analysis and our playing together. This is very serious, but somehow it has to do with play, my hairbrush, my smell, my feeling like I am over your knee too."

"Yes, it also feels to me as though it is quite serious. We are looking into something or for something that has been important and perhaps in some way hidden for a long time."

"Using an analytic colonoscope or sigmoidoscope is sort of like what I do with my work," he says.

"Are you in the colonoscopic position now?" I ask.

"Yeah, I guess so, I think that we can look at what's in there."

"On the other side of the wall," I say.

"China, man, this is very frightening to me. But less so with your being able to see. Maybe you can see what I can't. I know that I have to direct your gaze. Sounds like gays, ha ha."

"I notice that you say ha ha, and I know that you often hear the multiple meanings of a word, but do you think that you make the pun as a kind of diversion?" I ask.

"Are you mad at me?"

"Why?"

"That felt critical. It's just what came to mind. There is something about this that is gay, you know G-Y-M, G-O-M—maybe. It is a diversion, because what is in that dream—knifing, throwing Mistral out, hurting women—isn't gay; at least I don't think so. Now I have the thought that you just spanked me because I needed it. Do you think so?"

"I just wondered if it isn't very difficult to talk about these things and if it wouldn't help us to note what happens as we try to look into it, into a place where you cannot look so easily by yourself."

As the session ended, I felt that maybe I was spanking him but more likely that I was following the flow of his thoughts and how his multiple associations might be either deepening or disguising or both. I hoped that I was not involved in a discouraging enactment.

FIFTH HOUR

"It really bothered me what you said about gays yesterday. Have I misjudged you?"

"What do you mean?" I ask.

"Is it all right to play this way? Are we singing a duet?"

"Do you mean are you safe?"

"Yeah," he says. "I feel so . . . actually as I talk I feel safe again. I got a headache when I left yesterday, thought Herzog could wreck me, he could go to the dean and tell him about the brush. I can see it on the front page of the gazette, crackhouse raid nets Jony. It really made me very anxious. like you were critical of what I told you."

"I am sorry that it seemed that way. When you said ha ha I thought that you were signaling that the topic was maybe too scary and that by looking at that maneuver together we might be able to continue our looking, be able to follow it more clearly."

"That makes sense. I guess I am just very easily discombobulated."

He starts to cry. "You know, I never have talked about this to anyone. I call my brush Jony, like me. I've had it for almost 30 years. I considered bringing it here for you to sniff. Then that seemed too intimate to me, also too risky. [I feel immensely relieved. This doesn't seem like the kind of thing one could fake, a very delicate matter.]

"It seems very personal," I say.

"Yes, even more than actually being over your knee. Then you would only see or smell today, not the last 30 years. Thank you for apologizing. I know that you are not trying to derail me. I know that you know that this is important and that if I need to dilute things or tell it my own way then that is O.K. too. Danny got the strap when he did something wrong, and his mom saw to it that he got his cheeks reddened. He said that it would really burn and sting. It would happen about once a week. He was afraid of the strap, but not of his father. I got the sense that there was something fun about it. like they were all in it together. It was different with my mom and me. And then when my dad got home, she would become cold to me and quiet with him. I thought that when Mr. Collucci got home things would really heat up, especially Danny's ass, but also both of them, like they were fucking or something. I'm feeling very sad. I really wanted to live in Danny's house, not in my own. This is sounding ridiculous to me now, like I'm saying that Mr. and Mrs. Collucci were perverts getting off on whipping their boy's butt. But I'm not saying that, something like that they were all together and that the spanking wasn't all that bad because they were all together."

"That it wasn't too high a price to pay?" I ask, thinking this is about sexual excitement in a threesome.

"Yeah, Danny loved his father and his father loved him, I think that they all loved each other. Now it's sounding perverted again, like I'm saying that they were all in bed together. I'm not. I'm getting confused, but when I talk about being over your knee, it's more like being spanked by Mr. Collucci."

"Than?"

"What I do to myself with the brush. Most of the times boys don't get their holes punished by their dads, I think."

"So you are not your dad when you are whacking your hole."

"It sounds weird when you say that, but also safe again, like we are playing together. I've never thought about who I am, I guess it's like a Jony–Jony dialogue, the Jony brush and the Jony hole."

"You have mentioned that we are both Js," I say. "Is this a Jony–Jimmy dialogue?"

"Well, maybe yesterday when you asked about my defense, that's what you said we're doing isn't it? It felt like you were saying get back in there, don't let it come out. I think that's what I am doing when the smell is too strong, like some crude form of titration, get back in there, keep the cage closed."

"Like you are slamming the cage door?" I ask.

"Exactly. I do it very fast. *Schnell*." "*Schnell*?" I ask, using his word, which is German for fast.

"Yeah versus when I rub it when it smells good. Then I do it slowly afterward, like a reward. It's funny that you said *schnell*."

"Why?"

"Because I often think of that, *schlage schnell*. How did you know that?" (*Schlage schnell* is German for "beat fast.)

I reply, "I didn't. Until you mentioned it, I was just remembering that Herr Brandt said that after he said stink in that dream you were telling me about before you went to London."

"When you remember things like that it makes me feel that we are on the same wavelength, that you are really listening, and that you want to hear. My father never listened to me. He never wanted to hear, and he used to conduct these rounds from hell, shooting down everything I would try to say. That's when I would become so flustered, I think that's how I felt when you asked if I were trying to distract myself. That's transference right? I actually call the brush the Herr brush, *schnell* brush when I hit my hole, and *langsam* brush when I rub it as a reward, I don't know the German word for brush, do you?"

"No. Why do you have to slam the cage door shut so fast and so hard. What's in there?" I ask.

"I don't know, my shit. That doesn't sound right, something scary. What did Cicero say to Cataline, your unbridled audacity. [I think that this might be a distraction, too, but am not about to say so.] Something Jonyish, which is terrible, which even *you* would want to slam shut."

"Even me?"

"Well, I just said that."

"You also said that in the over-the-knee position I might get to see it and not beat your hole."

"Yeah, look, you might actually see it. I don't know what this is about. Maybe the Chinaman is in there, the part of me that is dressed to kill that wants to do in women. My father really wasn't very nice to my mother. I am trying to be nice to Marge, I am. We are working on making a baby, and I don't want to feel beaten on and like I am going to empty my gut, shit on everything, and just check out. I don't want to be destroyed by this relationship destroying something. It's like a prehistoric worm. [I thought of that with the sushi reference.] It's like Fafnia in the ring of the *Niebelungen*. My father and I have something evil and women hurting in our bowels. My uncle, too. This sounds like a delusion doesn't it?"

"Why shouldn't you think that you have some of your father in you, especially as your mother told you that you and your father were cut from the same dark, mean cloth?"

"Yes, and that's when it comes out, when I drink. Then I go on the fuck and rip cunt. I just cannot do that. Marge and I are not drinking at all, fetal alcohol syndrome prevention for both of us, no birth defects. Please don't say this is a defense, but berth defect comes to mind, like a berth in a boat, you know a bed. I just had the thought that it's about being thrown out of bed."

"Whose?"

"Well, the woman now, Marge's, God forbid."

"And then?"

"Theirs. We've been here before, haven't we?"

"Have we?"

"It feels that way, strangely familiar, almost uncanny."

"Have you read Kleist's *Prinz von Hamburg*? [I have been waiting to hear what would come next.] This guy is almost executed for falling asleep and thus getting a military maneuver wrong. He is dreaming about making love."

I think that perhaps Jonah is remembering falling asleep, seeing something, or having a dream and somehow the memory requires or at least threatens him with, execution. I wonder if this was the primal scene? What did he see? Why is it now located in the gut? What is its connection to his father, and how is his body connected to his mother and hers? Is the notion of the threesome, as in the Colluccis, a depiction of the traumatic event or a masking of it with a wish?

SIXTH SESSION

"I feel quite good. We have been working on the baby, and according to Marge's temperature chart we made love twice at just the right time. It feels like our chances are good. I feel like I can become a father. You know how much I have worried about that? It is an enormous relief to have finally told you about the brush. I just couldn't do it before."

"What made it possible now?"

"I don't know, trusting you. No, it's that I have been so fucking ashamed of it, always. Sort of like it is the embodiment of all the crap my father handed out to me, you know, literally. It could cake the brush a mile deep. This is probably premature, but I have felt less of a need to use the brush over the last week. I have taken a look at it several times, even sniffed it, but I haven't done it, the rubbing and the hitting. This feels really good, not having to do it."

"As though bringing it here helps?"

"Well, I didn't actually bring it here."

"In words and with all those thoughts about us, perhaps."

"I actually wanted to bring it in here."

"Yes."

"But then I thought, well I don't know what I thought. Well, that it is private. It's bad enough that it exists, but I don't have to rub your nose in it, too."

"Was that the thought?"

"Yeah—well, sort of. Make you sniff it, really bury your beak in there. It sounds so little boyish."

"What are you feeling?" I ask.

"Ashamed."

"Anything else?"

"I don't think so, maybe, I just thought again about Der Prinz."

"Why do you think that is?"

"Free association, what do you think?"

"Well, I asked you what you were feeling after you mentioned making me bury my beak in the smell on your brush."

"So, Kleist comes to mind."

"Yes, and I am sure for good reason, but do you think that it is also to get away from this feeling that you are going to make me do it?"

"But I didn't."

"I know, it was only a thought or a feeling."

"Yes, that isn't so bad is it?" he says.

"Perhaps you think it is too bad to stay with?"

"I have to think about this, but this Kleist business feels quite pressing. You know that the prince was dreaming about a woman with whom he was in love. Then he missed the father's orders and fucked up completely in a decisive battle." (An oedipal defense against something else?)

"I always have been concerned that no one else can make me do anything. Now we are talking about my making you do it. I remember how much that used to infuriate me, having to be here on time. I just couldn't be or, as you used to point out, wouldn't be."

"You seem to be talking about making me or my making you do it."

"I can remember your exact words, almost, that not getting here on time was of course related to externals, but if we could also look at the internals we might be able to see something of how I operate not only here but elsewhere. It would always make me furious, that, and when you would say that I perhaps worked at keeping my feelings about you cool and that we might try to find a way for me to bring them in here. I would feel, there he goes again trying to make me with his psychobabble, and it sounds ridiculous, but I just wouldn't."

"What does make me mean?" I ask.

"I think bury your beak in it. That makes me think of the archeopteryx, force you or me. I wasn't going to let you force me or something. I feel very confused, almost flustered. Like, if I say much more, who knows what will come out, like I have to slam it shut."

"As with the brush?"

"Yeah, but, I wanted to point out that you could spell that with two 't's, but that's my use of distraction, right? But this phrase, bury your beak in it, keeps repeating. It's such a strange thing for me to have thought. It's not only that I want you to smell me, be that close, but it's like I want you to see inside of me, you know analyze. But still that's not it. There's something like fuck you, I hate you, eat shit and die. (His voice rises and the last phrase, eat shit and die is almost screamed.)

"I'm sorry, really sorry." He is crying. He sobs, "No I'm not, I'm really not. I'm not going to say uncle!" [More of Jony is now here.]

"Well, what are you thinking?" I ask.

"That you said what you feel. It almost feels out of control, somewhere between fucking lethal and too good to be true. That's actually I—somewhere between fucking lethal and too good to be true. I used to think that Dr. F____ would throw me out if he knew that I slammed myself, although he slammed me. Remember how I used to tell you that he would say you do this and you do that and these are the reasons that you are behaving in such a way, cut your hair, don't cut classes, become a doctor? Look what you're doing, look. He was always hammering at me. I felt like I had to stand up straight and fly right, or he would throw me out. It actually got to be sort of funny, not telling him about the brush. I used to think 'Do onto yourself what others do onto to you or something.' Then, when I saw you the first time, I didn't know whether or not I would say anything, I had so much fucking trouble and things got so much better. It became like a superstition, don't rock the boat or something. When I went to Stanford, I would sometimes think about coming back and telling you, but then it felt like I couldn't stand it if you couldn't."

"Did it feel like I couldn't stand it?"

"Well it must have, but, two 't's again. I couldn't stand it, it made me so ashamed. It's funny, not so much with Dr F____ because he was so huffy. It seemed like it would be almost fun to shock him, but not you. With you I felt ashamed that I had a perversion or a fetish or whatever this is. I felt like you would never do anything like this, sniff the brush, I mean; you were married and a professor and seemed to have your shit together. Odd choice of words. Now it seems that you can take it, including my wishing to make you bury your beak in it. I never told you that I think you have a big nose, too, not as Jewish looking as mine, but you might have had trouble in *Deutschland* during the *Nazizeit,* too. There might just be a few drops of Jewish blood in those veins of yours."

"Does that make it easier to talk about this now?"

"Your nose, well, you seem less perfect than the last time and somehow that is connected to my being able to share this, I couldn't let it show before, not that part of me. If you had asked about the brush directly, I would have denied it."

"How could I ask about it?"

"I mean if you had known."

"How could I have known?"

"Well, if you could have read my mind."

"Did it seem that I could?"

"No, never, except when you were so fucking good at figuring things out, it made me feel fucking nervous. I am just remembering how my father used to grill me at the table, and then he would tell me what I was doing as I tried to squirm out of it—now you are lying, now you are exaggerating, now you are provoking. This is how your mind works, I know because I am the greatest professor in the world, and you, pipsqueak, you can't put anything over on me. [I have thoughts about defense analysis, mind reading, the father–son dialogue, and the fact that he had put something over on me. Did he have to? Is this the therapeutic enactment?] I hated it so much, I hated him so much. I used to think about killing him slowly so that I could watch him squirm and scream. I . . . can you stand this?"

"What is your thought?"

"I used to think about his being on the john all unsuspecting and my sneaking in there and ripping out his fucking guts, like all blood and shit and that being the end of the grand inquisitor."

"Sometimes you worried that I would bayonet you, eviscerate you, you said."

"That would be mild compared to what I had in mind for him. But you are right, it's in the same vein."

"You must have felt very injured by him and very, very angry."

"I used to feel till I went away to school that I was like a ticking time bomb, that I could just lose it and blast him. Then, when I left, I felt so much better."

"Didn't you say that that is when you started to use the brush?"

"Yeah, I remember the first time. I started out thinking that I would brush my pubic hair, Herr Brush. At the moment I can't imagine why, and then I just moved my way back and then I found the hole."

"And started beating it?" I asked.

"Yeah, something like that. So do you think it's connected?"

"At least in time, as you tell it today, you were a ticking time bomb waiting to go at your father's ass or gut in a murderous way, and then when you got out of there you started to go at yours."

"You don't understand," he says, very agitated and distressed. "He ripped my guts out. Every fucking night he would belittle me, show me to be a jerk, just wreck it for me in front of everyone, eat shit and die."

"Does it feel like I don't understand that you were very pained and very angry?"

"I was fucking abused, man." He is shouting. "Not just very pained and angry. I feel furious with you. You just don't get it. I think you are quite a bit like Dr. F____. Why didn't you tell me that you are a member of the John Birch society?"

"When did it begin to feel as though I had joined?"

"What, wait, what did you say?" he says.

"When did it begin to feel like I had joined the John Birch society?"

"When you were making a case about the brush and slamming him, like it just made me see red."

"Why?"

"I don't know, but, look, you are getting to see more and more of me, I can fly off the handle like that. This has happened with Marge and it's like . . . [sobbing] when I threw Mistralbel out of my life. [Jonah used to call his wife this pet name in moments when he felt the closest to her.] I feel like I'm trapped and that I'm fighting for my life, that you are going to or that she is going to kill me. This is crazy, but it's how desperate I used to get at home. It happens so rarely now, thank God. I hate it, I am terrified of it. Are you?"

"Strong, very strong feelings can be shared. They don't always have to be slammed back in."

"I know, but I don't really know, not in my gut anyway. Now I'm getting cramps again. This is just like that time a month ago. All of a sudden it just has to come out, like there's no warning. The thought is that this is my uncle's irritable bowel or even a cancer."

"I wonder if it isn't your terror and fury and what you sometimes have to slam back. Or if some feeling or something that we don't yet know about is somehow mobilized and sets this violent peristalsis in motion."

"Do you think it's bad that I have given up the brush? Do you think that I need it in order not to explode at you?"

"Why isn't it all right to explode at me?" I ask.

"I sounded fucking paranoid, man, like a freak."

"A little boy who is abused might really be ready to explode with his pain and rage. Why call that fucking paranoid?"

"I wanted to say, are you sure that this isn't too much for you, I mean for us? I guess it isn't. Look, this is like a colonic miracle I haven't had to rush to the bathroom."

"Do you need to?"

"It is not exigent, and I am, well, I am liking that I can wait. It's like we are showing me that I can." And here he becomes silent.

"Why do you stop?" I ask. "I don't know what to say. I've told you to eat shit and die. I think things are changing with the brush, and my uncontrollable peristalsis has spontaneously remitted. I am having quite a bit of trouble seeing how these things are connected."

"Are they?"

"I don't want you to answer. I'm afraid that I will become enraged again. Another cramp."

"What is to be afraid of?"

"I still don't know, something in there, no, in this, not requiring colonoscopy, but hopefully analysis."

"You seem to be very afraid of what is in there, but more able now to bring it here," I say.

"It's connected with this over-your-knee business, right? I am excruciatingly embarrassed about all of this, bare ass again, the spanking, the wanting you to sniff me."

"You've said that the Collucci stuff seems preferable to the carving up your father stuff."

"I still don't feel that I understand how all this is connected, the brush, hating him, telling you. I just notice that I feel very easily riled, like I am on really thin ice and one wrong word from you and I explode."

"Like my pointing out how you seem to manage strong feelings?"

"Yeah, it's like I can't tell the difference between your helping me to see, and being the judge and sentencing me to death. Wait, I can see the difference really, but it's like being dropped from one level of functioning to another, as though I regress right before our eyes. I think that this is what I was always afraid of."

"Does it seem so scary now?"

"More like we can manage it and, I know that this sounds crazy, but like I can give you the brush. I think I mean leave it here, not have to use it."

"Tolerate what you feel?"

"Is that it?" he asks. "I still feel like I can't make the connection, but I'm not giving up yet, not by a long shot. I may need two analyses but—there's the word again. What is the matter with that?"

"Nothing," I assure him, mindful that dangerous, slamming men still lurk: uncle, father, brush Jony, maybe myself.

SEVENTH HOUR

"I'm very upset. I had this long talk with my father, and he said that my brother and sisters are in much worse financial shape than I am and therefore he will leave all his money to them. I asked if I could at least have one of the books he had written. He said that I am being ridiculous. I told him that I felt as though he were disinheriting me. It felt as though he could read my mind, as though he knew that I was shrieking, 'Eat shit and die' here and that he was retaliating. I know that that isn't true, but that's how it felt."

"You shouted eat shit and die at me."

"Yeah, but it's transference, isn't it. I really meant it about him."

"Really?"

"Don't play mind games with me. If you thought I meant it about you, you'd be up out of your chair and throttling me. I wouldn't have gotten out of here alive yesterday. I'd be dead meat. My ass would be grass and you the mower."

"Is that how it feels?"

"I just told you, it was about my father. I actually know that what he said makes financial sense and that he doesn't know about here, but that's how it feels."

"I think that you did explode at me yesterday and that calling it transference may have some meaning," I say, "but it also is your way of taking it back, saying that it is not what you felt here."

"So, well, what if it is? Do you think that only a woman can change her mind?"

"We might be interested in what makes you change your mind."

"Nothing ever makes me do anything. At least that's what I would like to believe. I get so frightened at the idea that there is something inside that makes me. I am getting confused again. I hate this. I did scream at you, and it was about your telling me how my head works, just the way he did. I can't stand that. Do you get it? I can't stand it."

"And when you can't stand it, naturally you try to change it."

"Yeah, I can see that."

"Sometimes you slam it back, and sometimes you use other methods," I say.

"Now I feel a little calmer, not so flustered. We made love again last night. Marge thinks that she is pregnant. I picked up a kit this morning and tonight we will know. Feeling disinherited is like feeling that my father doesn't recognize me. Who are you if your father doesn't recognize you?" He begins to cry. "I have always felt disinherited, like I was given away by him. This is very strange. I felt recognized by you during the analysis but always as if you would disinherit me if you really knew me. You used to say that I could bring all of myself here, but I knew that that wasn't true. The more you asked what we could do, the more I felt that it was a trap. Now that has changed, I feel that we are recognizing what is inside of me. It stinks, right? I am a killer, a brush with the law, indeed. I deserve to be executed, not just beaten. Kleist's play is actually about that, isn't it? *Der Prinz* gets a reprieve; he is not executed. There is some connection here which I only dimly perceive. I can make a child if I share my demons with you, if I can see what is there; otherwise I can't. This is too formulaic. Analysis has no place at the academy for good reason. Who would believe it? Listen, are you going to retaliate? Is my ass grass?"

"What do you mean?"

"I just wonder if you aren't excessively cruel. You'll get me to believe that I can say whatever I feel here and then 'pop goes the weasel.'"

"You mean I'll slam you."

"Yeah, something like that."

"Unless you slam the door shut first."

"Yeah, walk out or say it just isn't true."

"Like transference."

"It is sort of strange, I have always insisted that there is no such thing as transference and now I invoke it."

"You must feel desperate."

"You aren't mocking me, are you? You see, I really can't believe that this is all right. It has not ever been all right. It's why I haven't been able to stay in a relationship up until now, this feeling that these feelings are lethal. But that isn't right, I have stayed in this relationship with you, I came back, I could come back. I counted on being able to come back, to bring you my brush. Don't be nervous, I don't mean actually. Do I?"

"Do you?"

"I think it would be gross. It doesn't seem necessary to actually do it right now, but if you were to give me grief, whatever that means, then I could actually bring it in."

"Make me bury my beak in it."

"Yeah, make you."

"That seems to be a critical part of this, the making me or you."

"As you just said, I thought of my aunt making me watch her rub herself in the bathtub. That's abuse, I don't know what this is about. She actually did make me; it wasn't a fantasy—it happened."

"And the brush isn't a fantasy. It is real, although it seems to be connected to all sorts of fantasies about what can come out, what you just get a whiff of."

"A whiff was all right, but when it actually stank . . . Is that the past tense? I just had the wonderful feeling that this might actually become the past tense. You know I wipe myself so hard that I sometimes bleed. This is connected too, right? I was always flunking his exams, and now he has actually disinherited me. Well, that isn't quite right. He has not actually disinherited me, but the first part is absolutely true."

"And when you wipe yourself so hard you actually bleed, I think that this actually doing it is important."

"What does it mean? Why do I do it? Funny, I don't feel so attacked at the moment. I think that this is what I mean or meant by being over your knee. It's a paradox, but it's like the safest seat in the house. Sounds like I'm punning again. I think that means, or you would say that means, I'm anxious, right? Well, I am but—two 't's—I'm also interested and I'm here. I have just had another peculiar thought. I don't think that I've told you about this, but in Palo Also, I had on arthroscopic exam at the orthopod's. He started an IV valium drip; it felt wonderful. I considered going back to him for a second examination. I think I am seeing something about actually doing it. This is not the same sensation as IV valium but it is related. From looking inside, from feeling eat shit and die, it's doing the feeling, not the drip or the brush. What's the Golden Rule? Do onto others what you would have them do onto you. I have the feeling that doing it is related to that. Like you learn that mode by having it done to you or something about the intensity of what you have felt. I am not very good at making a theory, but of course not. I prefer doing it, in my work too."

"As you say, having a feeling like eat shit and die is real."

"But it's not actually doing it."

"True, and I wasn't made to eat it or bury my beak in it, and I don't have to retaliate in action," I say.

"This is really interesting. I did feel like you should eat shit and die, and now I feel like, like that was all right and we can go on?"

"Yes."

In these seven hours, Jonah and I participated in a process in which the material at least in content resembled some of the things that Michael talked to me about. It was about the father, aggression, anality and the bottom and made references to aroma and spanking. Michael had brought up these topics with me, even briefly suggesting that they might involve play between us, but then shifted to his fantasy life outside of the analysis. Unlike Michael, Jonah said that he wanted to do it with me. His play seemed to be all in the room rather than involving a Rob or an Erik or a Hans. I was to spank him or sniff him. Soon it became apparent, however, that this invitation was also symbolic. He was describing a "safe-enough" position for a furthering of our analytic "colonoscopy." We were both to regard this verbal play as totally real but as confined to the use of words. Much associative material was stirred in me by what Jonah was saying. My way of being present was to resonate, wonder, move away, and then notice my movement and try to return. The reality of the verbal play and its evocativeness stirred anxiety, which necessitated defense. Something was trying to come out. How to participate so as to permit its emergence and to contain the intense affects which appear to account for its sequestration and accompany this transition? This was my task. I was asked by the process and by the interaction to feel these intense affects too and thus to deal with them on my own and as my way of accompanying Jonah.

From this sharing of the difficult to tolerate intense affect, what emerged was the sharing of the existence and meaning of the brush and the behavior associated with it. This behavior included rubbing both to sample and to categorize the stimulation it afforded, and then the administration of consequence. We came to understand this as not only a punishment involving pain, but also as a pushing back inside of something that was too dangerous or too reprehensible to gain egress. Here, too, we saw that the phenotypic meaning of symbol choice and activity was not the same as the genotypic significance that is always idiographic.

Jonah's analysis did not bring to light the kind of physical assault that Michael sustained. Nor was his memory access and lack of access arranged in a comparable manner. Jonah was spanked in reality. He contrasted this experience with what he was describing and also with his father's experience of being strapped. Both of these experiences may have informed the evolution of his perverse behavior, but neither represented an exact antecedent. We cannot, of course, rule out the possibility that the terror that needed to be dealt with was not some aspect of transmitted trauma from two generations before him, but this was not established in the material he shared. The defenses that are mustered to deal with transmitted trauma are often even more convoluted than those which arise in the effort to deal with first-hand trauma. As a consequence of this phenomenon, both the defensive behavior and the consequences of its disruption are often considerably more disturbing to the patient and, in a sense, more ego dystonic in so-called second-order, or transmitted, trauma.

Jonah had a problem with the modulation and organization of his aggressive drive and fantasy, and he, too, elaborated its "containment" in an anally organized structure. He employed an actual object and prescribed activities that were actually carried out; neither object nor activity was confined to fantasy. This fantasied object and activity was separate from his sexual life with his wife and with his other women friends, nor did it involve his male friends. It was not a part of a conscious masturbatory fantasy, nor did it intrude into his mind during intercourse or foreplay. Rather, it was kept in a separate place, his nighttable drawer. We came to learn that its function was simultaneously to keep present and to keep away feelings and fantasies that were unacceptable to him and yet constantly pressing on him.

The correspondence of the appearance of the rubbing, sniffing, and hitting with the brush to his leaving home and not being with his father and his mother are quite interesting. Once present, this behavior and this brush, this action and this object, remained stable and unchanging. The brush was never changed. It was taken wherever Jonah went. He even had a special carrying case for it that was like, he said, a large leather sock. It accompanied him on both of his honeymoons and quite literally everywhere. This companionship was discreet. No one knew of the second Jonah, the brush-Jonah. No one was aware that it, and what he did with it, was a feature of every day.

What does this mean, when an object and activity come to play this kind of invariant role in a life, separate from other activities and modes, but necessary? What would be the result of the involuntary separation of Jonah and the brush-Jonah?

During the first period of analytic work, the brush and what he did with it were never mentioned. I wondered about a beating fantasy from some of the material that Jonah presented, but as it did not emerge, I did not pursue my question. For him to bring the brush into our *Spielraum*, it seemed to be necessary for Jonah to feel safe enough both to initiate a different kind of play with me, the so-called safest seat in the house, and to feel that he was chaperoned as well, that is, that he had a wife on whom he could count and with whom he could stay. Here, too, there was the question: Would he bring it by telling me or bring it actually and make me "bury my beak in it?"

Again, to compare with Michael, Michael's quest for the father was organized around scent and seat. His quest appeared to be informed by the joint search with the mother. The developmental stage in which this search occurred, the second half of the second year, with its attendant issues of gender, impulse, control and dyscontrol, and anal erogeneity, all influenced the architecture of the evolving fantasy. Mother and he approached potential father-candidates from the rear, *nicht Gesicht*, so as to preserve for the longest possible time the possibility that they had found their man. His mother's interest in this route must have also been pivotal. The father's actual return was shocking in its amalgam of disruption, displacement, and assault. Finding the father, in the context of the antecedent search, now involved *terrorizing the end*, the spanking motif, as well as sniffing out the man as a toddler in the anal phase might do it.

Jonah's father was present, not away in the war, but a participant in another kind of war at home. During the period of development when Michael's father was away, Jonah's whole family was in Japan so that the father might pursue his work. Jonah had his mother when he and she were alone, and then on a daily basis lost her when his father returned. Moreover, his father would call him to task, flustering him and enraging him on a practically nightly basis. Jonah and I conjectured that his rage, perhaps egged on by the mother, had festered and grown throughout his childhood. It was held in check by the father's interrogations and by occasional spanking and frequent reference to the family's strap, which was actually visible when Jonah visited his aunt and uncle. We were to learn that the so-called abuse of watching his aunt rub herself in the bath was related to the simultaneous presence of the very strap that was used on his father in this very bathroom, where he had felt imprisoned. When Jonah freed himself from the external controls of his fury that the father's actual presence and the grandfather's strop conveyed, he became very anxious and in fact was unable to stay at the school he had wanted to attend. Simultaneously, the ritual of rubbing, sniffing, and hitting his anus with the brush began.

Notice that for each man, as a part of what might be called an *analized* solution to his father problem, what I shall call *aromaticity* played a role. By this, I mean that the smell of a man, domiciled according to the period of its inception in the anal period, came to serve as a symbol for the man himself and for one of his functions— some aspect of aggression and its discharge, modulation, or control—

and as a symbol for some blending of being with the mother or being approved of by the mother.

This use of smell and place involves a complicated process in which the olfactory function is appropriated to stand for more than simple odor or its absence. It might be noted that a man may smell the strongest in the locale of the anus, at least in an unwashed state, but its selection as the icon for masculinity betrays, reveals, I think, considerable ambivalence, as well as reflecting the period of inception. Thus, in the selection of scent and, in particular, some aspect of anal scent, as the male marker, each man, Michael and Jonah, shows us something of how a sensory function itself or a component of it can come to have a dual significance. For those men, scent symbolized both that which was longed for in a developmentally nutritive form and that which was abhorred in a way that reflected persistent and unintegrated problems in the extant selfobject representation. It is almost as if the part-object schema articulated by some theorists found voice—or aroma—in the sensory self, with other schemata denoting the problematic aspects of the relationship and the putative solution. Both Michael and Jonah suffered from persistent nasal congestion and other interruptions of the capacity to smell; each seemed to manifest a pattern of overextension of the meaning of smell and its use in the most highly convoluted but cathected activities, in fantasy or in fact, affected the more general use of this sensory mode in a deleterious fashion.

William Carlos Williams had the following to say about smell. His poem "The Smell" describes the way in which the part can stand for the whole and yet be whole onto itself.

> Oh strong-ridged and deeply hollowed
> nose of mine! what will you not be smelling?
> What tactless asses we are, you and I, boney nose,
> always indiscriminate, always unashamed.
>
> —William Carlos Williams, "The Smell"

Michael strove to pursue his father fantasy. Being very troubled by it while simultaneously finding it exciting, he kept it in a private place, only allowing himself access in the masturbatory sphere. Thus, the spanking and sniffing part of the fantasy was totally private, although shared with Anne, and falling in love with men was also kept to himself until the advent of his friendship with Rob.

Jonah kept the father's prohibitive function present with his action, beating his anus for its bad smell and beating back what the smell's intensity signaled was coming out. This behavior was the vehicle for an unconscious fantasy that involved the escape and emergence of his unmodulated rage and its descent, in archeopteryx-like fashion, on his father and his mother. The behavior and the fantasy together reveal the presence in his inscape of the way his father was with him, its internalization, and his efforts to stay on top of all this, to keep it down and out of his awareness. I think that Jonah was very right in noting that the meaning of the ritual with the brush needed very urgently to be known to him before he actually became a father, before the "badness that was being beaten back" reemerged in the father–child dialogue in another way.

Jonah also needed me to feel the combination of excitement and horror that he felt. By talking to me about being over my knee, about his spanking and sniffing in that position, and about my need to say "yes," he was reenacting an aspect of the universal father–son dialogue, albeit in a form that reflected his own experience. Sons use their likeness to their father and his to them to own their own aggression and its incendiary nature. Often this process involves aggressive episodes between them in which recognition of sameness is a component of mastery, limit setting, and eventual self-control, even if it begins as control of the self by the other. To bring the brush, Jonah needed me to feel the terror that he had felt. Thus he and I both felt the fear, even though there was also an opportunity for each of us, as both the active party and the recipient, to feel, as well, the aggression. I was invited, even taunted, to squash the proceedings, to push the aggression back into unconsciousness, where it was kept by the perverse, secret activity. In order for this not to happen, I had to be interested enough to continue. My interest was sustained, I think, through my using my own associations, which were related, and, in a certain sense, by my lending Jonah enough of my own available aggression for him to proceed. Jonah was provoking me to respond, as a little boy sometimes does with his father.

In such a developmental dialogue and in an analogous analytic one, the father/analyst needs to be able to use his roused aggression in a kind of lend-lease fashion so that it energizes something otherwise not available to the child/analysand, rather than squashing him. This is precisely what did not happen for Jonah in his own growing up. He needed to bury his own beak, so to speak, while harboring an ever-growing rage that he could not discharge, or acknowledge, or organize in any tolerable or productive fashion.

Again, let me point out that Jonah found a way to use me that was quite different from the way I could be most useful to Michael. Jonah needed to have a brush with the law, my now being the analytic law. First, he needed to negotiate a number of issues with me that had to do with claiming his anatomy and his rightful place with a woman. Only then could he bring forth the underpinnings of his place as a man with a man, not sexualized only or as a defense against oedipal dilemmas and their inherent risks, but around the basic issue of how to organize and modulate his aggressive drive and fantasy and still remain a member of the human race. This was a task with which he, like every other boy, needed help.

Michael, on the other hand, did not need to enact this drama with me, nor, in a sense, perhaps, could he. His sense of the terror that could befall one at the maddened father's hands or at the hands of the Nazis was too vivid to allow for a libidinal or aggressive skirmish with me in which no holds (or holes) were barred. Instead, we were "comrades in arms," using intense feeling for others and taking the joint-investigator approach. There were transference issues, and I was often viewed as prohibiting and disapproving. All this was bounded, however, by Michael's insistence that the alliance had to be maintained. This insistence was another manifestation of the meaning of his needing to see X-rays in order to remember. Had the abusive situation that Michael had known been recreated in the *Spielraum*, he might not have needed to "rebreak" his shoulder in the gym or seen the previous fracture on film. He felt, however, that a guarantee of enough safety to prohibit such an occurrence was the sine qua non of his being able to be in the analytic setting. Michael, of course, did his analysis as he needed to do it; so did Jonah. Doing it and not doing it as one's father is searched for, located, sequestered, displaced, and relocated as he is or is not in the past and now within the self is always a unique and complex undertaking. For Jonah, needing the brush or needing actually to have something reexperienced in the *Spielraum* was as valid a way to do the work as was not permitting a fantasy to reach fruition or keeping the alliance intact even if the transference had to be carefully muted so that the redoing with an analytic companion involved the participation of still others.

Both Jonah and Michael did the analytic work. Both reworked their pasts to find and integrate self-with-father with the other components of the self-system. Each played as he must, and each expanded the play repertoire as a result of the analytic experience. In so doing, both Jonah and Michael have shown us how self-with-father is represented and how that representation has functioned and shaped subsequent functioning in the service of both securing more and amending what is present. For each man, knowing what is there allowed for a more balanced approach to bearing his history and inscape, repairing what could be shifted in the interactive world where each dwells, and abiding that which shifts in the interactive world do not remedy.

AFTERWORD

HERE I SHOULD LIKE TO PRESENT SOME LATER material from both Michael and Jonah. Each of these revisits illuminates the continuity of certain kinds of inner experience and the changes and potential for growth and repair that the analytic experience affords.

Some seven years after the conclusion of the second part of our work, Michael came back to tell me of his current situation and to talk over with me an important career change. He spoke with me about the ongoing difficulties with his shoulder, his continuous effort to "work through" his past grief and assaults, and his helpful, but ultimately limited, attempts at working out and building himself up into a big enough and strong enough man to withstand whatever was meted out to him. This process was never-ending, he told me, but he had come to take a certain amount of pleasure in the knowledge that he had chosen to do it.

He told me of a recent experience in Greece, where he had gone swimming and then realized that he needed preferentially to use his right arm in order to protect his weaker left shoulder. It had taken an amazing act of will power to swim the last half-mile in this asymmetric fashion, and, when he finally reached the dock, he needed to be assisted out of the sea. Three women and a man hoisted him out of the water. "Much is involved for me in tolerating this, and yet" he said, "it has become almost second nature for me to do it this way and to feel that it is all right. The postures that they all assumed in helping me out of the water were like a bonus for me. I got to see a lot of butt and body. You know, I am still very interested in that part of the anatomy. I'm comfortable with it and not as fixated on particulars as I used to be. I guess I'll always be an ass man of sorts. I hope that you can hear that this is an evolution from where we left off. I have a lot more freedom, in fantasy and in actual play even with my physical limitations."

A little later, he told me that he and Rob were still very close friends. "The intensity has mellowed, I think I would say," Michael continued. "We talk together once or twice a week and are involved in a work collaboration. He is a very good friend, and I have others as well. I think that it would be accurate to say that some part of the extreme intensity I felt for Rob has returned to my feelings for Anne. This re-equillibration is quite comfortable for all of us."

Jonah called me after the birth of his second child, a daughter. He was worried that something of the see-saw nature of his relationship with his first wife and the other women he had known before he and Marge married might be reawakened by the arrival of little Natasha. As we talked, he told me about his father's death and about his friendship with Josh, a new colleague and workout buddy. He and Josh often talked about very intimate things, and he thought they were of considerable help to one another. Josh had been particularly important in helping Jonah when his and Marge's first child, Greg, had been in the terrible twos.

"You know, I really didn't know how to set limits, or at least I thought I didn't. In fact, my instincts are quite good, something I attribute to our work. Josh would agree with my thinking about how to help Greg when I ran things past him. It was sort of like talking with you, but friend to friend. Josh has a son, too, and he had a good father. He doesn't have a daughter though and I think that that is why I wanted to talk with you. This isn't true exactly, but I wanted to check in with the person who was my . . ." He began to cry, ". . . analytic father to make sure that I am O.K. I guess the real reason that I came back, though, is that I wanted to tell you that the hairbrush has now been retired for five years. It's quite amazing. I packed it up in an old gym bag in our attic. Somehow I thought that it should stay packed rather than be discarded. It feels wonderful to be able to leave it there, because it is not needed. I can, even though I needed to check in with you—you know, having a daughter is truly amazing—manage myself without it. I mean that I can tolerate my anger and my shit and not have to beat it back in or back away from it. Again, thanks."

Each man is proceeding with his life and with his play. Each has used the analytic play to recognize his inscape features and to try and remove those constrictions and limitations which play mode deformation conveys. This lifting of inner restriction has necessitated the acceptance of reality constraints in the past and in the present. The continuous paradox of loss and search, of seeing and knowing what is not there continues. Life after analysis is like life before. Pain remains, and an ongoing inner analytic process permits an examination of why, when, where, and how. Working on, working out, working with, and working through remains the only viable modus operandi, not that this is ever easy. Analytic accompaniment facilitates the continuation of this mode: seeking help and utilizing assistance. The beat goes on, but it is better.

I do not have follow-up on the three children of the T. family, but I do know that Tommy, he of Kryptonite and the black lions, continues to prosper. Feeling that it was necessary to work with an analyst of each gender, Etta, meanwhile, sought further treatment with a female analyst in her adolescence. She wanted that analyst to be in communication with me as she sought to consolidate her hold on a triadic reality (Herzog and Herzog, 1998) rather than two noncommunicating dyadic ones. This happened and has been fruitful. Ali is a psychoanalyst. Dr. C is doing well, and his wife remains in remission. Natalia is a creative artist and enjoys the company of many admirers. Bart entered the field of law enforcement. Dr. G., who would not change her appointment, rose to the very top of her profession and feels considerably better able to play. Nathan's career also goes well; he decided to move his family back to Germany and accept a professorship there. Davey, who was a "nosey nose," is the father of three; as a otolaryngologist he specializes in ear, nose, and throat. I thank each of them—and other patients mentioned more briefly—for enriching my life and teaching me about the many ways to play as we all try to manage our pain and our selves.

ORDNUNG, ORDNUNG, PAPA IS COMING

Roethke described the fatherless world of the lost son and the organizing, modulating, and integrating function that the father's return provides. "Ordnung, Ordnung, Papa is coming; order, order, Papa is coming," is meant to convey, I think, the father's optimal role in

helping the son to recognize his masculinity and claim it function-
ally rather than succumb to its inherent capacity to disorganize and
destroy. In this book, I have tried to show something of the way in
which fathers perform their role, an often *hit or miss* process in
which and by which drive pressure is harnessed in the service of
ego growth and play versatility is maintained in the face of derailing complexity.

In the spirit of Loewald (1960) and other "developmental" psy-
choanalysts, I have tried to show how this process brings together
powerful gender and generational specificities, processes, and designs.

> The parent/child relationship can serve as a model here. The
> parent ideally is in an empathetic relationship of under-
> standing the child's particular stage and development, yet
> ahead in his vision of the child's future and mediating this
> vision of the child in his dealing with him. This vision,
> informed by the parent's own experience and knowledge of
> growth and future, is ideally, a more articulate and more inte-
> grated version of the core of being that the child presents to
> the parent. This "more" that the parent sees and knows, he
> mediates to the child so that the child in identification with
> it can grow. The child, by internalizing aspects of the parent,
> also internalizes the parent's image of the child—an image
> that is mediated to the child in the thousand different ways
> of being handled bodily and emotionally—the bodily han-
> dling of and concern with the child, the manner in which the
> child is fed, touched, cleaned, the way it is looked at, talked
> to, called by name, recognized and re-recognized—all these
> and many other ways of communicating with the child, and
> communicating to him his identity, sameness, unity and indi-
> viduality, shape and mold him so that he can begin to iden-
> tify himself, to feel and recognize himself as one and separate
> from others and yet with others. . . . In analysis, if it is to be
> a process leading to structural changes, interactions of a com-
> parable nature have to take place [pp. 229–230].

By presenting normative and restitutive narratives, I have tried to
convey the continuous processes of inside-to-outside and outside-to-

inside dialogue and trialogue that characterize the self in its growth, in its derailment, and in its attempts at repair and recovery. For a child, the father is always relevant, always consulted as he appears in the inscape and as he is sought in the *Umwelt*, including in the analytic *Spielraum*. In this regard, the importance of internal enactment, by which I mean mobility among the three basic self-representations—self-with-mother, self-with-father, and self-with-mother-and-father together—is that a neurotic level of psychic functioning is then possible. The relationship of this internal-enactment mode to external enactments is delimited, at least in part, by the motivating and sustaining power of father hunger.

> *Long ago, I was wounded. I lived*
> *to revenge myself*
> *against my father, not*
> *for what he was—*
> *for what I was: from the beginning of time,*
> *in childhood, I thought*
> *that pain meant*
> *I was not loved.*
> *It meant I loved.*
>
> —Louise Glück, "First Memory in Ararat"

REFERENCES

Abelin, E. (1975), Some further observations and comments on the earliest role of the father. *Internat. J. Psychoanal,* 56:293–302.

Alexander, F. (1954), Some quantitative aspects of psychoanalytic technique. *J. Amer. Psychoanal. Assn.,* 2:685–701.

Benedek, T. (1970), The psychobiology of pregnancy. In: *Parenthood: Its Psychology and Psychopathology,* ed. E. Anthony & T. Benedek. Boston: Little, Brown.

Bentham, J. (1964), *The Theory of Legislation.* New Haven, CT: Yale University Press.

Bergmann, M. & Jucovy, M., eds. (1982), *Generations of the Holocaust.* New York: Basic Books.

Bettelheim, B. (1954), *Symbolic Wounds.* Glencoe IL: Free Press.

Bibring, G., Dwyer, T. F., Huntington, D. S. & Valenstein, A. F. (1961), A study of the psychological processes in pregnancy and the earliest mother–child relationship. *The Psychoanalytic Study of the Child,* 16:9–72. New York: International Universities Press.

Bolton, F. G., Lane,R. H. & Kane, S. P. (1980), Child maltreatment risk among adolescent mother:A study of reported cases. *Amer. J. Orthopschiat.,* 50:489–505.

Burlingham, D. (1973), The preoedipal infant–father relationship. *The Psychonanalytic Study of the Child,* 28:23–48. New Haven, CT: Yale University Press.

Casement, P. (1982), Some pressures on the analyst for physical contact during the reliving of an earlier trauma. *Internat. Rev. Psycho-Anal.,* 9:279–286.

Celan, P. (1972), *The Poems of Paul Celan,* trans. M. Hamurger. New York: Persea Books.

Chasseguet-Smirgel, J. (1985), *The Ego Ideal.* New York: Norton.

Cooper, S. (1993), Interpretive fallibility and psychoanalytic dialogue. *J. Amer. Psychoanal. Assn.,* 41:95–126.

des Pres, T. (1976), *The Survivor*. New York: Oxford University Press.

Deutscher, M. (1971), First pregnancy and family formation. In: *Psychoanalytic Contributions to Community Pyschology*, ed. D. Milman & G. Goldman. Springfield, IL: Thomas.

Earls, F. (1980), The prevalence of behavior problems in three year old children: Comparison of the reports of fathers and mothers. *J. Amer. Acad. Child Psychiat.*, 19:439–452.

Eisler, K. (1953), The effect of the structure of the ego on psychoanalytic technique. *J. Amer. Psychoanal. Assn.*, 1:104–143.

Erikson, E. (1950), *Childhood and Society*. New York: Norton, 1963.

Fraiberg, S. (1975), Ghosts in the nursery: A psychoanalytic approach to the problem of impaired infant-mother relationships. *J. Amer. Acad. Child Psychiat.*, 14:387–424.

Freud, A. (1965), *Normality and Pathology in Childhood*. New York: International Universities Press.

Freud, S, (1905), Three essays on the theory of sexuality. *Standard Edition*, 7:125–243. London: Hogarth Press, 1953.

Freud, S. (1909), Analysis of a phobia in a five-year-old boy. *Standard Edition*, 10:3–149. London: Hogarth Press, 1955.

Furman, E. (1986), On trauma: When is the death of a parent traumatic? *The Psychoanalytic Study of the Child*, 41:221–238. New Haven, CT: Yale University Press.

Geertz, C. (1973), *The Interpretation of Cultures*. New York: Basic Books.

Goethe, J. (1954), *Faust*, trans. S. Kaufman. New York: Anchor Books.

Goffman, E. (1959), *The Presentation of Self in Everyday Life*. Garden City, NY: Doubleday Anchor Books.

Greenberg, M. & Morris, N. (1974), Engrossment: The newborn's impact upon the father. *Amer. J. Orthopsychiat.*, 44:520–531.

Gurwitt, A. (1976), Aspects of prospective fatherhood. *The Psychoanalytic Study of the Child*, 31:237–272. New York: International Universities Press.

Herzog, J. (1977), Patterns of parenting. Presented to American Academy of Child Psychiatrists, Houston, TX.

———— (1978), Patterns of expectant fatherhood. Presented at meeting of American Psychoanalytic Association, Dec., New York City.

———— (1980), Adult–aAdult Interaction Predicts Adult–Child Interaction. Presented at meeting of American Psychoanalytic Association, May, San Francisco.

———— (1991), Die Muttersprache lehren: Aspekte des Entwicklungsdialoges zwischen Vater und Tochter [The mother tongue: Aspects of the developmental dialogue between father and daughter]. *Jahrbuch der Psychoanalyse*, 27:29–41.

———— (1992), *The Many Meanings of Play in Child Analysis.* New Haven, CT: Yale University Press.

———— (1993), Play modes in child analysis. In: *The Many Meanings of Play,* ed. A. Solnit. New Haven, CT: Yale University Press.

———— (1995), Finding the mother and the father in the analytic play-space: Attributes of neurotic process and its subsequent analytic exploration— In honour of the 100th birthday of Anna Freud. *Bull. Anna Freud Centre,* 18:261–277.

Herzog, J. & Herzog, E. (1998), Die Welt des Selbst und die Welt der anderen—Entwicklung und Behandlung narzisstischer Storungen [The world of the self and the world of the other—The development and treatment of a narcissistic disturbance. *Kinderanalyse,* 3:209–227.

Herzog, J. & O'Connell, M. (submitted), Operating with a full deck: How to use innate aggressive endowment in the optimal pursuit of organizational goals.

Hesse, E. & Main, M. (2000), Disorganized infant, child and adult attachment: Collapse in behavioral and attentional strategies. *J. Amer. Psychoanal. Assn.,* 48:1097–1128.

Hetherington, E. (1979), Divorce: A child's perspective. *Amer. Psychol.,* 34:851–858.

Hopkins, G. (1937), *Notebooks,* ed. Humphrey House. London: Norton.

Inhelder, B. & Piaget, J. (1958), *The Growth of Logical Thinking from Childhood to Adolescence.* New York: Basic Books.

Jessner, L., Weigert, E. & Foy, J. (1942), The development of parental attitudes during pregnancy. In: *Parenthood,* ed. E. Anthony & T. Benedek. Boston: Beacon Press, 1971.

Kennedy, H. (1986), Trauma in childhood: Signs and sequelae as seen in the analysis of an adolescent. *The Psychoanalytic Study of the Child,* 41:209–220. New Haven, CT: Yale University Press.

Kestenberg, J. (1974), Notes on parenthood as a developmental phase with special consideration of the roots of fatherhood. Presented at meeting of the American Psychiatric Association, spring.

———— (1975), Parenthood as a developmental phase. *J. Amer. Psychoanal. Assn.,* 23:154–166.

———— (1976), Regression and reintegration in pregnancy. *J. Amer. Psychoanal. Assn.,* 24:213–251.

Kinard, E. M. & Klerman, L. U. (1980), Teenage parenting and child abuse: Are they related? *Amer. J. Orthopsychiat.,* 50:481–489.

Klaus, M. & Kennell, J. (1976), *Maternal-Infant Bonding.* St. Louis, MO: Mosby.

Kris, E. (1956), The recovery of childhood memories in psychoanalysis. *The Psychoanalytic Study of the Child,* 11:54–89. New York: International Universities Press.

Loewald, H. W. (1951), Ego and reality. *Internat. J. Psycho-Anal.*, 32:10–18.

Lucas, A. (1977), Treatment of depressive states in psychopharmacology. In: *Childhood and Adolescence*, ed. J. Weiner. New York: Basic Books.

Maccoby, E. (1966), *The Development of Sex Differences.* Stanford, CA: Stanford University Press.

Mahler, M. S. (1955), On symbiotic child psychosis. *The Psychoanalytic Study of the Child*, 10:195-212. New York: International Universities Press.

Main, M. (2000), The organized categories of infant, child and adult attachment: Flexible vs. inflexible attention under attachment-related stress. *J. Amer. Psychoanal. Assn.*, 48:1055–1096.

Marcel, G. (1962), *Homo Viator.* New York: Harper & Row.

Mussen, P. & Distler, L. (1960), Childbearing antecedents of masculine identification in kindergarten boys. *Child Dev.*, 31:89–100.

Parke, R. D. (1981), *Fathers.* The Developing Child Series. Cambridge, MA: Harvard University Press.

Renik, O., Spielman, P. & Afterman, J. (1978), Bamboo phobia in an eighteen-month-old boy. *J. Amer. Psychoanal. Assn. Suppl.*, 26:255–282.

Ross, J. M. (1977), Toward fatherhood: The epigenesis of paternal identity during a boy's first decade. *Internat. J. Psycho-Anal.*, 58:327–347.

———— (1979), Fathering: a review of some psychoanalytic contributions on paternity. *Internat. J. Psycho-Anal.*, 60:317–328.

Rutter, M. (1979), Maternal Deprivation, 1972–1978. New findings, new concepts, new approaches. *Child Devel.*, 50:283–305.

Sandler, J. (1960), The background of safety. *Internat. J. Psycho-Anal.*, 41:352–356.

———— (1967), Countertransference and role-responsiveness. *Internat. Rev. Psycho-Anal.*, 3:43–47.

Shengold, L. (1989), *Soul Murder: The Effects of Childhood Abuse and Deprivation.* New Haven, CT: Yale University Press.

Slade, A. (2000), The development and organization of attachment: Implications for psychoanalysis. *J. Amer. Psychoanal. Assn.*, 48:1147–1174.

Tessman, L. (1978), *Children of Parting Parents.* New York: Aronson.

Tooley, K. (1976), Antisocial behavior and social alienation—Postal divorce: The man in the house of his mother. *Amer. J. Orthopsychiat.*, 46:33–43.

Vendler, H. (1988), *The Music of What Happens: Poems, Poets, Critics.* Cambridge MA: Harvard University Press.

Wallerstein, J. & Kelly, J. (1960), *Surviving the Break-Up: How Children and Parents Cope with Divorce.* New York: Basic Books.

Winnicott, D. W. (1958), The capacity to be alone. In: *The Maturational Processes and the Facilitating Environment: Studies in the Theory of Emotional Development.* Madison, CT: International Universities Press, 1965, pp. 29–36.

———— (1968), Communication between infant and mother, mother and infant, compared and contrasted. In: *What Is Psychoanalysis?* London: Balliere, Tindall & Cassell.

Yorke, C. (1986), Reflections on the problem of psychic trauma. *The Psychoanalytic Study of the Child*, 41:221–238. New Haven, CT: Yale University Press.

INDEX